Tort Law
Concentrate

3rd edition

Carol Brennan

**Senior Lecturer in Law,
University of Buckingham**

OXFORD
UNIVERSITY PRESS

Great Clarendon Street, Oxford, OX2 6DP,
United Kingdom

Oxford University Press is a department of the University of Oxford.
It furthers the University's objective of excellence in research, scholarship,
and education by publishing worldwide. Oxford is a registered trade mark of
Oxford University Press in the UK and in certain other countries

First edition 2011
Second edition 2013
Impression: 2

Published in the United States of America by Oxford University Press
198 Madison Avenue, New York, NY 10016, United States of America

British Library Cataloguing in Publication Data
Data available

Library of Congress Control Number: 2015931984

ISBN 978–0–19–872969–3

Printed in Great Britain by
Bell and Bain Ltd, Glasgow

Contents

Table of cases   vi
Table of legislation   xvi

1   Tort and the tort system: general overview   1

2   Negligence: duty of care   11

3   Duty of care: further issues   22

4   Pure economic loss and negligent misstatement   33

5   Psychiatric injury   49

6   Breach of duty: the standard of care   62

7   Causation in fact   75

8   Causation: intervening acts and remoteness   89

9   Employers' liability and vicarious liability   101

10   Product liability   118

11   Intentional torts   127

12   Nuisance and *Rylands v Fletcher*   140

13   Occupiers' liability   158

14   Defamation   172

15   Privacy   189

16   Defences and limitation   201

17   Remedies and principles of compensation   215

Exam essentials   A1
Outline answers   A5
Glossary   A12
Index   A14

Table of cases

A v B plc [2003] QB 195, CA ... 193, 195

A v Hoare [2008] 2 All ER 1 ... 211, 212

A v National Blood Authority [2001] 3 All ER 289 ... 120, 121, 124, 125

AAA v Associated Newspapers Ltd [2013] EWCA Civ 554 ... 195

AB v South West Water Services [1993] 1 All ER 609 ... 217

AB v Tameside and Glossop Health Authority [1997] 8 Med LR 91 ... 57

ABC v Lenah Game Meats [2001] 208 CLR 199 ... 198

Abouzaid v Mothercare [2001] EWCA Civ 348 ... 121, 124

AD v United Kingdom (2010) 51 EHRR 8 ... 30

Adams v Rhymney Valley DC [2000] 39 EG 144 ... 67

Adams v Ursell [1913] 1 Ch 269 ... 144

Addie v Dumbreck [1929] AC 358 ... 164

Alcock v Chief Constable of South Yorkshire Police [1991] 4 All ER 907 ... 49, 50, 54–6, 58–60, 106, A2, A6

Allen v Gulf Oil Refining Ltd [1981] AC 1001 ... 147

Allied Maples Group v Simmons [1995] 1 WLR 1602, CA ... 78

Allin v City and Hackney HA [1996] 7 Med LR 167 ... 57

Allsop v Church of England Newspaper [1972] 2 QB 161, CA ... 174

American Cyanamid v Ethicon [1975] AC 396 ... 221

AMF International Ltd v Magnet Bowling Ltd [1968] 1 WLR 1028 ... 160

Anderson v Newham College of Higher Education [2002] EWCA Civ 505 ... 204

Anns v Merton LBC [1978] AC 728 ... 14–16, 19, 26, 28, 35, 36, 37, 46, 47, A5

Arthur JS Hall v Simons [2000] 3 All ER 673; [2002] 1 AC 615 ... 15

Ashley v Chief Constable of Sussex Police [2008] UKHL 25 ... 135, 138, A8

Ashton v Turner [1981] QB 137 ... 208, 212

Associated Newspapers v Burstein [2007] EWCA Civ 600 ... 179

Attia v British Gas [1988] QB 304 ... 55

Attorney General v Hartwell [2004] UKPC 12 ... 113

Attorney General v PYA Quarries [1957] 2 QB 169 ... 148

Austin v Commissioner of Police for the Metropolis [2005] EWHC 480 (QB) ... 133

Austin v Commissioner of Police for the Metropolis [2009] 1 AC 564 ... 133, 136

Austin v United Kingdom (39692/09) [2012] ECHR 459 ... 133, 138, A3

Bailey v Ministry of Defence [2008] EWCA Civ 883 ... 81, 82, 83, 85

Baker v TE Hopkins and Sons Ltd [1959] 3 All ER 225 ... 207, 212

Baker v Willoughby [1970] AC 467 ... 84, 85

Bank of Montreal v Dominion Guarantee [1930] AC 659 ... 67

Banque Bruxelles Case *see* Lambert SA v Eagle Star Insurance Co Ltd

Barber v Somerset County Council [2004] 1 WLR 1089, HL ... 106

Barker v Corus UK [2006] UKHL 20 ... 83

Barkway v South Wales Transport Co Ltd [1950] AC 185 ... 71

Barnett v Kensington & Chelsea Health Management Committee [1968] 2 WLR 422 ... 76, 86

Barr v Biffa Waste Services Ltd [2012] EWCA Civ 312 ... 143

Barrett v Ministry of Defence [1995] 3 All ER 87 ... 25

Bellew v Cement Co [1948] IR 61 ... 144

Benjamin v Storr (1874) LR 9 CP 400 ... 149

Berkoff v Burchill [1996] 4 All ER 1008, CA ... 174

Bernard v Attorney General of Jamaica [2005] IRLR 398, PC ... 113

Bernstein v Skyviews [1978] QB 479 ... 134

Bici and Bici v Ministry of Defence [2004] EWHC 786 ... 129

Biddick (deceased) v Morcam [2014] EWCA Civ 182 ... 25

Bird v Jones (1845) 7 QB 742 ... 131

Blyth v Birmingham Waterworks (1856) 11 Ex 781 ... 64

Bogle v McDonald's Restaurants [2002] UKHL 490 ... 122

Bolam v Friern Hospital Management Committee [1957] 1 WLR 582, QB ... 67, 72, 73

Bolitho v City and Hackney Health Authority [1998] AC 232 ... 67

Bolton v Stone [1951] 1 All ER 1078 ... 69, 72, A7

Bone v Seal [1975] 1 All ER 787 ... 142

Bonnard v Perryman [1891] 2 Ch 269, CA ... 184, 185

Bonnington Castings v Wardlaw [1956] AC 613 ... 81, 82, 85, 86

Bookbinder v Tebbitt [1989] 1 WLR 640, CA ... 178

Bourhill v Young [1943] AC 92 ... 17, 52–4, 56, 58, 59

Bourne Leisure v Marsdon [2009] EWCA Civ 671 ... 161

Brice v Brown [1984] 1 All ER 997 ... 53

British Chiropractic Association v Singh [2010] EWCA Civ 350 ... 179

British Railways Board v Herrington [1972] UKHL 1 ... 164

Brooks v Commissioner of Police for the Metropolis [2005] UKHL 24 ... 29, 30

Bryanston Finance v de Vries [1975] QB 703 ... 181

Buck v Nottinghamshire Healthcare NHS Trust [2006] EWCA Civ 157 ... 67

Bunt v Tilley [2006] EWHC 407 ... 177

Burnie Port Authority v General Jones Pty Ltd [1994] 179 CLR 520 ... 152

Burton v Islington AHA [1993] QB 204, CA ... 29

Burton v Winters [1993] 1 WLR 1077 ... 148

Butchart v Home Office [2006] EWCA Civ 236 ... 57

Bybrook Barn Garden Centre v Kent County Council [2001] BLR 55, CA ... 145

Byrne v Dean [1937] 1 KB 818, CA ... 174, 185

Cairns v Modi [2012] EWCA Civ 1382 ... 184

Calgarth, The [1927] P 93 ... 160

Cambridge Water Co v Eastern Counties Leather [1994] 1 All ER 53 ... 3, 150, 151, 153

Campbell v MGN [2004] UKHL 22 ... 189, 191, 194–6, 198, A4, A10

Caparo v Dickman [1990] 2 AC 605 ... 11, 16–20, 40–2, 46, 95, A5

Capital and Counties plc v Hampshire CC [1997] QB 1004, CA ... 25

Capps v Miller [1989] 1 WLR 839, CA ... 203

Carmarthenshire County Council v Lewis [1955] AC 549 ... 25

Carslogie Steamship Co Ltd v Royal Norwegian Government [1952] AC 292 ... 93

Carstairs v Taylor (1871) LR 6 Exch 217 ... 152

Castle v St Augustine's Links [1922] 38 TLR 615 ... 148

CC v AB [2006] EWHC 3083 ... 193

Century Insurance v Northern Ireland Transport Board [1942] AC 509 ... 110, 114

Chadwick v British Railways Board [1967] 1 WLR 912, QB ... 55, 59, 60

Charleston v NGN [1995] 2 All ER 313 ... 174, 186

Chatterton v Gerson [1981] QB 432 ... 135

Chaudhury v Prabhaker [1989] 1 WLR 29, CA ... 39, A6

Chester v Afshar [2004] UKHL 41 ... 80, 83, 86

Christie v Davey (1893) 1 Ch D 316 ... 144, A9

Claimants in Corby Group Litigation v Corby BC see Corby Group Litigation v Corby BC

Clunis v Camden and Islington Health Authority [1998] QB 978, CA ... 208

Co-operative Group (CWS) Ltd v Pritchard [2011] EWCA Civ 329 ... 136

Cole v Davis-Gilbert [2007] EWCA Civ 396 ... 8

Collins v Wilcock [1984] 1 WLR 1172 ... 130, 136, A8

Table of cases

✳✳✳✳✳✳✳✳✳✳✳

Colour Quest v Total Downstream UK Ltd [2009] EWHC 540 (Comm) ... 152

Coltman v Bibby Tankers [1988] AC 276 ... 104

Commission of the European Communities v UK (Case C-300/95) [1997] All ER (EC) 481 ... 124

Conarken Group v Network Rail Infrastructure [2011] EWCA Civ 644 ... 36

Condon v Basi [1985] 1 WLR 866, CA ... 66, 207

Connor v Surrey CC [2010] EWCA Civ 286 ... 27

Conway v George Wimpey [1951] 2 KB 266 ... 111

Cook v Cook (1986) 162 CLR 376 ... 65

Cook v Lewis [1952] 1 DLR 1 ... 78

Corby Group Litigation v Corby BC [2008] EWCA Civ 463 ... 149

Corr v IBC [2008] UKHL 13 ... 91

Coventry v Lawrence [2014] UKSC 13 ... 143, 154, 222, A9

Customs and Excise Commissioners v Barclays Bank plc [2007] 1 AC 181 ... 16, 19, 43, 48

D v East Berkshire Community Health NHS Trust [2005] UKHL 23 ... 27, 30

D & F Estates Ltd v Church Commissioners [1988] 2 All ER 992 ... 36

Dann v Hamilton [1939] 1 KB 509 ... 206

Darby v National Trust [2001] EWCA Civ 189 ... 163

Davie v New Merton Board Mills [1959] AC 604 ... 5, 103

Davies v Swan Motor Co [1949] 2 KB 291, CA ... 202

Daw v Intel [2007] EWCA Civ 70 ... 106

De Keyser's Royal Hotel Ltd v Spicer Bros Ltd (1914) 30 TLR 257 ... 141, 147

Delaware Mansions Ltd v Westminster City Council [2001] 3 WLR 1007 ... 145, 148

Dennis v Ministry of Defence [2003] EWHC 793 ... 146, 147, 154, 222

Derbyshire CC v Times Newspapers [1993] AC 534 ... 177

Derry v Peek (1889) 14 App Cas 337, HL ... 37

Dickens v O2 plc [2008] EWCA Civ 1144 ... 81

Donachie v Chief Constable of Greater Manchester [2004] EWCA Civ 405 ... 57

Donoghue v Folkestone Properties [2003] EWCA Civ 231 ... 166

Donoghue v Stevenson [1932] AC 562 ... 11–14, 16, 17, 19, 38, 95, 119, 125, A5, A8, A11, A13

Douglas v Hello! [2001] QB 967, CA ... 193, 196, 198, 222

Douglas v Hello! [2005] 4 All ER 128 ... 192, 196

DPP v K [1990] 1 WLR 1067, QB ... 129

Dubai Aluminium Co Ltd v Salaam [2003] 2 AC 407 ... 113

Duchess of Argyll v Duke of Argyll [1967] Ch 302 ... 192

Dulieu v White [1901] 2 KB 669 ... 51, 52, 58, 59

Dunne v North Western Gas Board [1964] 2 QB 806 ... 152

Durham v BAI (Run-Off) Ltd [2012] UKSC 14 ... 83

Easson v London & North Eastern Railway Co [1944] KB 421, CA ... 71

Edwards v Railway Executive [1952] AC 737 ... 160

Ellis v Sheffield Gas Consumers Co (1853) 2 E&B 767 ... 108

Esso Petroleum v Mardon [1976] EWCA Civ 4 ... 39

Evans v Triplex Safety Glass [1936] 1 All ER 283 ... 119, 122, 125

F v West Berkshire HA [1989] 2 WLR 1025, HL ... 130, 135, 136

Fairchild v Glenhaven Funeral Services [2002] UKHL 22 ... 82, 83, 86

Ferguson v Welsh [1987] 1 WLR 1553, HL ... 160

Fitzgerald v Lane [1987] QB 781, CA ... 204, 205, A7

Flood v Times Newspapers [2012] UKSC 11 ... 182, 186

French v Chief Constable of Sussex [2006] EWCA Civ 312 ... 106

Froom v Butcher [1976] QB 286 ... 202, 203, 212, A7, A11

Furmedge v Chester-le-Street DC [2011] EWHC 1226 ... 160

Fytche v Wincanton Logistics Ltd [2004] UKHL 34 ... 107

Galli-Atkinson v Seghal [2003] EWCA Civ 697 ... 54

Gee v Metropolitan Railway Co (1873) IR 8 QB 161 ... 70

General Cleaning Contractors v Christmas [1953] AC 180 ... 104, 114, 162

General Engineering Services Ltd v Kingston and St Andrew Corporation [1989] 1 WLR 69 ... 110

George v Eagle Air Services [2009] 1 WLR 2133 ... 71

Giles v Walker (1890) 62 LT 933 ... 151

Gillingham BC v Medway (Chatham) Dock Co [1993] QB 343 ... 143, 154, A9

Glaister v Appleby-in-Westmoreland Town Council [2009] EWCA Civ 1325 ... 43, 164

Glasgow Corporation v Muir [1943] AC 448 ... 64, 72, A6

Glasgow Corporation v Taylor [1922] 1 AC 44 ... 160, 161, 168

Godfrey v Demon Internet Ltd [2001] QB 201 ... 176, 183, 186

Goldman v Hargrave [1967] 1 AC 645; [1966] 2 All ER 989 ... 26, 145, 154

Gough v Thorne [1966] 1 WLR 1387 ... 203, 212

Grant v Australian Knitting Mills [1936] AC 85 ... 119, 125

Gray v Thames Trains [2009] UKHL 33 ... 209, 210, 212, 213

Greatorex v Greatorex [2000] 1 WLR 1970, QB ... 56

Greene v Associated Newspapers [2005] QB 972 ... 185

Gregg v Scott [2005] 2 AC 176 ... 79, 80, 83, 86

Gregory v Kelly [1978] RTR 426 ... 203

Grobbelaar v News Group Newspapers [2001] EWCA Civ 33 ... 179, 184

Gwilliam v West Herts NHS Trust [2002] EWCA Civ 1041 ... 164

Hague v Deputy Governor of Parkhurst Prison [1992] 1 AC 58 ... 133, 136

Haley v London Electricity Board [1965] AC 778 ... 18, 19

Halsey v Esso Petroleum [1961] 1 WLR 683 ... 149, 154

Hambrook v Stokes Bros [1925] 1 KB 141, CA ... 52, 59

Harris v Birkenhead Corp [1976] 1 WLR 279 ... 160

Hartman v South Essex Mental Health NHS Trust [2005] EWCA Civ 6 ... 106

Harvey v O'Dell [1958] 2 QB 78 ... 111

Haseldine v Daw [1941] 2 KB 343 ... 163, 168

Hatton v Sutherland [2002] EWCA Civ 276 ... 58, 105, 106, 114, 116, A2

Haynes v Harwood [1935] 1 KB 146, CA ... 92, 207

Haystead v Chief Constable of Derbyshire [2000] 3 All ER 890, QB ... 129

Heaven v Pender (1883) 11 QB 503, CA ... 12

Hedley Byrne v Heller [1964] AC 465 ... 33, 37–43, 45, 46, A6, A13

Heil v Rankin [2001] PIQR Q3 ... 219

Henderson v Merrett Syndicates [1995] 2 AC 145 ... 42, 44, 46

Herd v Weardale Steel Coal and Coke Co [1915] AC 67 ... 132

Hicks v Chief Constable S Yorkshire Police [1992] 2 All ER 65 ... 223

Hill v Chief Constable of West Yorkshire [1989] AC 53 ... 16, 20, 28, 29

Hilton v Thomas Burton (Rhodes) Ltd [1961] 1 All ER 74 ... 111

Hinz v Berry [1970] 2 QB 40, CA ... 50, A6

HL v United Kingdom (45508/99) (2005) EHRR 32 ... 131

Holbeck Hall Hotel Ltd v Scarborough Borough Council [2000] 2 All ER 705 ... 145

Hollywood Silver Fox Farm Ltd v Emmett [1936] 2 KB 468 ... 144, 154

Home Office v Dorset Yacht Co [1970] AC 1004 ... 14, 20, 25, 26, 93

Hopps v Mott MacDonald and the Ministry of Defence [2009] EWCA Civ 1881 ... 70

Table of cases

✱✱✱✱✱✱✱✱✱✱✱✱

Horrocks v Lowe [1975] AC 135 ... 180

Hosking v Runting and Pacific Magazines Ltd (2005) 1 NZLR 1, CA ... 198

Hotson v East Berkshire AHA [1987] AC 750 ... 79, 80, 86, A7

Hudson v Ridge Manufacturing [1957] 2 QB 348, CA ... 103, A7

Hughes v Lord Advocate [1963] AC 837 ... 95–7, 100

Hulton v Jones [1910] AC 20 ... 175, 186

Hunt v Severs [1994] 2 AC 350 ... 218

Hunter v Canary Wharf [1996] 1 All ER 482 ... 142, 154, 157

Hussain v Lancaster City Council [1999] 4 All ER 125 ... 143

Huth v Huth [1915] 3 KB 32, CA ... 176

ICI v Shatwell [1965] AC 656 ... 206

Imbree v McNeilly (2008) 236 CLR 510 ... 65

Jain v Trent SHA [2009] UKHL 4 ... 43

Jameel v Wall Street Journal Europe (No 3) [2006] UKHL 44; [2007] 1 AC 359 ... 182, 186

James McNaughton Paper Group Ltd v Hicks Anderson & Co [1991] 2 QB 295, CA ... 41, 46

Janvier v Sweeney [1919] 2 KB 316, CA ... 133

Japp v Virgin Holidays Ltd [2013] EWCA Civ 1307 ... 65

JEB Fasteners v Marks Bloom & Co [1981] 3 All ER 289 ... 39, A6

JGE v The Trustees of the Portsmouth Roman Catholic Diocesan Trust [2012] EWCA Civ 938 ... 109

JIH v Newsgroup Newspapers Ltd [2011] EWCA Civ 42 ... 198

Jobling v Associated Dairies [1981] 2 All ER 7 ... 84, 85, 87

Joel v Morrison (1834) 6 C&P 501 ... 111

John v MGN [1997] QB 586, CA ... 184, 186, 217

Jolley v Sutton LBC [2000] 1 WLR 1082 ... 96, 98, 162, 168

Jones v Boyce (1816) 1 Stark 493 ... 204, A7

Jones v Livox Quarries Ltd [1952] 2 QB 608 ... 203, 212

Junior Books v Veitchi [1983] 1 AC 520 ... 14, 36

Kadir v Mistry [2014] EWCA Civ 1177 ... 223

Kaye v Robertson [1991] FSR 62 ... 129, 190, 191, 198, A10

KD v Chief Constable of Hampshire [2005] EWHC 2550 ... 219

Kemsley v Foot [1952] AC 345 ... 179

Kennaway v Thompson [1981] QB 88 ... 144, 222

Kent v Griffiths [2001] QB 36, CA ... 25, A5

Keown v Coventry Healthcare NHS Trust [2006] EWCA Civ 39 ... 165, A10

Keppel Bus Co Ltd v Ahmad [1974] 2 All ER 700 ... 112

Khorasandjian v Bush [1993] 3 All ER 669 ... 142

Kirkham v Chief Constable of Greater Manchester [1990] 2 QB 283, CA ... 91

Knight v Home Office [1990] 3 All ER 237 ... 68

Knightley v Johns [1982] 1 All ER 851 ... 28, 92, 98

Knowles v Liverpool City Council [1993] 1 WLR 1428 ... 104

Knupffer v London Express Newspapers [1944] AC 116 ... 175, 187

Kralj v McGrath [1986] 1 All ER 54 ... 219

Kubach v Hollands [1937] 3 All ER 907 ... 119

Kuddus v Chief Constable of Leicestershire Constabulary [2001] UKHL 29 ... 217

Lagden v O'Connor [2003] UKHL 64 ... 97, 98

Lamb v Camden LBC [1981] QB 625, CA ... 93

Lambert SA v Eagle Star Insurance Co Ltd ('Banque Bruxelles') [1997] AC 191 ... 99

Lane v Holloway [1968] 1 QB 379, CA ... 135, 136, A8

Latimer v AEC [1953] AC 643 ... 69, 104

Lawrence v Pembrokeshire CC [2007] EWCA Civ 446 ... 27

Leakey v National Trust [1980] QB 485 ... 145

Lemmon v Webb [1894] 3 Ch 1 ... 222

Les Laboratoires Servier v Apotex [2014] UKSC 55 ... 209

Letang v Cooper [1965] 1 QB 232, CA ... 128, 136, 202, 211, 212

Lewis v Daily Telegraph [1964] AC 234 ... 174

Lim v Camden and Islington AHA [1980] AC 174 ... 217, A11

Limpus v London General Omnibus Company (1862) 1 H&C 526 ... 111

Lippiatt v South Gloucestershire County Council [1999] 4 All ER 149 ... 143

Lister v Hesley Hall [2002] 1 AC 215 ... 112, 115

Lister v Romford Ice and Cold Storage [1957] AC 555 ... 113

Lloyd v Grace Smith & Co [1912] AC 716 ... 112, 115

LMS v Styrene Packaging and Insulation [2006] EWHC 2065, TCC ... 153

Loutchansky v Times Newspapers (No 2) [2001] EWCA Civ 1805 ... 177, 182

Lowery v Walker [1911] AC 10 ... 160

McDermid v Nash Dredging & Reclamation [1987] 2 All ER 878 ... 103, 114

McDonald's Corp v Steel (No 4) [2005] ECHR 103 ... 177

McFarlane v EE Caledonia [1994] 2 All ER 1 ... 55, 59

McGeown v Northern Ireland Housing Executive [1995] 1 AC 233 ... 168

McGhee v National Coal Board [1973] 1 WLR 1, HL ... 81, 82, 83, 86, 87

McHale v Watson (1966) 115 CLR 199 ... 72

McKennitt v Ash [2006] EWCA Civ 1714 ... 195, 197, 198, A10

McKew v Holland [1969] 3 All ER 1621 ... 90, 91, 98, 99

McKinnon Industries v Walker [1951] 3 DLR 577 ... 144

McLoughlin v Jones [2001] EWCA Civ 1743 ... 57

McLoughlin v O'Brian [1983] AC 410 ... 49, 53, 54, 60

McManus v Beckham [2002] EWCA Civ 239 ... 176

McWilliams v Sir William Arrol & Co [1962] 1 WLR 295 ... 78, 87

Maga v Archbishop of Birmingham [2010] EWCA Civ 256 ... 113

Majrowski v Guys and St Thomas's NHS Trust [2007] 1 AC 224 ... 108, 134, A2

Malone v Laskey [1907] KB 141 ... 142

Mansfield v Weetabix [1998] 1 WLR 1263, CA ... 65

Marc Rich & Co v Bishop Rock Marine Co Ltd ('The Nicholas H') [1996] AC 211 ... 16, 20

Marcic v Thames Water Utilities [2002] 2 All ER 55, CA; [2003] UKHL 66 ... 146, 154

Market Investigations Ltd v Minister of Social Security [1969] 2 QB 173 ... 109, 115

Mason v Levy Autoparts (1967) 2 QB 530 ... 150

Mattis v Pollock [2003] 1 WLR 2158 ... 113

Meering v Grahame-White Aviation [1919] 122 LT 44 ... 132, 137, A8

Melville v Home Office [2005] ICR 782 ... 106

Merrett v Babb [2001] QB 1172, CA ... 42

Mersey Docks and Harbour Board v Coggins & Griffiths [1947] AC 1 ... 110, 115

Metropolitan International Schools Ltd v Designtechnica Corp [2009] EWHC 1765 ... 177

Miller v Jackson [1977] QB 966 ... 144, 146, 147, 222

Ministry of Defence v AB and others [2012] UKSC 89 ... 211

Mitchell v Glasgow City Council [2009] UKHL 11 ... 25

Morgan v Odhams Press (1971) 1 WLR 1239, HL ... 175

Morgan Crucible Co plc v Hill Samuel Bank Ltd [1991] Ch 295, CA ... 41

Morris v Martin & Sons [1966] 1 QB 716 ... 112

Morris v Murray [1991] 2 QB 6, CA ... 206, 213, A11

Mosley v News Group Newspapers [2008] EMLR 20 ... 195, 197, 199

Muirhead v Industrial Tank Specialities Ltd [1985] 3 All ER 705 ... 36

Table of cases

****

Mulcahy v Ministry of Defence [1996] QB 732, CA ... 104

Mullin v Richards [1998] 1 WLR 1304, CA ... 65, 72

Murphy v Brentwood DC [1991] 1 AC 398 ... 33, 35, 36, 37, 46, 47, 168

Murray v Ministry of Defence [1988] 1 WLR 692, HL ... 132

Mutual Life & Citizens' Assurance Co Ltd v Evatt [1971] AC 793, PC ... 39, A6

Nettleship v Weston [1971] 2 QB 691 ... 64, 65, 72, 73, 206, A11

Network Rail v Morris [2004] EWCA Civ 172 ... 144

Newstead v London Express Newspapers [1940] 1 KB 377 ... 175, 187

Ng Chun Pui v Lee Chuen Tat [1988] RTR 298, PC ... 71

Nichols v Marsland (1876) 2 Ex D 1 ... 152

Ogwo v Taylor [1988] AC 431 ... 207

Oropesa, The [1943] 1 All ER 211 ... 92

O'Shea v MGN [2001] EMLR 40, QB ... 175

Osman v Ferguson [1993] 4 All ER 344 ... 29, 30

Osman v United Kingdom [1998] EHRR 101 ... 29

Overseas Tankship (UK) Ltd v Morts Docks and Engineering Co Ltd ('The Wagon Mound (No 1)') [1961] AC 388, PC ... 69, 94–6, 98, 168

Overseas Tankship (UK) v The Miller Steamship Co ('The Wagon Mound (No 2)') [1966] 2 All ER 709, PC ... 69, 72, 73, 94, A7

Owens v Brimmell [1977] QB 859 ... 202, 206, A7

Owens v Liverpool Corp [1939] 1 KB 394 ... 55

Page v Smith [1995] 2 All ER 736 ... 49, 51–3, 56, 58, 60, A6

Palsgraf v Long Island Railroad (1928) 162 NE 99 ... 17, 18, 53

Pamplin v Express Newspapers (No 2) [1988] 1 WLR 116, CA ... 184

Paris v Stepney BC [1950] 1 KB 320, CA ... 65

Patchett v Swimming Pool & Allied Trades Assn Ltd [2009] EWCA Civ 717 ... 43

Peck v United Kingdom [2003] EMLR 15 ... 196, 199

Performance Cars v Abraham [1962] 1 QB 33, CA ... 84, 87

Perry v Kendricks [1956] 1 WLR 85, CA ... 151, 152

Phelps v Hillingdon LBC [2001] 2 AC 619 ... 27, 30

Phillips v William Whiteley [1938] 1 All ER 566 ... 65–6

Phipps v Rochester Corporation [1955] 1 QB 450 ... 161, 169

Pickford (AP) v Imperial Chemical Industries plc [1998] 1 WLR 1189 ... 77

Piper v JRI (Manufacturing) Ltd (2006) 92 BMLR 141, CA ... 122

Pitts v Hunt [1991] 1 QB 24, CA ... 204, 208, 213

Polemis, Re [1921] 3 KB 560, CA ... 94

Pollard v Tesco Stores [2006] EWCA Civ 393 ... 121, 125

Prince Albert v Strange (1849) De G & Sm 652 ... 192, 195

HRH Prince of Wales v Associated Newspapers [2006] EWCA Civ 1776 ... 192, 194, 195, 199

R v Bournewood etc NHS Trust, ex p L [1999] 1 AC 458 ... 131

R v Governor of Brockhill Prison, ex p Evans [2001] 2 AC 19 ... 132, 133, 137

R v Ireland [1998] AC 147, HL ... 130

R v Meade (1823) 1 Lew CC 184 ... 130

R v Rimmington [2006] 1 AC 459 ... 149

Rabone v Pennine Care NHS Trust [2012] UKSC 2 ... 30

Rahman v Arearose [2001] QB 351 ... 58, 97

Rantzen v MGM [1986] 4 All ER 975 ... 184

Ratcliff v McConnell [1999] 1 WLR 670 ... 166, 169, A10

Read v Lyons [1947] AC 156 ... 150, 151

Reeves v Metropolitan Police Commissioner [2000] 1 AC 360 ... 91, 98, 202, 204, A7

Reid v Rush & Tompkins Group [1990] 1 WLR 212, CA ... 104, 114

Revill v Newbery [1996] QB 567, CA ... 165, 169, 170

Reynolds v Times Newspapers [2001] 2 AC 127 ... 177, 178, 181–3, 186–7, 216, A4

Rickards v Lothian [1913] AC 263 ... 140, 155

Rigby v Chief Constable of Northamptonshire [1985] 3 All ER 87 ... 28, 151

Roberts v Ramsbottom [1980] 1 WLR 823, QB ... 65

Robinson v Balmain Ferry Co Ltd [1910] AC 295 ... 132, 137

Robinson v Kilvert (1889) LR 41 Ch D 88 ... 144, 155

Robinson v Post Office [1974] 2 All ER 737, CA ... 97

Roe v Ministry of Health [1954] 2 QB 66, CA ... 65

Roles v Nathan [1963] 1 WLR 1264 ... 162, 169, A10

Rondel v Worsley [1969] 1 AC 191 ... 15

Rookes v Barnard [1964] AC 1129 ... 217, 224, A11

Rose v Miles (1815) 4 M&S 101 ... 149

Rose v Plenty [1976] 1 WLR 141 ... 111, 115, 116

Rothwell v Chemical & Insulating Co Ltd [2007] UKHL 39 ... 53, 56, 60

Rylands v Fletcher (1866) LR 1 Ex 265; affd (1868) LR 3 HL 330 ... 2, 3, 140, 150–3, 155, 156, A3, A9, A13

S (A Child), Re [2004] UKHL 47 ... 195

St Helen's Smelting Co v Tipping (1865) 11 HL Cas 642 ... 141, 143, 155, A9

Scally v Southern Health and Social Services Board [1992] 1 AC 294 ... 105

Scott v London and St Katherine's Dock Co (1865) 3 H&C 596 ... 70

Scout Association (The) v Barnes [2010] EWCA Civ 1476 ... 8, 70, 164

Sedleigh-Denfield v O'Callaghan [1939] 1 All ER 725 ... 142, 155

Shelfer v City of London Electric Lighting Co [1895] 1 Ch 287 ... 147, 148, 222, 224

Sidaway v Board of Governors of Bethlem Royal Hospital [1985] AC 871 ... 67

Sienkiewicz v Grief [2011] UKSC 10 ... 83

Sim v Stretch (1936) 52 TLR 669, HL ... 173, A10

Simaan General Contracting Co v Pilkington Glass [1988] QB 758, CA ... 36

Sion v Hampstead Health Authority [1994] Med LR 170, CA ... 51

Slipper v BBC [1991] 1 QB 283, CA ... 176

Smith v Baker [1891] AC 325 ... 206

Smith v Chief Constable of Sussex Police [2008] UKHL 50 ... 29

Smith v Eric S Bush [1990] 1 AC 831 ... 6, 40, 45, 47, 208

Smith v Leech Brain [1962] 2 QB 405, CA ... 97, 99

Smith v Littlewoods [1987] 1 AC 241 ... 23–4, 26, 30, A5

Smith v Ministry of Defence [2013] UKSC 1341 SC ... 17

Smith v Stages [1989] AC 928 ... 111, 115

Spartan Steel & Alloys v Martin [1973] QB 27, CA ... 34, 35, 47

Spencer v Wincanton (2009) EWCA Civ 1404 ... 91

Spicer v Smee [1946] 1 All ER 489 ... 141

Spiller v Joseph [2010] UKSC 53 ... 179

Spring v Guardian Assurance plc [1995] 2 AC 296 ... 43, 44, 47, 105

Stannard v Gore [2012] EWCA Civ 1248 ... 152

Stansbie v Troman [1948] 2 KB 48 ... 24, 93, A5

Staples v West Dorset DC (1995) 93 LGR 536 ... 163

Stapley v Gypsum Mines [1953] AC 663 ... 202, 204

Stennett v Hancock and Peters [1939] 2 All ER 578 ... 119

Stephens v Myers (1830) 4 C&P 349 ... 130, 137

Stevenson Jordan & Harrison Ltd v McDonald & Evans [1952] 1 TLR 101 ... 109

Storey v Ashton (1869) LR 4 QB 476 ... 111, 115

Stovin v Wise [1996] AC 923 ... 24, 26, 30

Stubbings v Webb [1993] AC 498 ... 211, 212

Sturges v Bridgman (1879) 11 Ch D 892 ... 143, 146, 147, 155

Table of cases

✱✱✱✱✱✱✱✱✱✱✱✱

Sullivan v New York Times (1964) 376 US 254 ... 183

Swinney v Chief Constable of Northumbria Police [1997] QB 464, CA ... 29

Swinney v Chief Constable of Northumbria Police (No 2) (1999) 11 Admin LR 811, QB ... 29

Tamiz v Google Inc [2013] EWCA Civ 68 ... 174, 177

Tate & Lyle Industries v GLC [1983] 2 AC 509 ... 148, A9

Tetley v Chitty [1986] 1 All ER 663 ... 143

Theaker v Richardson [1962] 1 WLR 151 ... 176, 187, A10

Theakston v MGN [2002] UKHC 137 ... 196

Thomas v National Union of Mineworkers [1986] Ch 20 ... 130, 137

Thompson v Commissioner of Police for the Metropolis [1997] 3 WLR 403 ... 217

Thompson v James [2014] EWCA Civ 600 ... 174

Thompson v Tameside and Glossop Acute Services NHS Trust [2008] EWCA Civ 5 ... 220, 224

Times Newspapers v UK (2009) EMLR 14 ... 177

Tolley v Frye [1931] AC 333 ... 174, 187

Tomlinson v Congleton DC [2003] UKHL 47 ... 166, 169, A10

Topp v London Country Bus Ltd [1993] 1 WLR 976 ... 26, 31

Transco plc v Stockport MBC [2003] UKHL 61 ... 150, 151, 155, A9

Tremain v Pike (1969) 3 All ER 1303 ... 96

Tuberville v Savage (1669) 1 Mod 3 ... 130

Twine v Beans Express [1946] 1 All ER 202 ... 111, 116

Van Colle v Chief Constable of Hertfordshire Police [2009] UKHL 50 ... 29, 31

Various Claimants v Catholic Child Welfare Society [2013] UKSC 56 ... 113

Venables v News Group Newspapers [2001] 2 WLR 1038 ... 197

Vernon v Bosley (No 1) [1997] 1 All ER 577 ... 51

Viasystems (Tyneside) Ltd v Thermal Transfer (Northern) Ltd [2005] EWCA Civ 1151 ... 110, 116

Victorian Railway Commissioners v Coultas (1888) 13 App Cas 222, PC ... 51

Von Hannover v Germany [2004] EMLR 21 ... 196, 198, 199, A10

Von Hannover v Germany (No 2) [2012] ECHR 228 ... 197, 198

Vowles v Evans [2003] 1 WLR 1607 ... 66

W v Essex County Council [2000] 2 All ER 237 ... 56

Wainwright v Home Office [2004] 2 AC 406 ... 134, 137, 196

Walker v Northumberland County Council [1995] 1 All ER 737 ... 58, 105, 106, 114

Walters v North Glamorgan NHS Trust [2003] PIQR 16, CA ... 51

Wandsworth LBC v Network Rail [2001] 1 WLR 368 ... 149

Warren v Henleys [1948] 2 All ER 935 ... 112

Watkins v Secretary of State for the Home Department [2006] UKHL 17 ... 216

Watson v British Boxing Board [2001] QB 1134, CA ... 207

Watt v Hertfordshire CC [1954] 1 WLR 835 ... 69

Watt v Longsdon [1930] 1 KB 130 ... 180, 181, 187

Weller & Co v Foot and Mouth Disease Research Institute [1966] 1 QB 569 ... 34

Wells v Cooper [1958] 2 QB 265, CA ... 66

Welton v North Cornwall DC [1997] 1 WLR 570, CA ... 39

West Bromwich Albion Football Club v El-Safty [2006] EWCA Civ 1299 ... 43

West v Shephard [1964] AC 516 ... 219, 224, A11

Wheat v Lacon [1966] AC 552 ... 159, 169

Wheeler v Saunders [1996] Ch 19 ... 143

White v Blackmore [1972] 1 QB 651, CA ... 208

White v Chief Constable of the South Yorkshire Police [1999] 1 All ER 1 ... 49, 55, 56, 60, A2

White v Jones [1995] 2 AC 207 ... 44, 45, 47

Wieland v Cyril Lord Carpets [1968] 3 All ER 1006 ... 91, 99

Wilkinson v Downton [1867] 2 QB 57 ... 127, 133, 134, 137, 196, A3

Williams v Humphrey, The Times, 12 February 1975 ... 129, 137

Williams v Natural Life Health Foods Ltd [1998] 1 WLR 830, HL ... 42

Wilsher v Essex Area Health Authority [1988] AC 1074, HL; [1987] QB 730, CA ... 66, 73, 82, 87, A7

Wilson v Pringle [1987] QB 237, CA ... 66, 73, 82, 87, 130, 137, A7, A8

Wilsons and Clyde Coal v English [1938] AC 57 ... 102, 114, A7

Wise v Kaye [1962] 1 QB 638, CA ... 218

Wong v Parkside Health NHS Trust [2003] 3 All ER 932 ... 133

Woodland v Swimming Teachers' Association [2013] UKSC 66 ... 109

Woodward v Mayor of Hastings [1945] KB 174 ... 164, 169

Wooldridge v Sumner [1963] 2 QB 43, CA ... 66, 73, 207

Wright v Cambridge Medical Group Ltd [2011] EWCA Civ 669 ... 93

Wright v Lodge [1993] 4 All ER 299, CA ... 92

X v Bedfordshire CC [1995] 2 AC 633 ... 27, 31

Yachuk v Oliver Blais [1949] AC 386 ... 203

Yuen Kun Yeu v Attorney General of Hong Kong [1988] AC 175 ... 15

Z v United Kingdom [2001] ECHR 333 ... 4, 27

Table of legislation

UK Primary Legislation

Administration of Justice Act 1982
  s 1(1)(b) ... 223
  s 6 ... A11

Civil Evidence Act 1968
  s 11 ... 70
Civil Liability (Contribution) Act 1978 ... 78,
    113, 201
  s 1 ... 78, 205
  s 2 ... 78, 205
Compensation Act 2006 ... 1, 8, 9, 70
  s 1 ... 8, 70, 164, A3
  s 3 ... 83
Congenital Disabilities (Civil Liability) Act
    1976 ... 29
Consumer Protection Act 1987 ... 118–19,
    123–6, A3, A8, A13
  Part 1 (ss 1–9) ... 120–3
  s 1(2) ... 120, A8
  s 2(2) ... 120
  s 3 ... 121, A8
  s 4 ... 122, A8
  s 4(1)(d) ... 122
  s 4(1)(e) ... 124, A8
  s 5 ... 122, A8
Countryside and Rights of Way Act
    2000 ... 165, 168
Courts Act 2003 ... 224
  s 100 ... 220
  s 101 ... 220
Courts and Legal Services Act 1990
  s 8 ... 184

Damages Act 1996 ... 220
  s 2 ... 220, A11
Defamation Act 1952 ... 173
  s 1 ... 176
  s 2 ... 173, A10
  s 5 ... 178
  s 6 ... 180

Defamation Act 1996 ... 178
  s 1 ... 176, 183, 186
  s 2 ... 175, 178, 183, 187, A10
  ss 3–4 ... 175, 178, 183, A10
  s 5 ... 210
  s 13 ... 180
  s 15 ... 180
  Sch 1 ... 180
Defamation Act 2013 ... 173, 177
  s 1 ... 172
  s 1(1) ... 172, 173, A10
  s 1(2) ... 177
  s 2 ... 178, A10
  s 3 ... 177, 179
  s 4 ... 178, 181, 182, 187
  s 5 ... 177, 178, 183
  s 6 ... 180
  s 8 ... 177
  s 10 ... 177, 183
  s 11 ... 172, 184
  s 13 ... 183
Defective Premises Act 1972 ... 37, 168
  s 1 ... 37
  s 4 ... 168

Employers' Liability (Compulsory Insurance)
    Act 1969 ... 5, 102
Employer's Liability (Defective Equipment)
    Act 1969 ... 103
  s 1 ... 103, A7
  s 1(1) ... 103
Environmental Protection Act 1990 ... 153

Factories Act 1961 ... 106
Fatal Accidents Act 1976 ... 215, 223
  s 1(3) ... 223
  s 5 ... 223
Fires Prevention (Metropolis) Act 1774
  s 86 ... 152

Health and Safety at Work Act 1974 ... A2

Health and Safety at Work etc. Act 1974 ... 106

Human Fertilisation and Embryology Act 1990 ... 29

Human Rights Act 1998 ... 4, 5, 26, 146, 177, 189–91, 222, A4, A10
s 12 ... 190, 191
s 12(3) ... 185, 197, 221, A10
s 12(4) ... 191, 221

Law Reform (Contributory Negligence) Act 1945 ... 201, 204, A11, A12
s 1(1) ... 202
s 4 ... 202

Law Reform (Miscellaneous Provisions) Act 1934 ... 215
s 1(1) ... 223

Legal Aid, Sentencing and Punishment of Offenders Act 2012 ... 8

Limitation Act 1980 ... 201, 210
s 2 ... 210
s 11 ... 210, 211
s 11A(4) ... 124, 211
s 14 ... 211
s 33 ... 211
s 33(1) ... 211

Local Government Act 1972
s 222 ... 148

Mental Health Act 1983 ... 209

Mines and Quarries Act 1954 ... 106

Occupiers' Liability Act 1957 ... 96, 158–64, 165, A3, A9
s 1(1) ... 159
s 1(2) ... 159, 160
s 1(3)(a) ... 160
s 2(1) ... 164, A9
s 2(2) ... 160
s 2(3) ... 164
s 2(3)(a) ... 161, A9
s 2(3)(b) ... 162, 169, A9
s 2(4)(a) ... 162, A9

s 2(4)(b) ... 163, 168, 169, A9
s 2(5) ... 164

Occupiers' Liability Act 1984 ... 158, 162, 164–8, A3, A10
s 1(1)(a) ... 165
s 1(3) ... 166, A10
s 1(3)(a) ... 166, 167
s 1(3)(b) ... 166, 167
s 1(3)(c) ... 166, 167
s 1(4) ... 166, 167, A10
s 1(5) ... 166
s 1(6) ... 166, A10

Offices, Shops and Railway Premises Act 1963 ... 106

Police and Criminal Evidence Act 1984
s 24 ... 132
s 24A ... 132, A8
s 28 ... 132

Protection from Harassment Act 1997 ... 127, 130, 134, 219, A3

Public Order Act 1986 ... 132

Rehabilitation of Offenders Act 1974
s 8 ... 178

Road Traffic Act 1988 ... 5
s 149 ... 206, 208, A11

Road Traffic (NHS Charges) Act 1999 ... 218

Senior Courts Act 1981 ... 220
s 32A ... 220

Social Security (Recovery of Benefits) Act 1997 ... 220

Theatres Act 1952 ... 173

Unfair Contract Terms Act 1977 ... 38, 45, 46, 47, 159, 164, 208, A3, A9
s 1(3) ... 208
s 2 ... 45, 208
s 2(2) ... 45
s 11 ... 45
s 11(3) ... 45

Workman's Compensation Act 1897 ... 102

Table of legislation
✼✼✼✼✼✼✼✼✼✼✼

UK Secondary Legislation

Consumer Protection Act 1987 (Product Liability) (Modification) Order 2000 (SI 2000/2771) … 120

Management of Health and Safety at Work Regulations 1999 (SI 1999/3242) … 106

Personal Protective Equipment at Work Regulations 1992 (SI 1992/2966) … 107

European Secondary Legislation

Directive on Product Liability 1985 … 120
  Art 7(e) … 123, 124

International Legislation

European Convention on Human Rights 1950 … 4, 175

Art 2 … 5, 30, 31

Art 3 … 5, 27

Art 5 … 5, 133, 136, 138

Art 5(1) … 131

Art 6 … 5, 29

Art 8 … 5, 30, 146, 154, 190, 191, 193, 195–7, 199, A3, A10

Art 8(2) … 195

Art 10 … 5, 172, 175, 177, 181, 185, 190, 191, 193, 195, 197, 199, A3, A10

Art 10(2) … 195

Art 13 … 27

Protocol 1, Art 1 … 146, 154

#1

Tort and the tort system: general overview

Key facts

- Tort law is the branch of civil law predominantly concerned with protecting a range of individual interests.

- The main interests protected concern the safety of person and property, the use and enjoyment of property, reputation and, to a limited extent, certain economic interests and privacy.

- Tort law is diverse and must be distinguished from other areas of law.

- Public policy and, more recently, human rights law must be taken into account in learning the law of tort.

- Remedies in tort are predominantly damages and, to a lesser extent, injunctions.

- Insurance plays a role in practice, if not in principle.

- The tort system is only one of many routes to compensation.

- Concerns about the growing 'compensation culture' have been reflected in the **Compensation Act 2006**, judicial decisions, and academic comment.

What types of loss or harm covered?

Any essay question regarding the 'law of tort' generally, or the 'tort system', will require you to master the definitional and policy issues raised in this chapter.

What is tort?

Tort can be described as the area of civil law which provides a **remedy** for a party who has suffered the breach of a protected interest. The word itself is derived from the Latin 'tortum', meaning twisted or wrong.

A wide scope of interests is protected by the law of tort. Currently, the tort which is the greatest source of litigation is that of **negligence**. Negligence concerns personal safety and interests in property, as well as some economic interests. Physical safety is also protected by the torts of **trespass** to the person while ownership of property is governed by trespass to property. Other kinds of property interests are the domain of the torts of **nuisance** and *Rylands v Fletcher*. Remedies for threats to one's reputation are provided by the tort of **defamation**. Recently, English law has seen significant developments concerning the protection of privacy from media intrusion.

Different torts for different types of harm

Tort is an extremely diverse field, which has been likened to 'a mosaic'. Different torts deal with different types of harm or wrongful conduct and the 'ingredients' for each of these torts are different; each with its own particular characteristics. For example, in order to succeed in the tort of **negligence** a claimant must show, not only that the defendant was at **fault**, but that he suffered damage as a result of the defendant's negligence. In terms of damage, the tort of negligence can be contrasted with the tort of libel where, once the publication of a defamatory statement is established, a claimant will be able to succeed without proof of damage. Thus it can be said that libel is *actionable per se*.

What types of loss or harm are covered?

Not all interests are protected by the law of **tort**.

Where a **loss** is suffered as a consequence of an infringement of an interest protected by the law of tort, the defendant will be liable to pay **damages** to compensate for that loss.

However, it is important to note that not all interests are protected by the law of tort, so that a person could suffer a loss as the result of another's conduct for which the law does not provide compensation. *Damnum sine injuria* is the Latin expression used to describe situations where harm is suffered but the interest is not one which is protected by the law of tort and the claimant has no **remedy** in tort.

For example, if you own a small bookshop on the High Street and a large chain newsagent lawfully opens a branch nearby, you may suffer a **loss** of business and reduced profit, but the loss is not recoverable in **tort** because no 'legal wrong' has been committed by the news-agent. Similarly, the pain and grief felt by someone whose spouse is killed by a negligent driver is generally unlikely to be covered by **damages** for the tort of **negligence**.

Competing interests

Many of the interests protected by law compete. The **tort** of **nuisance** provides an example; one resident may complain that the volume of his neighbour's music is so loud that it amounts to an interference with his use and enjoyment of his home or land. However, his neighbour may argue that it is he who is suffering the wrong, because he has the right to play his music in the privacy of his own home without complaint or interference. In these situations it is the role of the court to apply the law of tort in order to decide which of these competing interests should receive the legal protection under the tort of nuisance. Similarly, the clash between protection of reputation or confidence and freedom of expression is a key issue in the debate over the extension of the law of tort into the field of privacy.

Remedies

The law of **tort** deals with a wide range of activities and provides remedies for many different types of loss or harm. In cases of traffic accidents, injuries in the workplace and medical negligence, the **remedy** sought by the claimant is likely to be **damages**.

Tort also deals with disputes between neighbours about their use of land. If enjoyment of land is interfered with by noise or smells which are deemed to be unreasonable, this will constitute the tort of **nuisance**. Here, rather than seeking an award of financial compensation, the claimant may often request that the court grant an **injunction**, an order restraining the defendant from continuing to interfere with the claimant's enjoyment of his land.

Revision tip

At this stage, note must be taken of the overlapping nature of many torts. It is not uncommon to see a case brought in respect of more than one cause of action. An example is the important case of *Cambridge Water v Eastern Counties Leather* (1994) in which the original action was brought in **negligence**, **nuisance** and *Rylands v Fletcher* (see Chapter 12). In such actions, the judge will decide which cause of action (if any) best fits the facts of the case as presented. Should more than one be applicable then the claimant must elect one action with which to pursue a **remedy** prior to final judgment, to prevent double recovery.

Comparing tort to other areas of law

According to Winfield, a leading academic expert on the law of tort:

Tort is characterised by duties 'primarily fixed by law' and owed 'towards persons generally'.

Tort and contract

The ideal of the contractual obligation is that, rather than being imposed by law, it is negotiated by two parties. Instead of being owed to persons generally, it is specific to the two parties to the contract.

In contrast, in the tort of **negligence** you will see that duties and matching rights have evolved out of the operation of the common law (supplemented in some circumstances by statute), rather than by an agreement and that they tend to be applied to the population in general. We all have a duty not to drive carelessly and injure other motorists or pedestrians; and they all have the right to seek a **remedy** in **tort** if we breach this duty.

However, this basis for distinguishing contract and tort is not absolute. In the case of **pure economic loss** caused by a **negligent misstatement**, there are a number of instances in which the claimant has the choice of bringing his action in either contract or tort.

Tort and criminal law

The main distinction between **tort** and criminal law lies in the nature of their objectives. Simply put, the objective of the criminal law is to enforce the law by punishing those who break it. The objective of tort law, on the other hand, is to enforce the law by compensating those who suffer damage when the law is broken.

In tort, the primary focus is upon the **loss** or damage suffered by the claimant, rather than upon the individual personality and motivation of the criminal defendant. However, as with contract, the distinction described is not watertight.

There are instances, such as **defamation**, in which the law of tort allows punishment of defendants through the use of punitive **damages**. Equally, criminal courts now have extensive powers to award compensation to victims of crime. Additionally, some wrongs will constitute crimes as well as torts. Examples are **assault**, **battery** and public **nuisance**, and these torts can be prosecuted as criminal offences as well as being the basis for a civil **tort** action.

Tort and human rights

Prior to 2000, human rights law affected **tort** law only indirectly. Those claiming that a decision made in an English court was contrary to the **European Convention on Human Rights (ECHR)** could take their case to the European Court of Human Rights (ECtHR) in Strasbourg. A decision of the ECtHR would then influence further development of the common law. See for instance *Z v United Kingdom* (2001), in Chapter 3.

The right to appeal to Strasbourg still exists; however, with the coming into force of the **Human Rights Act 1998 (HRA)** in October 2000, key articles of the Convention became binding in the United Kingdom. Statutes and case law must be interpreted and applied in a sense which is compatible with Convention rights, as far as it is possible to do so. More specifically relevant are the articles of the **ECHR** which the **HRA** has incorporated into United Kingdom law. This enables individuals to seek remedies when public authorities act in ways incompatible with Convention rights. The rights which are relevant to **tort** law and have had an impact on the development of case law are as follows:

- Article 2: Right to life
- Article 3: Right to freedom from inhuman and degrading treatment
- Article 5: Right to liberty and security
- Article 6: Right to a fair trial
- Article 8: Right to respect for private and family life
- Article 10: Right to freedom of expression.

As courts themselves are public authorities, the impact of the HRA can extend into all tort cases in which Convention rights may be involved.

Revision tip

A number of examples of cases with significant human rights implications can be found in Chapter 14, 'Defamation' and Chapter 15, 'Privacy'.

The influence of insurance

The vast majority of **tort** actions (approximately 94%) are based upon insurance, for the simple reason that it is only the insured defendant who is likely to be able to pay compensation should he be held liable. While the cases studied appear to be between individuals, in reality they are usually brought against the wrongdoer's insurer and are often brought by the claimant's insurer. One policy concern for judges is the potential impact which a decision might have on the insurance industry in the future.

Two areas of liability are noted for their statutory requirements of compulsory insurance. Employers are required by the **Employers' Liability (Compulsory Insurance) Act 1969** to hold liability cover for their employees and the **Road Traffic Act 1988** requires motorists to be insured for damage to third parties. It is, then, no surprise to hear that the **Pearson Commission** (which reported on the tort system in 1978) discovered that 47% of all tort claims concerned employers' liability and another 41% were for motor accidents.

Judges have not agreed on the extent to which the reality of insurance should be taken into account in determining tort liability. The traditional view is represented by Viscount Simonds in *Davie v New Merton Board Mills Ltd* (1959):

> It is not the function of a court of law to fasten upon the fortuitous circumstance of insurance to impose a greater burden on the employer than would otherwise lie upon him.

However, in the same way that judges have become more open about discussing the policy behind their decisions, they have also begun to cite, and at times to justify, their decisions at least partly upon insurance considerations. In *Smith v Eric S Bush* (1990), Lord Griffiths put it this way:

> There was once a time when it was considered improper even to mention the possible existence of insurance cover in a lawsuit. But those days are long past. Everyone knows that all prudent, professional men carry insurance, and the availability and cost of insurance must be a relevant factor when considering which of two parties should be required to bear the risk of a loss.

Lord Griffiths was reflecting an awareness that one of the functions of **tort** is to *spread the cost of losses* efficiently. It is about more than simple blameworthiness.

The aims of the law of tort

The main objective of **tort** law is *compensation*, ie putting the claimant back into the position he would have been in, had the tort not occurred.

Tort also has two secondary objectives:

1. **Deterrence**—Awareness of possible tort liability may lead to more care being exercised and generally raise standards in a particular field, thereby preventing future loss. Insurance and punitive damages exercise opposing influences upon this objective.

2. **Justice**—Recognition that a wrong has taken place, and that this must be acknowledged and righted. This is particularly relevant to torts that are actionable without proof of damage. For example, in an action on false imprisonment the claimant may not be entitled to significant compensation but instead require recognition of the breach of his right to liberty.

Alternative routes to compensation

The process of claiming under the **tort** system has been likened to an 'obstacle race' which is slow, uncertain, and expensive. Lord Woolf's *Access to Justice*, in 1996, reported that for tort claims under £12,500, for every £1 claimed there was a cost of £1.35.

There are, of course, other ways that those who suffer **loss** due to different causes may be compensated.

No fault liability

In the case of many losses, either it is too difficult or impossible to prove **fault** or there is actually no-one to blame. The adoption of no fault liability was considered by the **Pearson Commission** but its limited recommendations in this area have not been implemented. New Zealand did implement a wide-ranging no fault scheme in 1974, which has been modified and restricted in recent years.

Social security

In our 'mixed system', social security benefits provide a significant and inexpensive form of protection for those in need which can be an alternative or a supplement to the tort system. Although the levels of payment will not be as generous as the high end of tort payments, they are largely granted as of right. Included is the Industrial Injuries Scheme.

Charity

Before the late 19th century, voluntary help provided by the church, community and individuals was the main source of support for the injured and bereaved. In modern times, we have seen the re-emergence of such efforts, particularly in relation to disasters such as the Ladbroke Grove rail crash and the London bombings.

'First party insurance'

Many losses suffered will be covered by 'first party' (or personal) insurance, taken out for his own benefit by the person who suffers the **loss**.

The Motor Insurers' Bureau

Established by the insurance industry, it provides compensation for those who suffer personal injury or property damage at the hands of uninsured or untraceable drivers.

Ex gratia or single issue compensation schemes

Occasionally situations occur involving widespread **loss** or **injury**, in which the government takes on the role of compensating its victims. Currently, such schemes apply to vaccine damage sustained by children and for those who have contracted Hepatitis C and the HIV virus from the NHS supply of contaminated blood products.

The Criminal Injuries Compensation Authority (CICA)

The Authority administers the statutory scheme, established in 1964, providing compensation for those who suffer **loss** due to violent crime. It is not necessary that the perpetrator be convicted, or even identified.

'A compensation culture'?

In the last several decades, there has been a perception that the British have become increasingly prone to resort to litigation following an adverse event. Despite the fact that research produced ambiguous results into how real this 'problem' is, the government felt that it was necessary to address it. The availability of legal aid has been progressively reduced; however, this has been replaced by the **conditional fee agreement** (CFA), sometimes known as 'no-win, no-fee'. The operation of CFAs has been investigated by the 'Review of Civil Litigation Costs' ('Jackson Review'—2010).

The **Legal Aid, Sentencing and Punishment of Offenders Act 2012** sets out to implement the recommendations of the Jackson Review in order to streamline civil justice litigation through reforms in procedure and costs.

Compensation Act 2006

Concern about the 'compensation culture' is reflected in the **Compensation Act 2006**, which, in addition to s 1, also deals with regulation of claims managers and asbestos-related **damages** actions.

Section 1 is a reminder to judges to consider carefully the impact that decisions about **negligence** liability might have in potentially deterring the pursuit of certain types of socially beneficial activities. There is a deterrent effect of potential liability:

The Compensation Act 2006, s 1

A court considering a claim in **negligence** or breach of statutory duty may, in determining whether the defendant should have taken particular steps to meet a standard of care (whether by taking precautions against a risk or otherwise), have regard to whether a requirement to take those steps might:

- prevent a desirable activity from being undertaken at all, to a particular extent, or in a particular way, or
- discourage persons from undertaking functions in connection with a desirable activity.

Although the Act has not often been cited in practice, the attitudes behind it can be seen in cases such as *Cole v Davis-Gilbert* (2007).

Cole v Davis-Gilbert [2007] EWCA Civ 396

Here, the claimant injured her ankle when she stepped into a hole left on the village green by a maypole. In holding that there had been no breach of duty, the Court of Appeal said that 'accidents happen'. A different outcome would threaten the future of fêtes and other village activities.

See further, *The Scout Association v Barnes* (2010), discussed in Chapter 13.

In 2010, the government commissioned a review of health and safety and the compensation culture entitled: 'Common Sense, Common Safety'. The aim was to explore ways of reversing some of the bureaucratic hindrances to activities, such as school trips, resulting from undue fears about tort litigation. www.cabinetoffice.gov.uk/sites/default/files/resources/402906_CommonSense_acc.pdf.

✅ *Looking for extra marks?*

In addition to 'Common Sense, Common Safety', you may wish to consult either the government's Better Regulation Task Force's *Better Routes to Redress*, a 2004 publication on research into the reality of the so-called 'compensation culture', or the House of Commons Constitutional Affairs Select Committee report of 2005–06, which preceded the 2006 Act.

ⓘ Conclusion

Studying the law of **tort** requires the honing of skills in accurately applying both case law and, to a lesser extent, statute law. Trends in the development of tort law will be best understood having assimilated the effects of policy and, more recently, human rights law.

Revision tip

The diversity of the law of **tort** may tempt some students to 'question-spot' or 'topic-spot', for instance focusing on one tort, such as **negligence**, to the exclusion of another, such as **nuisance**. This would be a mistake, however, because these torts overlap and interlink and good answers to exam questions must reflect this.

🔟 Key debates

Topic:	'Human Rights and Civil Wrongs: Tort Law under the Spotlight'
Author:	Lady Justice Arden
Viewpoint:	The speech reviews the impact of the **ECHR** on domestic tort law. It concludes that its impact has been variable, and that judges have had considerable discretion over which areas would be influenced by Convention rights and which would not.
Source:	The Hailsham Lecture 2009 www.judiciary.gov.uk/media/speeches/2009/speech-arden-lj-12052009
Topic:	'Insurance and the Tort System'
Author:	R. Lewis
Viewpoint:	Describes the importance of insurance for the **tort** system, and concludes that it is difficult to ascertain a specific impact of the doctrine of tort law itself.
Source:	(2005) 25 LS 85

Exam questions

✳✳✳✳✳✳✳✳✳✳✳

Topic:	'Spiralling or Stabilising? The Compensation Culture and Our Propensity to Claim Damages for Personal Injury'
Author:	A. Morris
Viewpoint:	Analyses the different factors which have contributed to the perception of the 'compensation culture', with particular focus on the role of the media.
Source:	(2007) 70 MLR 349

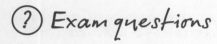 Exam questions

Essay questions

1. 'The objectives of the law of tort are unique.'

   Discuss.

   See the Outline Answers section in the end matter for help with this question.

2. Consider the extent to which alternative systems of compensation are preferable to the tort system.

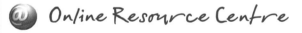 Online Resource Centre

To see an outline answer to this question visit www.oup.com/lawrevision/

#2
Negligence: duty of care

Key facts

- Duty is the first element in the 'negligence equation' and the primary means of limiting liability in negligence. (See Figure 2.1.)

- The first general principle for finding duty of care was the 'neighbour principle' of **Donoghue v Stevenson** (1932).

- Currently the three criteria for determination of duty of care in novel situations are: foreseeability; proximity; and fairness, justice and reasonableness. This is the 'three-stage' test set out in **Caparo v Dickman** (1990).

- Duty of care has a strong policy component.

- Duty must be established first in principle and then in respect of the particular claimant in question.

- There are limited duties of care in respect of defendants who are public bodies; also in respect of omissions.

- Duty of care may be problematic when the damage is pure economic loss or psychiatric injury.

Assessment

Figure 2.1 Negligence equation

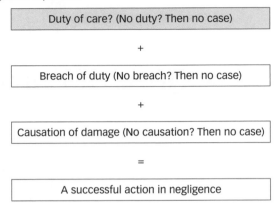

Duty of care? (No duty? Then no case)

+

Breach of duty (No breach? Then no case)

+

Causation of damage (No causation? Then no case)

=

A successful action in negligence

Assessment

The issue of duty may be disputed in some problem questions (where the claim is 'novel') but unproblematic in others. It is a popular subject for essay questions, which may ask you to trace the development of the case law leading to the present approaches to determining when **duty of care** is held to exist. The essay question may, on the other hand, ask you to discuss the influence of judicial policy-making in this area.

Introduction to the tort of negligence

Negligence is usually the largest subject in any **tort** course and is a relatively new tort. It began to develop substantially in the early 19th century when liability for careless acts was founded upon 'a duty to take care' owed by the defendant to the plaintiff. The early cases concerned personal injury and death and damage to property, with these still forming the most readily recognized type of damage in negligence.

The 'duty to take care' was originally linked to contractual relationships, but throughout the 19th century its reach widened. On a case-by-case basis duty was found to exist owing to the relationship between the parties, for example that of employer and employee. Attempts such as that in *Heaven v Pender* (1883), to set out a more general concept of duty had failed, until the iconic case of *Donoghue v Stevenson* in 1932.

↳starting point.

Donoghue v Stevenson [1932] AC 562 ✗

FACTS: Mrs Donoghue drank from a bottle of ginger beer, purchased for her by a friend at a seaside café. When she poured the remainder from the opaque bottle into her glass she was shocked to see that it had contained a decomposed snail, which allegedly caused her to become sick. As there was

> no contractual relationship between Mrs Donoghue and the beer manufacturer, her only possibility for compensation lay in the **tort** of **negligence**.
>
> **HELD:** The House of Lords concluded that the defendant manufacturer had been under a **duty of care** not to cause her **injury**.

This decision included the **neighbour principle**, as prescribed by Lord Atkin, which must be considered in full:

> The [Biblical] rule that you are to love your neighbour becomes in law, you must not injure your neighbour; and the lawyer's question, 'Who is my neighbour?' receives a restricted reply. You must take reasonable care to avoid acts or omissions which you can reasonably foresee would be likely to injure your neighbour. Who then, in law, is my neighbour? The answer seems to be—persons who are so closely and directly affected by my act that I ought reasonably to have them in contemplation as being so affected when I am directing my mind to the acts and omissions which are called into question.

Duty of care can be broken down into *two questions*: the first one being general and determined as a matter of law and policy; followed by the second one, which is specific and fact-based:

1. Is this a case of the *type* to which the law of **negligence** is applicable?

If so:

2. Was it foreseeable that *this* claimant would be harmed by the defendant's act?

Question 1: the neighbour principle

The **'neighbour principle'**, with its requirements for **foreseeability** and **proximity**, provides the answer to the first question and forms the basis of the finding of **duty of care**—the first step in every case of **negligence**. Duty of care can be said to serve the function of *controlling* the reach of the law of negligence—without it the potential for liability would be virtually unlimited.

Revision tip

Remember that the *type* of damage suffered can be an important factor in determining **duty of care**. The most acceptable types are personal injury and death and property damage. When the damage is only **pure economic loss** (such as loss of profit) or psychiatric injury, duty will be more difficult to establish. These types of damage are dealt with in Chapters 4 and 5 respectively.

Developments in the duty of care

Following *Donoghue v Stevenson*, the courts, in a number of key cases, used and adapted the concept of **duty of care** in ways which at first expanded and later contracted the **tort** of **negligence**.

Developments in the duty of care

✳✳✳✳✳✳✳✳✳✳✳

> ### Home Office v Dorset Yacht Co [1970] AC 1004 🐟
>
> **FACTS:** The boys escaped from a weekend outing and damaged the plaintiff's yacht. The question was whether a **duty of care** was owed by the prison authorities in respect of the actions of youth offenders in custody.
>
> **HELD:** The House of Lords held by a majority of four to one that there was a duty of care owed by the Home Office to the plaintiff. It was recognized that in so doing, it was extending the *Donoghue v Stevenson* **neighbour principle** into circumstances which were novel for two reasons. First, because the wrong against the plaintiff had not been committed directly by the defendant (or his employees) but rather by a third party, the boys. Any liability of the defendant would then be based upon an *omission*—that is, his failure to control the actions of the boys. Second, the defendant was a public body and thereby subject to statutory and resource constraints.

In *Anns v Merton LBC* (1978) Lord Wilberforce set out what has been described as a 'two-stage' test by which **duty of care** was to be determined.

1. First one must ask, 'whether, as between the alleged wrongdoer and the person who has suffered damage there is a sufficient relationship of **proximity** or neighbourhood such that, in the reasonable contemplation of the former, carelessness on his part may be likely to cause damage to the latter—in which case a *prima facie* duty of care arises'.

2. If so, 'are there are any considerations which ought to negative, reduce or limit the scope of the duty in the circumstances?'

Compare The *Anns* test appeared to diverge from that of *Donoghue v Stevenson*. Here, the concept of **proximity** in the first stage was treated as having been effectively established wherever there was **foreseeability** of damage, rather than being treated as a factor to be established in its own right. Also, despite the potentially limiting nature of the policy considerations in the second stage, a *prima facie* **duty of care** appeared to indicate almost a presumption of duty, which was felt to over-extend the reach of **negligence** liability.

> ### ✅ Looking for extra marks?
> You may wish to consider *Junior Books v Veitchi* (1983), possibly the high-water mark of **negligence** liability. It has not been overruled, but has not been followed and must now be regarded as confined to its own facts.

Policy

Compare In the second question suggested by Lord Wilberforce in *Anns*, the 'considerations' which may contradict the earlier presumption of duty can be described as *policy*. We can define policy as the non-legal effects of a decision; for instance, the ethical, economic or social implications of the finding of a **duty of care**. One of the most frequently invoked policy issues is whether a decision in favour of a duty of care would lead to a large increase in litigation, perhaps to an unmanageable extent. In shorthand this is often referred to as the 'floodgates' problem. Policy may also include reference to alternative options available to the client for obtaining redress.

The question of whether a duty of care should be owed by a barrister to his client for the conduct of a court case provides a good illustration of the effect of policy upon judicial decision-making. In the 1969 case of *Rondel v Worsley* the House of Lords held that no such duty existed between barrister and client. Its reasoning for this view was based upon the following policy factors:

- the advocate's overriding duty lies not to his client but to the court;
- to permit actions in **negligence** might result in the effective retrial of a number of cases, with a consequential impact on confidence in the administration of justice;
- there is a 'cab-rank rule' whereby the barrister is not at liberty to pick and choose which cases are accepted; and
- the advocate must exercise his skill with complete independence, rather than in fear of a negligence claim.

Thirty years later the House of Lords had the opportunity to reconsider the position in *Arthur JS Hall v Simons* (2000). This time, the consensus on the matter was different. The Law Lords reflected on the changes over the years in both professional culture and public attitudes and concluded that the effective immunity enjoyed by barristers from **negligence** liability for the conduct of a court case could no longer be justified. There was now a greater public expectation of legal redress for carelessness in professional situations and this was said to outweigh the policy considerations described in *Rondel*.

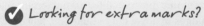

✔ Looking for extra marks?

Legal commentators differ on whether **proximity** is a factual determination or is rather more concerned with issues of policy. To learn more of the latter view you may wish to read P. Cane, 'Another Failed Sterilisation' (2004) 120 LQR 189.

The narrowing of duty/negligence

In the period between 1985 and 1991 the courts in a number of cases indicated that the problematic *Anns* 'two-stage' test should be applied restrictively in order that the **duty of care** not be too extensive. For instance, in *Yuen Kun Yeu v Attorney General of Hong Kong* (1988), a case which dealt with purely economic loss, Lord Keith in the Privy Council observed, 'that for the future it should be recognized that the two-stage test in *Anns* is not to be regarded as in all the circumstances a suitable guide to the existence of a duty of care'.

Developments in the duty of care

✱✱✱✱✱✱✱✱✱✱✱

Hill v Chief Constable of West Yorkshire [1989] AC 53

FACTS: It was claimed that the **negligence** of the police caused the death of Jacqueline Hill, the last victim of the 'Yorkshire Ripper', Peter Sutcliffe.

HELD: Applying the *Anns* test, the House of Lords held that no **duty of care** had been owed to her. Although death as a type of damage was foreseeable there was not sufficient **proximity** between the police and Miss Hill. She was no more identifiable as a potential victim than any other young woman in a wide geographical area.

Additionally there were a number of policy arguments indicating that the police, in their role of investigation and prosecution of crime, should not be under a duty of care to potential victims. Among these were the potential detrimental effects of 'defensive policing' and the existence of preferable mechanisms for monitoring the efficiency of the police.

You will see in Chapter 3 that *Hill* is also an example of a case involving an omission and liability of public bodies; and also that this apparent immunity acquired by the police came to be questioned in the context of human rights law.

Lord Macmillan, in *Donoghue v Stevenson*, said: 'The categories of negligence are never closed.' When no comparable category exists, it can be said that the possible duty situation is a novel one.

The current test for **duty of care** in a novel situation was laid down by Lord Bridge in the case of *Caparo v Dickman* (1990). According to Lord Bridge three criteria must be satisfied before a duty can be found:

1. the damage must be *foreseeable*, and
2. there must be *proximity* of relationship between the parties, and
3. it must be *'fair, just and reasonable'* for such a duty to exist. This third element is the one in which *policy* comes to be considered.

This test is more difficult for the claimant to satisfy than that in *Anns* and you will note that, here, **proximity** is separated from **foreseeability**. It remains questionable to what extent the three-stage test provides dependable assistance to judges in novel duty situations, however.

According to Lord Bingham in *Customs & Excise Commissioners v Barclays Bank* (2007), 'the three-fold test itself provides no straightforward answer to the vexed question whether or not, in a novel situation, a party owes a duty of care'.

Marc Rich & Co v Bishop Rock Marine Co Ltd ('The Nicholas H') [1996] AC 211

FACTS: This case demonstrates the application of Lord Bridge's three-stage test. The defendant was a marine classification society, whose function was to determine the seaworthiness of ships. One such ship had been certified by the defendant but soon sank, with the **loss** of the plaintiff's cargo.

HELD: When the House of Lords applied the three-stage test it concluded that there had been no **duty of care**. Although there had been **proximity** of the parties and **foreseeability** of the

---

damage, ɩ ᴥ e requirement that a duty be fair, just and reasonable had not been met. The risk between the parties had been governed by the rules of international shipping law and the introduction of a common law duty of care could not be permitted to override these.

In *Caparo* Lord Bridge endorsed an *incremental* approach to determining duty of care, according to which each case should be considered on the basis of analogy with earlier comparable categories of duty. See *Smith v Ministry of Defence* (2013) in which the Supreme Court upheld lower courts' refusal to strike out claims which raised the prospect that a duty of care could be owed to soldiers when being trained and equipped for combat.

Revision tip

You may find it helpful to revise the history of the differently phrased judicial tests for **duty of care**, beginning with *Donoghue v Stevenson* and to learn the key cases which illustrate the expansion and contraction of the law of **negligence**. As you do this, the significance of the underlying policy objectives may become apparent.

Question 2: duty to *this* claimant?

Having established in the answer to Question 1 that the case is one of the *type* in which a **duty of care** can be imposed, the second question which must be answered is fact-specific: was it foreseeable that *this* claimant would be harmed by the defendant's act? It is necessary to consider this because a duty to one party does not necessarily entail a duty to all—otherwise **tort** liability could potentially be unlimited. At this stage, the characteristics of the particular claimant are more important than those of the defendant.

Palsgraf v Long Island Railroad (1928) 162 NE 99

FACTS: The American case of *Palsgraf v Long Island Railroad* (1928) provides an early example of the unforeseeable claimant. The defendant's employee, a porter, was assisting a passenger who was boarding a train. He jostled a package which the passenger dropped. Unfortunately the package contained fireworks, which exploded causing weighing scales to fall onto the plaintiff, who was some distance down the platform.

HELD: Her **negligence** action against the railroad failed because, although the defendant owed a **duty of care** to the nearby passengers regarding their person and property, it was unforeseeable that the plaintiff was at risk and therefore no duty was owed to her. This was because of the combination of the factors of her distance from the porter and the absence of any indication that the package contained explosives.

Bourhill v Young (1943), the facts of which are considered in Chapter 5, provides another illustration of the requirement of **foreseeability** of the particular plaintiff in question. The House of Lords concluded, 'duty is not to the world at large'.

Conclusion

Foreseeability of risk to the plaintiff, or a plaintiff of his type, was required in *Haley v London Electricity Board* (1965):

Haley v London Electricity Board [1965] AC 778

FACTS: A blind pedestrian fell on a tool which had been left guarding a trench in which the defendant was working. The barrier would have been obvious to a sighted person but the plaintiff's white stick did not detect it and he fell over it. His injuries left him almost completely deaf.

HELD: The House of Lords heard evidence about the numbers of blind people living in London and concluded that a member of that class should have been within the reasonable foresight of the defendant in considering obstacles on the pavement.

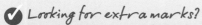 **Looking for extra marks?**

The question of whether a duty was owed to the particular claimant in question is closely related to that of remoteness. You will see in Chapter 5 that a question such as that considered by the court in *Palsgraf* in terms of **duty of care** could be looked at instead as a question of **causation**, ie by asking whether damage of *this kind* was reasonably foreseeable at the time of the defendant's **negligence**.

The striking out application

Duty of care is an aspect of **negligence** which is relatively rarely the subject of litigation. When it is contested, however, the role of duty of care as a control mechanism means that cases will often reach the Court of Appeal or Supreme Court (previously the House of Lords), where the policy aspects of the determination will be discussed. In many such cases, the defendant will bring a **striking out action**. This rule of civil procedure allows the defendant to argue that there are no reasonable grounds for the claimant's case; here, essentially that the defendant owes no duty of care to the claimant. The merits of the case are not adjudicated upon at this stage.

 **Conclusion**

Duty of care will be undisputed in a great number of **negligence** cases, but no case can proceed unless there is a duty of care. The current test for duty, in novel situations, is the three-stage test from *Caparo v Dickman*. Unfortunately, for both law students and judges, the test is not always easy to apply and can lead to more questions than answers.

Revision tip

When approaching **duty of care** questions it will be helpful to you to keep in mind the incremental approach favoured in *Caparo*, by which novel situations are first compared to previously existing categories of duty. To assist in this, you should remember that **negligence** situations can be categorized into those in which there tends to be a duty owed, for instance in motoring, and those in which it is less likely, for instance with some public bodies, further considered in Chapter 3.

 Key cases

Case	Facts	Principle
Anns v Merton LBC [1978] AC 728 *2 stage Test.*	A local authority was held liable for its failure to prevent the construction of a building which later cracked, causing economic loss to the plaintiffs.	The test for duty of care was restated by Lord Wilberforce in terms which created a strong presumption in favour of finding a duty. The two-stage test required establishing (1) 'proximity or neighbourhood' (founded upon foreseeability) plus (2) the absence of any policy considerations which would negative the finding of a duty. This expansive test is no longer in use: see *Caparo*.
Caparo v Dickman [1990] 2 AC 605 *Caparo Test*	In a negligence action against a firm of auditors for financial loss suffered due to the negligent compilation of company accounts, it was held that the defendant did not owe a duty of care to the investors.	Lord Bridge established the three-stage test for duty of care in novel situations, requiring (1) foreseeable damage, (2) proximity between the parties, and (3) that the existence of a duty would be 'fair, just and reasonable'. This is the current approach.
Customs and Excise Commissioners v Barclays Bank [2007] 1 AC 181	Customs and Excise had obtained 'freezing orders' on the bank accounts of two companies. The defendants had negligently contravened these orders and allowed funds to be withdrawn from the accounts.	The House of Lords held that the 'three-stage test' was insufficient in this factual situation and 'assumption of responsibility' had also to be considered. The order against the defendants had been compulsory and so they could in no way be said to have voluntarily assumed responsibility. No duty of care in negligence could be attributed.
Donoghue v Stevenson [1932] AC 562	Mrs Donoghue sued the manufacturers of ginger beer for damage she suffered when a snail was found in her bottle. It was held that the defendant had owed her a duty of care according to Lord Atkin's 'neighbour principle'.	The 'neighbour principle', based upon foreseeability, was the first general principle for determining duty of care in negligence. The so-called 'narrow ratio' from *Donoghue* established the liability of manufacturers to those injured by their products.
Haley v London Electricity Board [1965] AC 778	A blind pedestrian was injured when he fell on an obstacle which would not have posed a danger to those who could see. A duty of care had been owed to him.	The court considered statistics on the frequency of blind pedestrians and concluded that they were common enough that they should have been within the contemplation of the defendant. *Haley* illustrates that the duty must be owed to *this claimant*.

Key debates

*********** *

Case	Facts	Principle
Hill v Chief Constable of West Yorkshire [1989] AC 53	It was claimed on behalf of a victim of a serial killer that the police had owed her a duty of care and that their failure to conduct criminal investigations adequately had been the cause of her death. The House of Lords held that no such duty existed.	The foundation for this decision lay in the application of the *Anns* two-stage test. The plaintiff in *Hill* failed both owing to the absence of proximity between the defendant and the deceased victim but also due to a number of persuasive policy reasons.
Home Office v Dorset Yacht Co [1970] AC 1004	A group of young offenders on an outing escaped and caused damage to the plaintiff's yacht. It was held that the Home Office, whose employees should have been controlling the youths, owed a duty of care to the plaintiff.	The 'neighbour principle' was applied to extend duty of care to create liability for damage caused, not directly, but by a third party over whom the defendant had been expected to exercise control.
Marc Rich & Co v Bishop Rock Marine Co [1996] AC 211	A marine classification society certified as seaworthy a ship which later sank. There was held to be no duty of care owed to the owners of lost cargo.	The three-stage test from *Caparo* was applied. The House of Lords was satisfied that foreseeability and proximity existed but that it would not be fair, just and reasonable for the classification society to owe a duty of care.

(99) Key debates

Topic:	'Many Duties of Care—Or a Duty of Care? Notes from the Underground'
Author:	D. Howarth
Viewpoint:	Analyses **duty of care** in terms of political theory and concludes that the concept of 'one duty' is most conducive to simplicity and rational development of **negligence**.
Source:	(2006) 26 OJLS 449

Topic:	'On the Function of the Law of Negligence'
Author:	A. Robertson
Viewpoint:	Analyses the role of **policy** and the availability of alternative remedies in judicial decisions on **duty of care**.
Source:	(2013) 33 OJLS 31

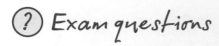 Exam questions

Essay questions

1. Why, and by what means, does the law of negligence prevent what Judge Cardozo described as 'liability in an indeterminate amount for an indeterminate time to an indeterminate class'?

   See the Outline Answers section in the end matter for help with this question.

2. Discuss the role of policy as reflected in the development of judicial tests for the existence of a duty of care.

 Online Resource Centre

To see an outline answer to this question visit www.oup.com/lawrevision/

#3
Duty of care: further issues

- There are a number of areas in which the existence of a duty of care is problematic. This chapter must be studied in conjunction with Chapter 2, and with Chapters 4 and 5, which concern cases where the type of damage suffered causes problems in determining duty of care.

- In the case of omissions, that is, when damage has resulted from the defendant's lack of action, rather than directly from a positive act, duty of care is often absent.

- When the defendant is a public body, policy may make it undesirable to impose a duty of care.

- An interesting case study of contested duty of care arises in relation to the conduct of the police in relation specifically to prevention and investigation of crime.

- The action in respect of damage done to an unborn child is regulated by both statute and the common law.

Assessment

Examiners may introduce the more problematic aspects of **duty of care** in either problem or essay questions. In a problem question, this is likely to be one component of a more wide-ranging **negligence** scenario. Possible essay questions may focus on the nature of omission or on policy issues around liability of public bodies.

Omissions

In English law there is generally no duty to perform an action to help someone or to prevent his **injury**. An illustration is often given in terms of the possible rescue of a non-swimmer struggling in the water. The general position is that **tort** law would impose no liability on someone who had the means to rescue a drowning person but chose not to do so.

There are a number of reasons behind the restriction of **duty of care** in the case of omissions:

- the heavy burden which would be placed on individuals by the general expectation that they be on guard for dangers to others,
- the indeterminacy of such a duty in terms of application and extent (or as Lord Hoffmann in *Stovin v Wise* (**1996**) put it, 'why pick on me?'), and
- economic inefficiency.

Before going on to review case law in this area and the very important exceptions to the above rule, it is necessary to recall what is meant by an omission in law. For example, in the medical context, the failure properly to examine a patient may in one sense consist in *not* doing something. However, this is not regarded as an omission but instead a careless way of treating patients.

Revision tip

We are often, here, looking at a defendant's failure to protect the claimant from a risk of harm caused by a third party or by himself. You may be assisted in this suggestion by Lunney and Oliphant: omission can be thought of as the difference between 'making things worse' (which may bring liability) and 'failing to make things better' (which usually does not).

Smith v Littlewoods [1987] 1 AC 241

FACTS: The defendant owned a disused cinema, which people began to enter and in which, several times, unknown to the defendant, they attempted to start fires, one of which spread and damaged adjoining properties.

Liability for omissions

✳✳✳✳✳✳✳✳✳✳

> **HELD:** The owners of those properties failed in their action against the defendant in **negligence** for his omission to secure the premises adequately. The reasoning in the House of Lords was based upon lack of duty, according to Lord Goff; while the others in the majority based their conclusion on lack of breach of duty.

In *Stovin v Wise* (1996) the cause of the danger to road users was a projecting bank of earth which, combined with negligent driving, resulted in a crash. A county council was sued for its failure, or omission, to enforce removal of the projection, of which it was aware. The fact that the council's wrong was an omission was the major factor, combined with the fact that the defendant was a public body (discussed later), in concluding that there should be a presumption against a **duty of care** in such cases.

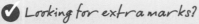

✅ *Looking for extra marks?*

The judgments in both *Smith* and *Stovin* referred to the need for 'something more' than **foreseeability** and **proximity** before there would be a **duty of care** regarding an omission. In *Stansbie v Troman* (1948), a decorator specifically undertook to the householder that he would lock the house when he left. He was held liable for the burglary which resulted when he neglected to do so.

Liability for omissions

It is suggested that you read the speech of Lord Goff in <u>*Smith v Littlewoods* (1987)</u>, where he set out exceptional situations in which there can be held to be a **duty of care** in respect of an omission.

- There is a <u>relationship between the parties which creates</u> an **<u>assumption of responsibility</u>** <u>on behalf of the defendant</u> <u>for the safety of the claimant.</u>
- There is a relationship of control between the defendant and a third party who causes damage.
- The defendant creates or permits a source of danger to be created, which is interfered with by third parties.
- There is a failure of a defendant to remove a source of danger of which he is aware; but note in *Stovin* the reluctance to impose a duty on a public body operating statutory powers.

Illustrations are as follows:

Relationships creating an assumption of responsibility

> **Barrett v Ministry of Defence [1995] 3 All ER 87**
>
> **FACTS:** This action arose in a Navy base where there was a culture of drinking and where the plaintiff's husband collapsed while drunk. The duty officer arranged for him to be taken to his room where he was left unsupervised and later died owing to choking on his own vomit.
>
> **HELD:** The Ministry of Defence was not held to be under a general responsibility to prevent its employees from excessive drinking; however, when the deceased had fallen ill, a relationship of care had been undertaken leading to a duty.

In *Mitchell v Glasgow City Council* (2009) the House of Lords did not find any **assumption of responsibility** by a local authority housing department to warn one of its tenants that they were aware of threats of violence to him by a fellow tenant. It was significant that the defendant here was a public body, upon whom the House of Lords felt it would not be '*fair, just and reasonable*' to place such a heavy burden.

See *Biddick (deceased) v Morcam* [2014] EWCA Civ 182 where B, a homeowner, was held to have assumed a duty of care to M, a contractor working in his loft, despite the fact that M had not actually been relied on by B.

> ✅ *Looking for extra marks?*
>
> You may wish to explore the reasoning behind two contrasting 'omissions cases' of *Capital and Counties plc v Hampshire CC* (1997) and *Kent v Griffiths* (2001). In the first case there was held to be no **duty of care** upon a fire service which failed adequately to respond to a fire, but in the second it was held that a duty was assumed by the ambulance service when it responded to a 999 call.

Existing relationship with wrongdoer involving control

> **Carmarthenshire County Council v Lewis [1955] AC 549**
>
> **FACTS:** A young child ran from his nursery school premises onto the busy road nearby. The plaintiff's husband swerved his car to avoid the child and was killed when he hit a tree.
>
> **HELD:** The defendant council and the teachers at the school were held to have been jointly in control of the children and therefore under a duty to take reasonable steps to prevent them becoming a danger to others.

> *Revision tip*
>
> You will recall the case of *Home Office v Dorset Yacht* (1970), which provides another illustration of this exception. Here, failure adequately to exercise control in the custodial relationship led to liability by the prison authorities for the vandalism created by the Borstal boys.

Creation of or failure to remove a danger which may then be involved in actions by third parties

We have seen that in *Smith v Littlewoods* (1987) the House of Lords concluded that the defendant could not be held liable for negligently failing to 'abate a fire risk created by third parties on their property without their fault', due in part to the lack of reasonable **foreseeability** of these vagrants and their actions.

In *Goldman v Hargrave* (1966), a **nuisance** case, the details of which are covered in Chapter 12, it was suggested that liability might lie in **negligence** for failure to extinguish a fire caused by lightning.

It would seem, however, that the courts are often reluctant to impose liability.

Topp v London Country Bus Ltd [1993] 1 WLR 976

FACTS: A driver left his bus, along with the ignition keys, in a lay-by near to a pub for a relief driver who never arrived. Later, the bus was stolen and, while being driven by the thief, hit and killed the plaintiff's wife.

HELD: The Court of Appeal held that no **duty of care** arose. The theft was not a foreseeable result of the defendant's **negligence**. **Proximity** between the bus company and the deceased was doubtful and, in any case, it would not be fair, just and reasonable to impose a duty. It would appear that it was crucial to the decision that the defendant had not been aware of the nature of the clientele of the pub!

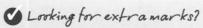 *Looking for extra marks?*

In order to distinguish between *Goldman* and *Topp*, it may be helpful to think about the distinction between the natural hazard of a lightning strike and the deliberate criminal act of a third party.

Public bodies as defendants

Negligence actions against public bodies, such as organs of government, schools, and the police, have in the past raised difficulties around the issue of **duty of care**. They are often operating under statutory or resource restrictions and case authority indicates that policy often has a significant impact here. The **Human Rights Act 1998** is also likely to be part of the decision-making process. You should also be aware that this type of liability often involves an omission on the part of the defendant, as in the case of *Stovin v Wise* (1996).

Judges have at times used public law concepts such as *ultra vires* to address the problem of **tort** liability of public bodies (see *Dorset Yacht*). Later, *Anns v Merton LBC* (1978) saw the adoption of the policy/operational distinction, with only the former being seen as '**justiciable**', that is open to judicial decision-making. Case law illustrates that it is not always easy to place activities into one category or the other.

X v Bedfordshire CC [1995] 2 AC 633

FACTS: The considerations behind the absence of duty in many such cases is illustrated by where a **negligence** action was brought against a local authority social services department by the plaintiffs who claimed to have suffered damage due to a negligent failure to remove them, when children, from their abusive parents.

HELD: The House of Lords held that, despite the fact that this decision-making process was **justiciable**, a **duty of care** would not be fair, just and reasonable.

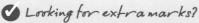 ✅ Looking for extra marks?

You should be aware that when this case was appealed to the European Court of Human Rights (ECtHR) in *Z v United Kingdom* (2001) judgment was given in favour of the claimants. The UK was held neither to have protected the children from inhuman or degrading treatment (a breach of **art 3 European Convention on Human Rights (ECHR)**) nor to have given them an effective legal **remedy** for this failure (a breach of **art 13 ECHR**).

Although there remains a degree of unpredictability about when courts will impose liability on public authorities, there appears to be a growing sympathy with claimants against education authorities.

Phelps v Hillingdon LBC [2001] 2 AC 619

The House of Lords heard a group of conjoined cases brought against local authority education departments for failures to diagnose and treat learning difficulties. It refused to strike out the claims on the basis of lack of duty, explaining that the policy reasoning in the *Bedfordshire* case did not lay down any wider presumption of immunity.

Revision tip

It is important to note that just because an issue is held to be **justiciable** and some types of duty are recognized, this does not mean that the public body will owe a **duty of care** to all parties concerned.

See also *D v East Berkshire Community Health NHS Trust* (2005) and *Lawrence v Pembrokeshire CC* (2007).

Also, you should remember that just because there is duty, this does not mean that there will be liability. The possibility has been considered, for instance by Lord Nicholls in the *East Berkshire* case, that liability could be restricted through the regulation of standard of care rather than by duty, although this alternative approach has not been widely adopted.

✅ Looking for extra marks?

In *Connor v Surrey CC* (2010) the Court of Appeal had to decide the extent to which a common law **duty of care** (that of an employer to an employee) could be fulfilled by the performance of a public law statutory power. It concluded that this was possible in exceptional situations and held an education authority liable for negligently failing to prevent an employee suffering psychiatric injury.

Duty of care and the police

The question of the liability of the police in **negligence** must be divided into two duty categories: first, the 'operational' and second, that concerning crime control. Studying the second category will focus upon policy, drawing parallels with decisions made in respect of omissions and public bodies.

'Operational' liability

It is well established that the police will be held to owe a **duty of care** when they directly cause damage as a result of a positive act or (in some cases) an omission. For example, there is a clear duty of care upon a police driver in relation to the safety of pedestrians and other road users.

> **Rigby v Chief Constable of Northamptonshire [1985] 3 All ER 87**
>
> The police used flammable CS gas in an operation to flush a suspect out of a building. They were liable in **negligence** for damage caused by the resulting fire because they had failed to take the usual precaution of having fire-fighting equipment standing by.

See also *Knightley v Johns* (1982).

Crime control

However, the situation changes when the question is one of police liability for harm arising from the 'investigation and suppression' of crime. Here, the courts have been slow to impose duties of care and have used a range of different devices to justify this position.

The facts of *Hill v Chief Constable of West Yorkshire* (1989) were outlined in Chapter 2 ('The narrowing of duty/negligence', p 15). You will recall that the House of Lords held that no **duty of care** was owed by the police to prevent victimization by the Yorkshire Ripper. This outcome was based on the *Anns* two-stage test: first on the absence of **proximity** but second due to a number of policy factors detailed by Lord Keith. These included:

- the police's general sense of public duty would not be reinforced by **negligence** liability;
- potential liability could lead to 'defensive policing';
- conducting murder investigations is a complex task involving decisions, often resource-dependent, on 'matters of policy and discretion';
- defending negligence actions would be demanding of money, time, and manpower and divert the police from their main function;
- negligence actions would effectively reopen formerly closed cases; and
- internal or public inquiries are the more appropriate means of supervising the efficiency of the police.

The policy of *Hill* was applied in the defendant's favour in the extreme case of *Osman v Ferguson* (1993); however, in *Osman v United Kingdom* (1998), the ECtHR held that giving a blanket immunity to the police was contrary to the **art 6** right of access to the courts.

In *Swinney v Chief Constable of Northumbria Police* (1997), the Court of Appeal held that there were strong policy reasons for finding a duty. It is interesting to note that following the initial **striking out action**, the substantive case was tried in *Swinney v Chief Constable of Northumbria Police (No 2)* (1999). Here, the facts were examined and it was held that, apart from the duty issue, there would be no liability because there had been no breach of duty.

✅ *Looking for extra marks?*

Reading the speech of Lord Steyn in *Brooks v Commissioner of Police for the Metropolis* (2005) provides a helpful summary of the current state of the law regarding police liability in **negligence** in the field of crime control. He reasserted the 'core principle' in *Hill* and its policy justifications.

The decision in *Smith v Chief Constable of Sussex Police* (2008) further reinforced the lasting effect of *Hill* and *Brooks*. Along with *Smith* the House of Lords heard a joined appeal, *Van Colle v Chief Constable of Hertfordshire Police*. *Van Colle* illustrates the application of human rights law to this aspect of **negligence**.

The unborn child as claimant

The question of legal liability for damage suffered by a child before birth came to pressing public attention with the Thalidomide crisis in the 1960s. Following recommendations by the Law Commission, the **Congenital Disabilities (Civil Liability) Act 1976** was passed. It applies to damage, to a child born alive, caused by **negligence**:

- during the birth process, or
- during pregnancy, or
- prior to conception, and
- was amended by the **Human Fertilisation and Embryology Act 1990** to include damage incidental to fertility treatment.

Liability of the mother is not included unless related to her driving of a car. Also, defences which would have applied to the parents will apply to an action by the child.

A common law **duty of care** in such situations was confirmed by *Burton v Islington AHA* (1993), but because the Act applies to all live births since 1976, common law actions are now unlikely.

 ① *Conclusion*

The more problematic aspects of these **duty of care** situations, particularly those regarding liability for omissions and defendants who are public bodies, often overlap in a way that makes it difficult

Key cases

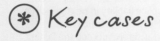

to predict what the outcome will be. You should learn the factors which the appeal courts have suggested should be taken into account, but most importantly, learn trends in the different 'species' of case law in this area: social services, education, police, highway authority, and emergency services. The influence of the ECtHR is growing and must always be considered. See, for instance, *AD v United Kingdom* (2010) where an **art 8** claim was successful in a childcare case with similarities to *D v East Berkshire Community Health NHS Trust*. In *Rabone v Pennine Care NHS Trust* (2012) the state's duty to take positive steps to protect life, an actionable right under **art 2**, was held to have been breached when a voluntary patient in a mental hospital committed suicide.

Key cases

Case	Facts	Principle
Brooks v Commissioner of Police for the Metropolis [2005] UKHL 24	A witness to the racially motivated murder of Stephen Lawrence, who was himself a victim, brought a negligence action against the police for the way they had behaved towards him.	Despite the fact that *Hill* could no longer be treated as having established a blanket immunity, its policy factors still led to the denial of a duty of care to this claimant.
Osman v Ferguson [1993] 4 All ER 344	Police failed to respond adequately to fears raised by a campaign of harassment against the plaintiff's family and murder resulted.	Despite proximity and foreseeability the *Hill* policy factors led to a finding of no duty of care. Note the contrary outcome of the case before the ECtHR.
Phelps v Hillingdon LBC [2001] 2 AC 619	A group of combined 'education cases' concerned with damage caused by failures to diagnose and provide for pupils' special needs gave rise to an arguable case for duty of care.	Despite recognizing the need for caution, the House of Lords did not find a strong enough policy reason to justify striking out these claims.
Smith v Littlewoods [1987] 1 AC 241	The defendant did not adequately protect his disused property. It was broken into by vandals who lit a fire which damaged neighbouring premises. The House of Lords held that there was no liability both for reasons of lack of duty and lack of breach.	Lord Goff set out the parameters of duty of care in cases where the defendant had failed to prevent his property facilitating a third party's tort.
Stovin v Wise [1996] AC 923	A local authority failed to remove a highway obstruction which later was involved in causing an accident.	There was no liability because the matter was within the discretion of the highway authority and, since the alleged wrong was an omission, 'something more' was required.

Case	Facts	Principle
Topp v London Country Bus Ltd [1993] 1 WLR 976	A bus driver negligently left the bus, with its keys, in a lay-by near a pub. A thief took the bus and caused an accident resulting in a death.	Applying the position of Lord Goff in *Smith*, it was held that, given the lack of foreseeability of the intervention by the thief and the lack of proximity with the victim, a duty of care would not be fair, just and reasonable.
Van Colle v Chief Constable of Hertfordshire Police [2008] UKHL 50	A prosecution witness notified the police of threats against him and was ultimately murdered. The negligence action against the police failed owing to the conclusion that there had been no apparent 'real and immediate risk'.	In some circumstances such a situation could give rise to a positive duty to provide protection, under the right to life in **art 2 ECHR**. Here, the facts did not support such a duty.
X v Bedfordshire CC [1995] 2 AC 633	A negligence action was brought against a local authority social services department in respect of damage suffered after failure to take children into care.	In finding in favour of the defendant the House of Lords gave a number of policy reasons according to which this public body should have the benefit of a presumption against a duty of care.

Key debates

Topic:	**'Public Authority Liability in Negligence: The Continued Search for Coherence'**
Author:	S. Bailey
Viewpoint:	Endorses the gradual disappearance of public law reasoning in this area, leaving liability of public authorities to be determined according to the ordinary principles of **negligence**.
Source:	(2006) LS 155

Topic:	**'Getting Defensive about Police Negligence'**
Author:	C. McIvor
Viewpoint:	Analyses the current status of the police immunity derived from *Hill*, arguing that it is too wide and in some circumstances unjustified.
Source:	(2010) CLJ 133

Exam questions

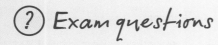

Problem question

Martin is leaving work late one evening when he hears an alarm bell ringing in the office of his manager, Raj. He does nothing about this until he returns home and then decides to ring the emergency services. Linda, who takes the call, does not give it priority status and when the police arrive to investigate two hours later it is discovered that thieves have escaped with most of the contents of Raj's office.

Advise Raj.

See the Outline Answers section in the end matter for help with this question.

Essay question

To what extent do concerns about 'defensive practice' govern the current state of the law regarding duty and standard of care in negligence?

To see an outline answer to this question visit www.oup.com/lawrevision/

#4

Pure economic loss and negligent misstatement

Key facts

- Pure economic loss, not linked to the causing of tangible damage, is generally not recoverable in negligence.

- It is an aspect of duty of care.

- Pure economic loss can be divided into that due to the acquisition of a defective product or property and that resulting from a negligent misstatement.

- It is an area of commercial and professional importance and has shown a trend towards expansion in the area of negligent misstatement.

- The two key cases in this area are *Murphy v Brentwood District Council* and *Hedley Byrne v Heller*.

- The concept of assumption of responsibility has been developed as a justification for imposition of duty of care.

- Pure economic loss must be studied in conjunction with duty of care in Chapters 2 and 3.

Assessment

In assessment, **pure economic loss** may arise on its own as an essay question focused on recent developments or policy. However it is more likely to take the form of a problem question. In order to answer a problem question accurately it is essential that you are able to distinguish pure economic loss from that which is merely the financial outcome of tangible damage. Remember: there can always be recovery for *consequential* economic loss without satisfying the following principles.

Introduction

Pure economic loss is that which is not derived from physical injury, death, or property damage. It comes in the shape of failure to receive expected future profit or receipt of some financial benefit, or it may result from the acquisition of an item of defective property, or be due to property damage sustained by a third party.

Along with psychiatric injury, it is one of the two types of damage in which **duty of care** is likely to be problematic, or absent.

There are two main reasons for this:

1. Pure economic loss has historically been seen as the province of the law of contract, whereas **tort** law has been concerned with property damage, personal injury, and death.

2. There have been concerns about the 'floodgates' in terms of potentially widespread and limitless losses.

Historical background

The two cases below will help to clarify exactly what is meant by **pure economic loss**.

Weller & Co v Foot and Mouth Disease Research Institute [1966] 1 QB 569

FACTS: The defendant had negligently allowed the spread of foot and mouth disease. The plaintiff was an auctioneer who lost money owing to quarantine restrictions which meant he was unable to hold his weekly cattle auctions.

HELD: The **negligence** action failed because only profit had been lost. The defendant would, however, have been liable to compensate farmers whose livestock became ill—this was regarded as property damage.

An especially helpful case to illustrate the sometimes elusive dividing line between physical and economic damage is *Spartan Steel & Alloys v Martin*.

Spartan Steel & Alloys v Martin [1973] QB 27

FACTS: The defendant negligently drove a power shovel through the cable (significantly, belonging to the utility company) which supplied electricity to the plaintiff's factory, causing a 14-hour power cut.

The plaintiff suffered losses under three headings:

- the reduced value of metal which had to be removed from Furnace One before it solidified and damaged machinery,
- profit which would have been made from that 'melt' had it been completed, and
- profit from four other future 'melts' in Furnaces Two and Three which would have been made but for the long power cut.

HELD: The Court of Appeal, by a majority, held that only the first two heads justified compensation; being treated as consequential to physical damage. The third constituted **pure economic loss** because it did not flow directly from physical damage to the plaintiff's property (see Figure 4.1).

Figure 4.1 *Spartan Steel & Alloys v Martin* (1973)

| No power | ORE | No power | (empty) | No power | (empty) |

Furnace One
Ore solidified and scrapped: consequential loss of sale. Claim successful.

Furnace Two
Out of use for 14 hours: pure economic loss. Claim unsuccessful.

Furnace Three
Out of use for 14 hours: pure economic loss. Claim unsuccessful.

Anns and *Murphy*

Anns v Merton LBC, which, it is important to note, was overruled in the later case of *Murphy v Brentwood DC*, illustrates the uncertainty which has existed around this concept, even within the courts themselves.

Anns and *Murphy*

✲✲✲✲✲✲✲✲✲✲✲✲

Anns v Merton LBC [1978] AC 728

FACTS: The plaintiffs occupied flats in a block which, some eight years after completion, began to develop cracks and unstable floors. This was caused by having been built on foundations which were too shallow, despite prior approval by the local council.

HELD: The House of Lords found that the plaintiffs had suffered 'material physical damage' and ordered the council to compensate for repair costs needed to avoid a danger to the health and safety of occupants of the building.

In *Anns*, the defendant's creation of *defective property* (basically the concern of contract law) was regarded as *damaged property* (for which there is a **duty of care** in **negligence**).

Revision tip

You will remember *Anns* as the case in which Lord Wilberforce set out his 'two-stage test' (see Chapter 2). At that time, when **duty of care** was expanding, *Anns* was accompanied by *Junior Books v Veitchi* (1983). *Junior Books* was distinguished in *Muirhead v Industrial Tank Specialities Ltd* (1985) and *Simaan General Contracting Co v Pilkington Glass* (1988), which reasserted the primacy of contract law in this area. *Junior Books* is now regarded as confined to its own facts.

Further doubt was cast on *Anns* in *D & F Estates Ltd v Church Commissioners* (1988) and in 1991 *Murphy v Brentwood DC* gave the House of Lords the opportunity to revisit the decision in *Anns*, in a case founded on very similar facts.

Murphy v Brentwood DC [1991] 1 AC 398

FACTS: The plaintiff was the owner of a house which had been built on inadequate foundations leading to cracked walls. He lost profit on the sale of the house, owing to the remedial work which was going to be necessary to restore the foundations, and sued the Council who had approved the original construction plans for the house.

HELD: The House of Lords held that *Anns* had been wrongly decided. The **loss** which had been described there as physical damage was in fact **pure economic loss** and was not recoverable. The building had never existed without its defective foundations and in a sense had been fundamentally flawed from the start.

The extent of consequential economic loss was linked to the *Wagon Mound* test of reasonable **foreseeability** in *Conarken Group v Network Rail Infrastructure* (2011). Here, the defendants who damaged railway property were held to also be liable to Network Rail for the contractual payments they owed to train operating companies while the track was unusable.

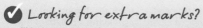 **Looking for extra marks?**

It will help you to understand this area of the law if you read the speech of Lord Bridge in *Murphy*. He also discussed the (unrealized) potential of the 'complex structure' theory (which is sometimes raised in problem questions) and the influence of the **Defective Premises Act 1972**.

The Defective Premises Act 1972, s 1

Section 1 of the **Defective Premises Act 1972** imposes a statutory duty upon builders and others (architects, etc.) undertaking work on dwellings to perform their role in a 'workmanlike or professional manner, and with proper material'. Until recently, the Act did not apply to the majority of newly built houses and still remains subject to a limitation period of six years, so would not have applied in the cases of *Anns* and *Murphy* in any event.

Negligent misstatement

Cases in which the claimant has suffered **pure economic loss** due to a negligent statement by the defendant provide a significant *exception* to the reluctance of the law to recognize a **duty of care**.

'Statements' may include:

- advice,
- references,
- provision of information, and
- services.

The case of *Derry v Peek* (1889) established a presumption that liability in **tort** was only possible for **loss** caused by a fraudulent (the tort of deceit) rather than negligent statement. This position changed significantly in 1964.

The special relationship

Hedley Byrne & Co v Heller & Partners gave the House of Lords the opportunity to reassess the position and the decision opened up a major new area of liability.

Hedley Byrne v Heller [1964] AC 465

FACTS: The plaintiff, an advertising agency, wanted to know about the financial status of Easipower, on whose behalf it was considering entering into a number of advertising contracts. Through its own bankers, the agency requested references from Easipower's bank, Heller & Partners. These were

---

Negligent misstatement

✳✳✳✳✳✳✳✳✳✳✳

supplied, confirming the creditworthiness of its client in a letter headed by this disclaimer: 'For your private use and without responsibility on the part of this bank or its officials.' On the strength of the reference, Hedley Byrne entered into contracts on behalf of Easipower and lost £17,000 when that company went into liquidation (Figure 4.2).

HELD: The House of Lords held that a duty of care could exist in respect of a statement leading to pure economic loss, if the parties were in a 'special relationship'. In this case, the duty had been avoided by the defendant's use of the disclaimer.

Figure 4.2 *Hedley Byrne v Heller* (1964)

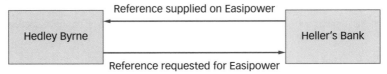

It was recognized that cases of **pure economic loss** were very different from those of physical damage as per *Donoghue* (see Chapter 2) but it was felt that the ingredients of **foreseeability** and **proximity** could be adapted into a general principle of proximity, to be based on a '*special relationship*' between parties which would give rise to a **duty of care** in making statements.

Although the requirements for a special relationship were fulfilled in *Hedley Byrne*, it is important to remember that the disclaimer at the top of the reference meant that there could be no liability on behalf of Heller. Note that in view of the **Unfair Contract Terms Act 1977** such disclaimers may no longer be so effective.

Duty of care as established by the Hedley Byrne v Heller 'special relationship'

- C relied on D's skill and judgement or his ability to make careful inquiry;
- D knew, or ought reasonably to have known, that C was relying on him; and
- it was reasonable in the circumstances for C to rely on D.

Revision tip

It is essential that you learn and understand the decision in *Hedley Byrne* as well as the cases which follow and apply it.

The *Hedley Byrne* duty

Defendant?

To apply *Hedley Byrne* you must know what sort of person is subject to this **duty of care** when making a statement. The accepted view is that of the minority opinions in *Mutual Life & Citizens' Assurance Co Ltd v Evatt* (1971): specific or professional expertise in giving advice was not required and it was sufficient that the plaintiff had consulted a businessman in the course of his business and made it plain that he sought considered advice and intended to act upon that advice. See, for example, *Esso Petroleum v Mardon* (1976).

Context?

A social setting or relationship does not normally fulfil the requirements for a special relationship. *Chaudhury v Prabhaker* (1989), where the defendant was asked by his friend to advise him about the purchase of a used car, should be treated as a rather narrow exception to this rule.

Silence and threats?

The duty can arise in cases in which the claimant alleges that his **loss** has been caused by the defendant's failing to warn him about a situation or pressuring him to do something. In *Welton v North Cornwall DC* (1997) threats by an environmental health inspector that he would close a bed and breakfast unless expensive renovations were done gave rise to *Hedley Byrne* liability.

> *Revision tip*
>
> The social or semi-social setting is a favourite of examiners for testing your understanding of the law on **negligent misstatement**.

Causation

It is important to remember that the *Hedley Byrne* special relationship only goes to establish **duty of care**. The claimant must also prove breach and **causation**. This is illustrated in *JEB Fasteners v Marks Bloom & Co* (1981), where it was held that the misstatement had not motivated the plaintiff to make his loss-making takeover bid. Effectively, the defendant's breach had not caused the plaintiff's **loss**.

Indirect statements

Liability under the *Hedley Byrne v Heller* exception has been extended to situations in which the statement or supply of information was not made directly to the claimant, or perhaps was made for purposes other than influencing the claimant.

Negligent misstatement
✱✱✱✱✱✱✱✱✱✱✱✱✱

Smith v Eric S Bush [1990] 1 AC 831

FACTS: A negligent surveyor's report led to the plaintiff purchasing a house which was later found to need expensive repair owing to subsidence. However, the report was given not to the plaintiff but to his building society.

HELD: The House of Lords found the relationship between the valuer and the purchaser to be very close, 'akin to contract'. The plaintiff had paid for the survey and it was foreseeable, reasonable, and fair for him to rely on it: **Hedley Byrne** applied (Figure 4.3).

Figure 4.3 *Smith v Eric S Bush* (1990)

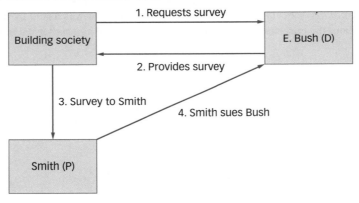

✔ Looking for extra marks?

It is interesting to note that in **Smith** it was indicated that the decision might have been in favour of the defendant had it not been a modest residential property.

Hedley Byrne refined

A key case which explains and arguably applies the *Hedley Byrne* principle is *Caparo v Dickman*. *Caparo* has already been discussed (see Chapter 2) in terms of the 'three-stage test' for **duty of care** in novel situations.

Caparo v Dickman [1990] 2 AC 605

FACTS: The plaintiff suffered **pure economic loss** following a successful takeover bid, which was based upon the company's valuation provided in its annual audited accounts. These were prepared

---

by the defendant accountants and sent to the plaintiff in its status as an existing shareholder of the company. The accounts had been negligently prepared and falsely represented the company as profitable.

HELD: The **negligence** action against the accountants ultimately failed. According to the House of Lords, in preparing the annual accounts the defendant had owed a duty to the company but not to the public at large. Effectively, there had not been sufficient **proximity** between the plaintiff and defendant.

Two cases provide significant examples of the *Caparo* approach

In *Morgan Crucible Co plc v Hill Samuel Bank Ltd* (1991) it was held that a duty could exist in a factual situation similar to that in *Caparo* but where the financial accounts had been revealed to an identified bidder.

In *James McNaughton Paper Group Ltd v Hicks Anderson & Co* (1991) an auditor's **duty of care** was held not to exist when the plaintiff relied on a company's draft accounts in his takeover bid, as they had not been prepared for that purpose or even for him. Here, six helpful pointers to the existence of a *Hedley Byrne* duty were set out:

1. *The purpose for which the statement was made.* In both *Caparo* and *James McNaughton*, this was the strongest factor against the finding of a duty.

2. *The purpose for which it was communicated.*

3. *The state of knowledge of the maker of the statement.* Did the maker know the purpose of the statement, to whom it would be communicated, and what sort of reliance there might be upon it?

4. *The size of the class to which the recipient belonged.* This is indicative of **proximity** and was a problem for the plaintiff in *Caparo*.

5. *The relationship between the maker, the recipient, and any third party.* Was there an additional source of information on the matter?

6. *Reliance by the recipient.*

Revision tip

You should note that the first two are the most helpful. Each of these criteria will not be relevant in every case and there is a degree of overlap between them.

Voluntary assumption of responsibility

During the last ten years, the *voluntary acceptance of responsibility* to the recipient by the maker of the statement (which was referred to in *Hedley Byrne*) has gained a growing importance in the establishment of the special relationship. It is a flexible concept and some say it has contributed to lack of consistency and predictability in this area.

The prime example of the use of the 'voluntary assumption of responsibility' is the key case of *Henderson v Merrett Syndicates Ltd*.

Henderson v Merrett Syndicates Ltd [1995] 2 AC 145

FACTS: This case concerned a complex group of actions against managing agents who were alleged to have been negligent in handling the investments of the plaintiff 'Names' in the Lloyd's insurance market. In many cases the parties were linked by contract but some contractual actions were time-barred. However, there were also instances in which there was no privity of contract between the parties because they were separated by a third party. In the absence of possible contractual remedies, the injured parties brought **negligence** actions for the **pure economic loss** which they had suffered.

HELD: The House of Lords held that there was a **duty of care** not to cause pure economic loss to both groups of plaintiffs for the following reasons:

1. The existence of contractual relationships between the parties did not exclude the possibility of a duty of care in negligence.
2. The *Hedley Byrne* special relationship did not apply only to the giving of information and advice but also to the provision of services.
3. The foundation of the duty of care in *Hedley Byrne* was, according to Lord Goff, the assumption of responsibility to the plaintiff by the defendant. Once this was established, it was unnecessary to apply the *Caparo* test of whether it was fair, just, and reasonable to impose a duty.

See *Williams v Natural Life Health Foods Ltd* (1998), where it was held that a company director had made no assumption of responsibility; but also *Merrett v Babb* (2001), where a property valuer was held solely liable owing to the assumption of responsibility.

✓ Looking for extra marks?

It is worth considering the policy issues behind decisions regarding **negligent misstatement**. If the decision in *Caparo* had extended the liability of the accountants this would have had major implications for the profession. In *Henderson* one of the many actions concerned liability by one managing agent and 42 members' agents to 1,000 plaintiffs and there was a potential liability of £200 million.

Recent developments in liability for negligent misstatements

The following case illustrates the way in which the courts often apply the *Henderson* test and the *Caparo* three-stage test (for general **duty of care**) either alternatively or so that they supplement one another.

> **Customs and Excise Commissioners v Barclays Bank plc [2006] 3 WLR 1**
>
> **FACTS:** Here, the 'assumption of responsibility' criterion did not provide a clear statement of duty in a situation with no precedents. The defendant negligently failed to implement freezing orders placed upon his clients by the claimant. Neither the **Hedley Byrne** special relationship nor **assumption of responsibility** fitted the FACTS: the defendant had merely been a passive recipient of a legally binding instruction.
>
> **HELD:** The case failed owing to the absence of an assumption of responsibility, combined with of a lack of **proximity** between the parties and the fact that it would not be fair, just, or reasonable to impose a **duty of care**.

Revision tip

It is suggested that you read the speech of Lord Bingham in the case, which will provide you with a helpful review of the law in this area.

The four following cases indicate the courts taking a cautious approach to extensions in liability for **negligent misstatement**:

1. *West Bromwich Albion Football Club v El-Safty* (2006),
2. *Patchett v Swimming Pool & Allied Trades Assn Ltd* (2009),
3. *Jain v Trent SHA* (2009), and
4. *Glaister v Appleby-in-Westmoreland Town Council* (2009).

Negligent misstatements relied on by a third party

In *Hedley Byrne*, the plaintiff (who sustained **loss**) was the recipient of the negligent statement (the reference). A **duty of care** has also been recognized when the *subject* of a statement suffers **pure economic loss** due to that statement being given without due care.

The following two cases illustrate this principle operating in two different contexts.

> **Spring v Guardian Assurance plc [1995] 2 AC 296**
>
> **FACTS:** The plaintiff was the subject of a negligently composed reference which damaged his job prospects. The facts did not fit neatly into the **Hedley Byrne** format, because Spring, the plaintiff, was the *subject* rather than the *recipient* of the reference. Further, it was inaccurate to say that he had *relied* on the statement, in terms of changing his behaviour because of it.
>
> **HELD:** The House of Lords found a **duty of care** based on an **assumption of responsibility** by the defendant and the close relationship between the parties (Figure 4.4).

Negligent misstatement

✱✱✱✱✱✱✱✱✱✱✱✱

Figure 4.4 *Spring v Guardian Assurance plc* **(1995)**

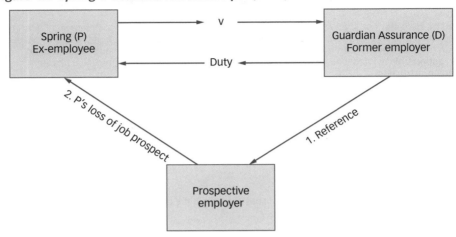

In *White v Jones* assumption of responsibility was used to give a **remedy** to the beneficiaries of a will.

White v Jones [1995] 2 AC 207

FACTS: Owing to the **negligence** of their father's solicitor, the plaintiffs were no longer legally entitled to the legacy he had intended to leave them in his will. As in *Henderson*, the case concerns the performance of a service and, as in *Spring*, the injured parties were not in a direct relationship with the defendant but were third parties.

HELD: The House of Lords found that a duty existed for the following reasons:

- Although it was difficult to describe the plaintiffs' expectation of benefit as reliance, there had been an **assumption of responsibility** to them by the undertaking of the drafting of the will.
- The potential for **loss** was foreseeable.
- It was fair, just, and reasonable because the situation indicated a gap in the law which should be filled.
- There was no conflict of interest between the solicitor's duty to his client and to the beneficiaries (Figure 4.5).

Revision tip

Spring, *White*, and *Henderson* are often considered together primarily because they involved detailed consideration of **'assumption of responsibility'**, but also because they were decided by the House of Lords within the same six-month period.

Figure 4.5 *White v Jones* (1995)

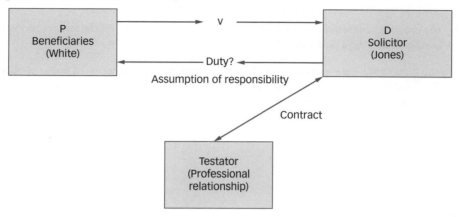

Disclaimers

You will recall that in *Hedley Byrne*, despite the finding of a **duty of care**, the defendant was not held to be liable because he had headed his reference letter with a disclaimer. This ability of an adviser to specifically limit or exempt liability was a potential restriction on the new *Hedley Byrne* duty for **pure economic loss**. This would now be subject to the *'reasonableness test'* according to the **Unfair Contract Terms Act 1977**.

Unfair Contract Terms Act 1977, s 2 and s 11

Section 2(2): a person cannot by means of any contract term or notice restrict his liability for **loss** or damage other than personal injury caused by **negligence** in the course of a business unless he shows that the term is *reasonable*.

Section 11(3): the requirement of reasonableness is that it should be fair and reasonable to allow reliance on it, having regard to all the circumstances obtaining when the liability arose or (but for the notice) would have arisen.

In *Smith v Eric S Bush* (discussed earlier) the valuer had included an exemption clause in the report. Factors that were taken into account in applying **s 2(2)** were:

- whether the parties were of equal bargaining power;
- whether it would have been practicable, in terms of costs and time, for the recipient to obtain independent advice;

- the difficulty of the task which was the subject of the disclaimer (a difficult or dangerous task would be more likely to make a disclaimer reasonable); and
- the practical consequences of upholding or striking down the disclaimer, in terms of costs and also the availability of insurance.

On the facts of the case, particularly given that the valuation concerned a house of 'modest value' and the parties were of unequal bargaining power, the court concluded that the disclaimer was unreasonable in the circumstances, and therefore ineffective according to the 1977 Act.

 *Key cases*

Case	Facts	Principle
Anns v Merton LBC [1978] AC 728	The local authority negligently approved plans which resulted in the plaintiff's building having inadequate foundations and cracked walls.	The cracked building was regarded as property damage and so compensation was awarded. See **Murphy**.
Caparo Industries v Dickman [1990] 2 AC 605	The plaintiff's takeover bid was informed by the annual audit of the company's accounts. They were faulty and he lost profit.	The accounts were not prepared for the plaintiff or for the purpose of informing investment decisions. No duty of care.
Hedley Byrne v Heller [1964] AC 465	An advertising agency lost money when it relied on a negligently compiled bank reference about a client.	This case founded the tort of negligent misstatement, but there was no liability here owing to the disclaimer. Duty of care was determined by finding the *special relationship*.
Henderson v Merrett Syndicates [1995] 2 AC 145	Concerned losses incurred by Names in the Lloyds insurance market due to negligent agents' investment decisions.	Assumption of responsibility for the provision of services can be the basis of a duty of care for negligent misstatement, even when there is also a contractual relationship.
James McNaughton Paper Group v Hicks Anderson [1991] 2 QB 295	The plaintiff's takeover bid was informed by draft accounts, prepared (not for him) at short notice.	No duty of care was owed. The court set out six key factors for consideration in determining duty.

Case	Facts	Principle
Murphy v Brentwood DC [1991] 1 AC 398	The faulty foundations on the plaintiff's house led to cracks and a loss in profit when he sold it after ten years.	**Anns** was overruled. This type of damage was pure economic loss and not recoverable. The only remedy would have been in contract.
Smith v Eric S Bush [1990] 1 AC 831	In a valuation conducted for mortgage purposes, the defendant negligently undervalued the plaintiff's home, so he incurred extra expenditure for repairs.	There was proximity between the parties and foreseeability, so in this professional context there should be a duty of care. The disclaimer was invalid according to the **Unfair Contracts Terms Act 1977**.
Spartan Steel & Alloys v Martin [1973] QB 27	The loss of power caused by cutting the cable to a factory affected the operation of three furnaces melting steel.	Compensation was permitted for the furnace containing the damaged ore but not for loss of profits linked to empty furnaces. Illustrates the difference between property damage and pure economic loss.
Spring v Guardian Insurance [1995] 2 AC 296	The plaintiff was the subject of a negligent employment reference written by his former employer.	A duty of care for a negligent misstatement to a third party can be owed to the subject of a negligent misstatement, when there has been an assumption of responsibility.
White v Jones [1995] 2 AC 207	Disappointed beneficiaries sued a solicitor who had been negligent in executing a will.	Although there had not been reliance by the plaintiffs in the **Hedley Byrne** sense, there was a duty of care based upon foreseeability, proximity, and an assumption of responsibility.

❞) Key debates

Topic:	'Wielding Occam's Razor: Pruning Strategies for Economic Loss'
Author:	C. Barker
Viewpoint:	Examines the four different strategies currently used by the Court of Appeal in economic **loss** cases and argues for a simpler single approach which focuses on policy rather than abstract principle.
Source:	(2006) 26 OJLS 289

Exam questions

✱✱✱✱✱✱✱✱✱✱ ✱

Topic:	'Professional Negligence: Duty of Care Methodology in the Twenty First Century'
Author:	K. Stanton
Viewpoint:	Analyses the tests for duty in cases of professional **negligence**, in view of the impact of *Customs and Excise Commissioners v Barclays Bank*.
Source:	(2006) 22 PN 134

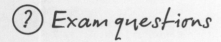 Exam questions

Problem question

Susan was at the gym when she met Lynne, an accountant. She told Lynne that she had recently been made redundant and given a large severance payment. Lynne said she had read a report the previous week which had been produced for VGP, a video games production company. The report stated that VGP shares were undervalued because 'the company was about to declare record profits'. Susan immediately invested all her money in VGP but within a matter of weeks she had lost her entire investment.

Advise Susan.

See the Outline Answers section in the end matter for help with this question.

Essay question

In *Hedley Byrne v Heller* the House of Lords adopted the concept of 'reasonable reliance' by the plaintiff on the defendant's skill and judgement as the basis of liability for negligent statement. More recently, this has additionally been restated on the basis of an 'assumption of responsibility' by the defendant.

Critically analyse the concept of assumption of responsibility.

 Online Resource Centre

To see an outline answer to this question visit www.oup.com/lawrevision/

#5
Psychiatric injury

Key facts

- Psychiatric injury which is not derived from physical injury is a type of damage which is not always recoverable in negligence.

- It was referred to in older cases as 'nervous shock'.

- It is an aspect of *duty of care*.

- The range of allowable actions has evolved through developments of *control mechanisms* in the common law.

- The four key cases are *McLoughlin*, *Alcock*, *Page*, and *White*.

- This has been the subject of consideration by both the English and Scottish Law Commissions.

- Psychiatric injury must be studied in conjunction with Chapters 2 and 3.

Assessment

This can be the subject of either a problem or an essay question. As a problem it might be one aspect of a general **negligence** scenario or, more commonly, the main focus of the scenario where you will be required to demonstrate knowledge of the different controlling approaches taken by the courts. Some of the more challenging aspects of psychiatric injury arise in the non-accident cases.

Introduction

Physical injury is often accompanied by psychological effects as well. When someone is injured in an accident, they may become depressed when they are out of work during recuperation. If they receive **tort** compensation for the accident, this will also cover any psychological effects of their injuries. But compensation becomes problematic when the victim has not suffered any physical injury but developed some psychological condition as a result of a narrow escape from **injury** or because they witnessed harm to someone else.

The law was reluctant to allow recovery for this type of injury for three main reasons:

1. A general lack of awareness or understanding of how the mind worked. For instance, post-traumatic stress disorder (PTSD) has only been recognized as such since the 1960s. Until recently, psychological injury was referred to in the law reports as 'nervous shock'.

2. Formerly, it was believed that psychological injury was very much more likely to be fraudulently claimed than the physical, which is usually visible and therefore somehow more 'real'. We now know that this is not always a meaningful distinction.

3. Lastly, there was a policy concern that allowing liability for psychological injury threatened to open the 'floodgates'.

Controlling factors

The requirement for a medically diagnosed psychiatric condition

This is a key control mechanism. Mere grief, distress, or anger is not enough (*Hinz v Berry* (1970)). According to Lord Oliver, in *Alcock v Chief Constable of South Yorkshire Police* (1991), grief, sorrow, deprivation, and the necessity for caring for loved ones who have suffered **injury** are all a necessary part of life which must be accepted. **Damages** will only be awarded for a *recognized psychiatric illness*.

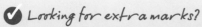

Looking for extra marks?

See **Vernon v Bosley (No 1)** (1994), where a father who watched his children drown was awarded damages, which did not distinguish between the aspects of his condition which were a normal grief reaction and those which were pathological.

A sudden event or its immediate aftermath

The condition must be the result of the impact of a sudden event or its immediate aftermath, hence the original term, 'nervous shock'. When it is the result of any sort of prolonged exposure, say to stress, it will not qualify under this category of legal claim.

In *Sion v Hampstead Health Authority* (1994), the effect on a father of spending two weeks sitting by the bedside of his dying son, who had been injured owing to the defendant's **negligence**, was not sufficient to found a claim.

For a more generous approach, see *Walters v North Glamorgan NHS Trust* (2003).

Primary and secondary victims

Victorian Railway Commissioners v Coultas (1888) confirmed the non-recoverability of compensation for psychiatric injury; however, the tide was turning and *Dulieu v White* (1901) saw the first successful such claim.

Dulieu v White [1901] 2 KB 669

FACTS: A barmaid was serving customers in a pub when she looked up and saw a horse and cart out of control, crashing through the wall of the pub. She was pregnant and the shock she sustained from the event caused her to suffer a stillbirth.

HELD: In an innovative decision, she recovered compensation in negligence. The basis of the plaintiff's reaction was a reasonable fear for her own physical safety.

A claimant who has direct involvement in the incident and is within the range of foreseeable physical injury would later be known as a *'primary victim'*. There is presumed to be a **duty of care** not to cause them physical injury and this is extended to include a duty not to cause mental harm.

A different approach is taken to the other category: that of the *'secondary victim'*. Nearly a century after *Dulieu*, the House of Lords in *Page v Smith* (1995) discussed in detail the implications of the distinction between primary and secondary victims. Remember that the distinction between the two categories is not always clear-cut.

Controlling factors

Page v Smith [1995] 2 All ER 736

FACTS: A claim was made by the driver of a car which was involved in a relatively minor collision, caused by the **negligence** of the defendant, the other driver. Although the plaintiff suffered no physical injury, he alleged that the accident caused a recurrence of chronic fatigue syndrome, from which he had previously suffered.

HELD: A majority of Law Lords held that a **duty of care** had been owed to the plaintiff for the type of damage suffered.
   The two key aspects of the decision in **Page v Smith** are:

1.   in the law, psychiatric injury is not to be regarded as injury of a different kind from physical injury; and

2.   for the primary victim, reasonable **foreseeability** of physical injury is sufficient to bring with it a duty in regard to psychiatric injury.

The developing case law

Following the landmark decision in *Dulieu*, the first significant case was *Hambrook v Stokes Bros* (1925).

Hambrook v Stokes Bros [1925] 1 KB 141, CA

FACTS: A mother suffered (fatal) shock when she saw a driverless lorry roll down a hill and around a bend where it crashed, out of her sight but in a place where she had recently taken her children.

HELD: The claim succeeded. The court felt that it would be unfair to allow recovery to someone like the barmaid in *Dulieu*, fearing for her own safety, but to deny a remedy to someone who unselfishly feared for the safety of a loved one.

Following the extension of liability in *Hambrook*, it became uncertain where the boundaries for nervous shock recovery lay. Some limits were set in *Bourhill v Young*.

Bourhill v Young [1943] AC 92

FACTS: A pregnant Edinburgh fishwife was getting off a tram when she heard the collision between the defendant's motorcycle and a car, some 40 yards away on the other side of the tram. The motorcyclist died at the scene and although the plaintiff saw neither the event nor the body, she later saw blood on the road but claimed that the shock she experienced was responsible for the eventual stillbirth of her baby.

HELD: In the House of Lords, the plaintiff's status as a mere bystander, who had not been in any physical danger, was a key reason for denying that a **duty of care** had been owed. **Injury** to her had not been reasonably foreseeable, owing to her distance from the accident but also because the law expects that members of the public will display a degree of fortitude.

Revision tip

It is important that you remember that the different components of the 'negligence equation' are not always fixed and can be interchangeable. Alternative reasons for denying Mrs Bourhill's claim could be that she was an unforeseeable plaintiff, as in *Palsgraf v Long Island Railway* (1928) (see Chapter 2), or on the basis of lack of causal link between the driver's **negligence** and her shock.

The 'thin skull' rule

You should note at this point that the '*thin skull' rule* applies to psychiatric injury in the same way as to physical injury. *Brice v Brown* (1984) confirms that if psychiatric injury would have been foreseeable in a person of ordinary fortitude, then if the plaintiff suffers excessive harm owing to the fact that she was prone to depression, recovery is available for that further **injury**.

Revision tip

For more on the 'thin skull' rule, see Chapter 8 (The 'thin skull' rule, p 96).

✅ *Looking for extra marks?*

The *Bourhill* requirement for normal fortitude operated against the claimants in *Rothwell v Chemical & Insulating Co Ltd* (2007). Former asbestos workers claimed that their employers' **negligence** in exposing them to asbestos had led to anxiety and depression due to fear that they could contract a serious asbestos-related disease in the future. The House of Lords did not consider that the exposure could count as a 'zone of danger' to make the claimants primary victims under *Page v Smith*.

The principles of liability emerge

From *Bourhill* onwards, the **foreseeability** of secondary victims began to be assessed in terms of:

- time,
- space or geography,
- **causation**, and
- relationship to the primary victim of the **negligence**.

The importance of these factors was stressed in *McLoughlin v O'Brian*.

McLoughlin v O'Brian [1983] AC 410

FACTS: The plaintiff was a mother who was told by phone of her family's involvement in a motoring accident. She arrived at the hospital two hours later to see their untreated injuries and to learn of the death of one child. She developed depression and a change of personality and sued the negligent driver who caused the accident.

Controlling factors

✳✳✳✳✳✳✳✳✳✳✳✳

> **HELD:** The House of Lords held that, as a secondary victim, her damage was foreseeable owing to her relationship with the direct victims and there was **proximity** to the accident because she was witness to its 'immediate aftermath', therefore her claim succeeded.

The defining House of Lords decision on **duty of care** to secondary victims arose from a very public event. In the Hillsborough football stadium disaster of 1989, 96 supporters were killed and another 400 injured in the spectator stands when crowd control broke down and barriers collapsed at the beginning of an FA Cup match between Liverpool and Nottingham Forest.

> ### *Alcock v Chief Constable of South Yorkshire Police* [1991] 4 All ER 907
>
> **FACTS:** The plaintiffs were relatives and associates of those caught up in the crush, who all suffered psychiatric illness as a result of what they experienced that day. None had been in any physical danger themselves: all were secondary victims. Some had watched events unfold on television; some, who were present at the ground, had feared for friends or relatives; and others had viewed bodies in the mortuary some nine hours later.
>
> **HELD:** The House of Lords, applying and expanding upon the **foreseeability** criteria of *Bourhill* and *McLoughlin*, unanimously held that none of the plaintiffs could recover.

It is essential that you understand and remember the three '*Alcock* criteria' of **foreseeability**, which are necessary for finding a **duty of care** to a secondary victim:

1. *A sufficiently close relationship of love and affection with the primary victim.* There is a (rebuttable) presumption between a husband and wife and parents and children; those in other relationships will have to convince the court.

2. *Proximity to the accident, or its immediate aftermath, which was sufficiently close in time and space.* Seeing bodies in the mortuary for the purpose of identification, some nine hours after the event, was held not to be sufficiently proximate in *Alcock*.

3. *Suffering nervous shock through what was seen or heard of the accident or its immediate aftermath* or, as Lord Ackner put it, 'sudden appreciation by sight or sound of a horrifying event which violently agitated the mind'. What is seen on television, or told by someone else, is not immediate enough.

✅ *Looking for extra marks?*

How far the immediate aftermath will extend is uncertain. In *Galli-Atkinson v Seghal* (2003), a mother came upon the scene where her daughter had been hit by a dangerous driver and was told that her daughter was dead. Part of the shock she suffered was due to this experience and the other part was caused when she saw her daughter's body in the mortuary some two hours later. This was a considerably shorter time than the insufficiently proximate mortuary viewing in *Alcock* and the Court of Appeal held that it was within the definition of 'immediate aftermath'.

'Rescuers'

Another key case, which derived from Hillsborough, involved the complex situation of police officers who had assisted in the aftermath.

White v Chief Constable of the South Yorkshire Police [1999] 1 All ER 1

FACTS: This was a **negligence** action brought by a number of police officers who suffered psychiatric illness following their experiences of the tragedy. Like the plaintiffs in *Alcock*, they were never in any physical danger but were still closely involved with the events of the day. Some had been on duty in another part of the ground but were called upon to tend to the injured and dying; others dealt with relatives of the dead at the mortuary. All were witnesses to gruesome and upsetting scenes and this led to their mental conditions. Their case was successful in the Court of Appeal, the establishment of **foreseeability** having been strongly assisted by the fact that they were employees of the defendant.

HELD: The Court of Appeal was reversed by the House of Lords, which strictly applied the *Alcock* criteria to the police officers as secondary victims, under the influence of the inevitable comparisons that would be made with the failure of the relatives' action in that case.

Prior to *White*, it had appeared that rescuers might form a special category of victims for the purposes of determining duty for psychiatric injury.

In *Chadwick v British Railways Board* (1967), Mr Chadwick successfully recovered compensation when he sustained what would now be termed serious PTSD following the night he spent attempting to rescue the victims of a terrible train crash which occurred near to his house.

Chadwick can be reconciled with *White* on the basis that, by putting himself into danger in the wrecked carriages, the plaintiff was a primary rather than secondary victim, but following *White* the status of rescuers suffering from psychiatric injury is now somewhat unclear.

✅ *Looking for extra marks?*

The decision in *McFarlane v EE Caledonia* (1994), which involved an explosion on an oil rig, may support the view that rescuers will not be treated as a separate category beyond the reach of *Alcock*.

'Unique' factual situations

There are two cases, which pre-dated *Alcock*, in which liability for psychiatric injury was imposed despite the fact that the 'primary victim' was an inanimate object.

In *Owens v Liverpool Corp* (1939), the successful plaintiffs were mourners at a funeral who were understandably shocked when, owing to a collision, the coffin fell out of the hearse and overturned, threatening to spill out its contents.

In *Attia v British Gas* (1988) it was held that there could be a **duty of care** owed to a homeowner in respect of the shock caused by witnessing the destruction of her home due to a fire negligently caused by employees of the defendant. W. Rogers, the current editor of *Winfield & Jolowicz on Tort*, points out that in fact the relevant duty breached in this situation was that owed by the defendant in respect of Mrs Attia's property and therefore the case does not fit the pattern of 'pure' psychiatric injury claims.

In contrast, in *Greatorex v Greatorex* (2000), public policy dictated that there should be no recovery by a father who attended an accident involving his son, who was also the **tortfeasor**.

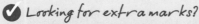

✅ Looking for extra marks?

You might want to consider whether it would be stretching the *Alcock* criteria to imagine feeling close ties of love and affection with one's home, possessions, or pet?

Primary or secondary victim?

It has been noted earlier that the categories of primary and secondary victims are not always clear-cut. In *Page v Smith* (1995), Lord Lloyd defined the two as follows:

- Primary victim: directly involved in the accident and well within the range of foreseeable physical injury.
- Secondary victim: in the position of a spectator or bystander.

We have seen that in *White* the argument was accepted in the Court of Appeal that while the police officers could not be described as spectators or bystanders, they could be treated as primary victims (although the House of Lords disagreed). You should be aware of other cases in which the classification was uncertain or in which the distinction appeared to produce an unsatisfactory outcome.

W v Essex County Council [2000] 2 All ER 237

FACTS: Here, an action was brought by parents who suffered psychiatric injury when they discovered that their children had been molested by a foster child, who had been placed in their care by the local authority. The parents were certainly never in any physical danger themselves, and so did not appear to be primary victims but, if secondary victims, they could not satisfy the second and third *Alcock* criteria.

HELD: The House of Lords held that a duty of care for psychiatric injury was owed to these claimants, most likely on the basis they were burdened with having unintentionally (and indirectly) been responsible for the abuse of their children.

We saw earlier in *Rothwell v Chemical & Insulating Co Ltd* (2007) that the claimants' condition, apprehension of illness, could not be fitted into either of the *Page v Smith* categories. Here, their Lordships did not feel moved to stretch principle to provide a **remedy** to the claimant owing to the influence of the *Bourhill* 'fortitude' policy, along with concerns about 'floodgates' implications.

Some cases have been based upon the claimant's imprisonment.

In *McLoughlin v Jones* (2001), the claimant's psychiatric condition developed out of a period of imprisonment due to his wrongful conviction, attributable to the **negligence** of his defence solicitors. Negligence liability was imposed, despite the fact that many of the usual criteria for this type of case were missing. Perhaps loss of liberty can be viewed as a form of physical injury; alternatively it is possible that the solicitor's professional status, bringing with it an **assumption of responsibility** to the claimant, was the basis for the **duty of care**.

See also *Butchart v Home Office* (2006), where the prison authorities were held liable to a prisoner whose cellmate committed suicide.

Employment

You have seen that, in most cases, the risk which the primary victim faces is of accidental **injury**; however, this is not the only type.

In *Donachie v Chief Constable of Greater Manchester* [2004] a police officer was responsible for fitting a surveillance device to the bottom of a suspect's car. Because his employer had supplied him with a device which did not function properly, the claimant had to return repeatedly to the car, increasing the danger that he would be seen by the criminal suspect. The stress of the experience led to high blood pressure, psychiatric problems, and eventually a stroke. The police officer's status as a primary victim was confirmed by the Court of Appeal.

In *Donachie* the psychiatric injury was caused by the breach of an employer's **duty of care** to his employee. Employment-related stress is an area of liability of psychiatric injury in which the **negligence** principles we have just been considering do not apply.

For more on employers' liability, including that for stress, see Chapter 9.

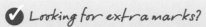 **✔ *Looking for extra marks?***

Damage caused by the giving of bad news has been the basis of **negligence** actions. Courts have been reluctant to impose liability for the *way* in which bad news has been delivered (see *AB v Tameside and Glossop Health Authority* (1997)), but less reluctant when the negligence lay in the giving of *wrong* information (see *Allin v City and Hackney HA* (1996)).

The future?

In 1998, the English Law Commission reported on the state of this aspect of **negligence** law. It recommended that for primary victims the development of the law could be left to the courts. However, as regards some secondary victims (other than rescuers or 'involuntary participants'), legislation would be proposed in order that:

- the requirement for sudden shock would be removed, thereby opening up possible liability to claimants whose condition has developed over time;

Controlling factors

- the second and third of the *Alcock* criteria would no longer be required, so that claimants might be successful even if they were not near to an event or its immediate aftermath and perceiving it with their own unaided senses; and

- close ties of love and affection with the direct victim (the first *Alcock* criterion) would be maintained as a condition for liability, but the category of those relationships in which these ties would be presumed would be expanded. The group would now include spouses, parents, children, siblings, and cohabitees of at least two years.

The Law Commission's proposals have *not* been acted upon, although the importance of this aspect of the law has been reinforced by the report of the Scottish Law Commission in 2004, which made its own extensive proposals.

Revision tip

Consideration of these proposals would be relevant in answering any essay question requiring analysis of policy or the possible future development of psychiatric injury in **negligence**. Law Commission, *Liability for Psychiatric Illness* (Law Com 249, 1999) (see Table 5.1).

Table 5.1 Psychiatric damage and duty of care

	'Bystander'			
Primary/ Secondary	'Accident' n/a	In danger: primary	Not in danger: Secondary	'Employee' n/a
Sudden shock required?	No	Yes	Yes	No
Foreseeability of physical injury required?	Yes	Yes	Yes	No
Foreseeability of psychiatric injury required?	No	No	Yes	Yes
Indicative cases	*Rahman v Arearose* (2001)	*Dulieu v White* (1901), *Page v Smith* (1996)	*Alcock v South Yorkshire* (1992), *Bourhill v Young* (1943)	*Hatton v Sutherland* (2002), *Walker v Northumberland* (1995)

 Key cases

Case	Facts	Principle
Alcock v Chief Constable of South Yorkshire Police [1991] 4 All ER 907	In one of a number of cases arising out of the Hillsborough Stadium disaster, a group of relatives and witnesses suffering psychological injury sued the responsible police in negligence.	All claimants were unsuccessful because they did not fulfil the three main criteria for finding a duty to a 'secondary victim'. These are a close relationship of love and affection to the victim, proximity to the event or its immediate aftermath, and direct personal perception of the event.
Bourhill v Young [1943] AC 92	A pregnant fishwife suffered shock leading to a stillbirth when she heard a motorcycle accident and later saw blood on the road.	The defendant had owed no duty to the plaintiff in respect of her injury, which was unforeseeable as she was outside the range of danger. The law must expect a degree of fortitude from the public.
Chadwick v British Railways Board [1967] 1 WLR 912	A member of the public assisted at the scene of a railway crash and sustained long-term psychological problems as a result.	The plaintiff's claim for compensation was successful. At the time, this case appeared to indicate that the law would take a generous stance towards non-professional 'rescuers' in such circumstances.
Dulieu v White [1901] 2 KB 669	A pregnant barmaid suffered shock when a horse and cart was driven through the window.	The plaintiff was awarded damages on the basis of her foreseeable fear for her own safety. This was the first successful English claim for psychiatric damage.
Hambrook v Stokes Bros [1925] 1 KB 141	A mother died following shock she sustained having seen a runaway lorry heading for her children and hearing things which led her to believe that they had been hit.	Following the authority of **Dulieu**, it was held that liability could be extended to shock suffered due to fear for the safety of others. It may have been significant that this fear was for her children and that she experienced the event at first hand.
McFarlane v EE Caledonia [1994] 1 All ER 1	The plaintiff suffered shock following his exposure to an oil rig explosion and fire.	Because he was not in danger, he was not a primary victim and did not involve himself sufficiently in the rescue to qualify as a rescuer. His claim was unsuccessful.

Key debates

✶✶✶✶✶✶✶✶✶✶✶

Case	Facts	Principle
McLoughlin v O'Brian [1983] AC 410	A mother arrived at the hospital two hours after her family had been injured in a car accident and the shock of what she saw led to severe psychological illness.	The House of Lords unanimously ruled in her favour on the basis that although she had not witnessed the accident, she had seen the 'immediate aftermath'.
Page v Smith [1995] 2 All ER 736	The plaintiff was involved in a motor accident, due to the defendant's negligence. He suffered a recurrence of chronic fatigue syndrome.	It was held that a duty was owed to him in respect of psychological injury. He was a primary victim due to the fact that he was in the range of possible physical injury, and therefore the *Alcock* criteria did not apply. Ultimately his claim failed, due to doubts about causation.
White v Chief Constable of South Yorkshire Police [1999] 1 All ER 1	Police officers suffered shock following their involvement in the rescue and aftermath of the Hillsborough disaster, but their claim failed.	The House of Lords found that they were not primary victims, calling into doubt the decision in *Chadwick*. Because they did not fulfil the *Alcock* criteria for secondary victims, their claim failed.

⑨⑨ Key debates

Topic:	'Liability for Fear of Future Disease?'
Author:	M. Jones
Viewpoint:	Analyses the current status of *Page v Smith* in the light of the decision in *Rothwell*. Concludes that the law on psychiatric injury remains in an uncertain and unsatisfactory condition.
Source:	(2008) 24 PN 13

Topic:	'Liability for Negligently Inflicted Psychiatric Harm: Justification and Boundaries'
Author:	H. Teff
Viewpoint:	Analyses the current state of the law following *Page* and *Alcock*. Argues for a more flexible and generous approach with an emphasis on **foreseeability** rather than **proximity** and primary/secondary distinction.
Source:	(1998) 5 CLJ 91

Problem question

Mike is attending the annual Borsetshire Carriage Driving Championship to support his wife, Wendy, who is a competitor. They have recently reconciled after Wendy's affair with Ken. The organizers mistakenly supply Wendy with a racehorse and it runs so fast that her carriage tips over, seriously injuring Wendy. The horse narrowly misses Ken, who was viewing the race from the sidelines. Mike watches the accident from the stands, then sits by Wendy's hospital bed while she recovers from her injuries. He later develops serious depression. Ken is having nightmares and flashbacks.

Advise Mike and Ken.

See the Outline Answers section in the end matter for help with this question.

Essay question

'The concepts of primary and secondary victims have not helped to bring clarity to the law regarding liability for psychiatric injury.'

Discuss.

To see an outline answer to this question visit www.oup.com/lawrevision/

#6

Breach of duty: the standard of care

- Standard of care is the second and the most fact-specific, evidence-based element in the 'negligence equation' (see Figure 6.1).

- To establish that the duty of care has been breached, first the standard of care must be found and then it must be decided if that standard was reached in the circumstances.

- The general standard of care is objective: the 'reasonable person' standard.

- There are exceptions to the objective standard: when the defendant is a child or exercising a special skill.

- The standard must be considered in 'all the circumstances of the case'.

- The circumstances often involve a balancing of risks and costs.

- Proof of breach must be established by the claimant on the balance of probabilities.

- *Res ipsa loquitur* may assist the claimant in proof of breach.

Figure 6.1 Negligence equation

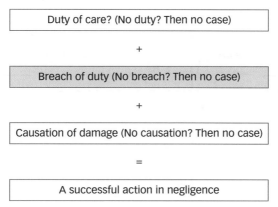

Duty of care? (No duty? Then no case)

+

Breach of duty (No breach? Then no case)

+

Causation of damage (No causation? Then no case)

=

A successful action in negligence

Assessment

Breach is a topic which rarely appears on its own but more commonly as one aspect of a larger **negligence** problem. Because determination is so dependent on the particular facts of each case, when answering a problem question it may be necessary for you to hypothesize if not all the information has been given to you, ie 'If the car had been travelling too fast and the driver had been drinking, then …'.

Be aware of the situations which diverge from the objective reasonable man standard and take into account the 'balancing factors': how might the issues of risk or extent of potential damage be approached? Always remember to consider the applicability of *res ipsa loquitur*.

Key features and principles

Having established that the defendant owed a **duty of care** to the claimant (see Chapters 2 and 3), the next element in a successful **negligence** claim requires that the defendant breached that duty. That is, that negligence took place and so, because the defendant was at **fault**, he may be liable. What level of carelessness constitutes negligence in law?

This must be addressed in two stages:

 1. What was the appropriate standard of care? How ought the defendant to have behaved in the circumstances?

This is a matter of law, based upon case and statutory authority.

 2. Did the defendant reach that standard?

This is a matter of fact and will depend upon what actually happened in each case.

Key features and principles
✳✳✳✳✳✳✳✳✳✳✳✳

Stage 1. Setting the standard of care—'the reasonable person'

In 1856 the standard of care in **negligence** was said, in *Blyth v Birmingham Waterworks (1856)*, to be that of the 'reasonable man'. The reasonable man (or person!) is neither excessively cautious nor unusually risk-taking. By applying this hypothetical standard, the law is taking an objective approach—that is, it is not generally concerned with the capacities of any particular defendant.

Glasgow Corp v Muir [1943] AC 448

FACTS: This is the prime authority for the objective test, which was applied to an accident which took place when an urn of boiling tea was spilled onto children in a public tea room.

HELD: The House of Lords stressed that it must assess what a reasonable person would do *in the circumstances* existing at the time, and to that extent there was a subjective element in setting the standard of care. Here, a reasonable person would not have foreseen the risk of the accident which occurred. In the absence of breach of duty, the defendant was not liable in **negligence**.

The **objective standard** can sometimes operate harshly upon defendants. Probably the most extreme example is illustrated in the case of *Nettleship v Weston* (1971).

Nettleship v Weston [1971] 2 QB 691 → learner driver.

FACTS: The plaintiff, who was not a professional driving instructor, agreed to give lessons to the defendant, a friend, having confirmed that she held fully comprehensive insurance. On her third outing, while driving in a car without dual controls and despite her instructor's attempts to avert the crash, she hit a tree. The plaintiff suffered a fractured knee. The key issue considered by the Court of Appeal was the standard of care to be expected of the learner driver.

HELD: By a two to one majority, it was held that the standard of care expected of the learner driver was, according to Lord Denning, that of: 'an experienced, skilled and careful driver'. The defendant was liable to her instructor on the grounds that she had breached that standard of care. The damages awarded were reduced by 50% on the grounds of the instructor's **contributory negligence**.

This controversial (and some would say, harsh) decision illustrates the way in which the application of the 'reasonable person' standard of care was here driven by policy considerations aimed at reducing danger on the roads and placing potential liability upon insured drivers.

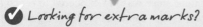

✅ Looking for extra marks?

In the Australian case of *Cook v Cook* (1986) it was held that the **duty of care** owed by a learner driver varied according to his relationship with the claimant. If the injured party was another road user, then the principle in *Nettleship* would apply but the relationship of learner and instructor necessarily carried with it a lower standard of care. The decision in *Cook v Cook* was not followed in 2008 in *Imbree v McNeilly* and Australian law is now consistent with *Nettleship*.

Knowledge

In cases where scientific and technical expertise may be involved, the defendant's actions will be judged in terms of the state of knowledge at the time of the incident in question. This was illustrated in *Roe v Ministry of Health* (1954), where developments in medical knowledge about potential cracks in glass ampoules between the date of the claimant's **injury** and the date of trial were ignored, leading to a finding of no breach of duty by the defendant. See also the recent case of *Japp v Virgin Holidays Ltd* (2013) in which the standard of care for building construction was held to be the safety standards and customs at the time of construction, rather at the later time of the accident.

On the other hand, regard must be had to any specific knowledge of the defendant. In *Paris v Stepney BC* (1950), where the employer knew that the claimant had already lost one eye, there was a higher expectation that the employer provide protective equipment.

Exceptions to the objective standard

In some situations, common sense has dictated that the **objective standard** must be modified.

Children

A child cannot be expected to attain the same standard of care as an adult. In *Mullin v Richards* (1998) two 15-year-old girls were fighting with plastic rulers in school. When a ruler snapped, one of the girls sustained an eye injury. The standard to be applied was that of the *reasonable child of that age*. Here there had been no breach.

Illness

To what extent will a defendant be liable for actions influenced by physical illness? This will depend on the extent of awareness of the illness and whether or not actions can be controlled. Two contrasting cases are *Roberts v Ramsbottom* (1980) and *Mansfield v Weetabix* (1998). In the former, the defendant was held to have breached his **duty of care** when he caused an accident having continued to drive while aware of the early effects of a stroke. The lorry driver in *Mansfield*, however, bore no liability for an accident which resulted when he unknowingly slipped into a coma.

Skill

When the defendant is performing a task which requires a level of skill, the standard set will vary according to context and how he presents himself. For example, in *Phillips v William*

Key features and principles
✳✳✳✳✳✳✳✳✳✳

Whiteley (1938) a jeweller piercing ears in a department store was not expected to reach a medical standard of cleanliness and in *Wells v Cooper* (1958) someone performing a 'DIY' job at home was not expected to reach the standard of a professional carpenter, but only that of the reasonably competent domestic handyman.

Experience

Some modification of the purely **objective standard** is necessary in cases involving the combination of professional skill and the impact of experience. This is best illustrated by *Wilsher v Essex AHA*.

Wilsher v Essex Area Health Authority [1987] QB 730, CA

In this medical negligence case it was held that the standard of care expected of a doctor was that appropriate to the post held (eg junior doctor or consultant), but within that level no further account would be taken of relative inexperience. On **causation** in *Wilsher*, see Chapter 7 ('One out of many', p 82).

Revision tip

Breach of duty by doctors and other professionals must be considered in conjunction with the '*Bolam* test', see later in the chapter.

Special standards

Sports

Here, those involved are frequently pushing themselves 'to go all out to win', in situations of physical contact and sometimes danger. The decision in *Wooldridge v Sumner* (1963) was that the duty of a rider to a spectator at a horse show had not been breached because he had not shown 'reckless disregard' for safety.

One aspect of the circumstances to be considered in setting the standard is the level at which the particular sport is being played. In *Condon v Basi* (1985), a reckless foul constituted **negligence** in a local league football match, whereas it might not have done had it taken place in the Premier Division. In *Vowles v Evans* (2003) the Court of Appeal recognized that a higher standard of care would be expected from a professional rugby referee than from an amateur.

Revision tip

Regarding sports cases, other issues which overlap with that of breach are consent, ruling out **battery** (see Chapter 11), and the defence of ***volenti*** (see Chapter 16).

Professional skills

When the defendant has held him or herself out as having particular professional skills, the relevant standard must be based upon comparisons with others of the same profession.

This principle was clarified in *Bolam v Friern Hospital Management Committee*.

Bolam v Friern Hospital Management Committee [1957] 1 WLR 582

Here, in the context of medical diagnosis and treatment, it was held that '[t]he test is the standard of the ordinary skilled man exercising and professing to have that special skill'. The ***Bolam*** approach contains both objective and subjective elements.

How do we know what the 'ordinary skilled' practitioner would do in certain circumstances? According to *Bolam*, 'A doctor is not guilty of negligence if he has acted in accordance with a practice accepted as proper by a responsible body of medical men skilled in that particular art.' In *Sidaway v Board of Governors of Bethlem Royal Hospital* (1985) the *Bolam* standard was applied to the medical duty to inform patients of risks.

✅ *Looking for extra marks?*

In *Bolitho v City and Hackney Health Authority* (1998) the House of Lords asserted the significant role of the courts in determining what constituted a responsible body of opinion: the view in question must be 'capable of being logically supported'.

Adams v Rhymney Valley DC (2000) serves as a reminder that the *Bolam* test can apply to the non-medical context as well. Here, the relevant skill pertained to the design of council house windows.

At times, in relation to a special skill it will be claimed that the action in question was *common practice* and therefore not negligent. The courts have not accepted this as a conclusive defence: 'Neglect of duty does not cease by repetition to be neglect of duty' (*Bank of Montreal v Dominion Guarantee* (1930)).

Best practice

Best practice, or professional guidelines, can be one piece of relevant evidence which the court will take note of in reaching its decision.

In *Buck v Nottinghamshire Healthcare NHS Trust* [2006] EWCA Civ 157 a **negligence** action was brought by psychiatric nurses who were injured by a patient. The Court of Appeal measured the defendant's behaviour against NHS regulations concerning the handling of dangerous patients and found that the **duty of care** to staff had been breached.

The restricted resources of the defendant may be taken into account.

Key features and principles
✳✳✳✳✳✳✳✳✳✳✳✳

In *Knight v Home Office* **[1990]** 3 All ER 237 the court recognized that the facilities available in a prison hospital would necessarily be limited in comparison to a specialist psychiatric hospital. Lack of funds would not be a complete defence to insufficient safety precautions in a **negligence** case; however, the court must accept the reality that resources for prison medicine are limited.

Stage 2. Applying the standard of care: a 'balancing' exercise

Now that you have decided upon the appropriate standard of care, it must be decided whether the defendant conformed to this standard in the specific case.

What would the reasonable person have done?

The answer to this question is one of fact and will be assisted by balancing two different aspects of the specific scenario (see Figure 6.2):

1. The magnitude of risk. This is comprised of the likelihood (or **foreseeability**) of **injury** occurring plus the severity of the injury should it occur. We can think of it as the *cost of running the risk*.

2. The importance of the activity undertaken by the defendant plus the practicability of taking precautions against the risk: the *cost of avoiding the risk*.

If the *cost of running the risk* exceeded the *cost of avoiding the risk* then it is likely that the defendant was negligent. If the *cost of avoiding the risk* was greater than the *cost of running the risk*, then it is likely that the defendant was not negligent.

Figure 6.2 The balance of risk

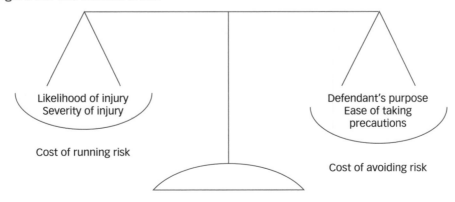

Likelihood of injury
Severity of injury

Cost of running risk

Defendant's purpose
Ease of taking
precautions

Cost of avoiding risk

Bolton v Stone [1951] 1 All ER 1078

FACTS: A **negligence** action was brought against a cricket club by a pedestrian who was struck by a ball which had been hit over the fence into the street along which she was walking. On one side of the balancing scale, it was found that the likelihood of this happening had been very slight and the severity of potential **injury** relatively minor. On the other side of the scale, a high value was given to the defendant being able to continue to play cricket on the site, and the cost of raising a fence to stop occasional balls flying into the road was prohibitive.

HELD: On the basis of these conclusions, the defendants' playing of cricket in the circumstances was held by the House of Lords to have been reasonable and therefore not negligent. They had reached the standard of the reasonable person.

The outcome in *Bolton v Stone* can be compared to that in *The Wagon Mound (No 2)*.

Overseas Tankship (UK) v The Miller Steamship Co [1966] 2 All ER 709, PC ('The Wagon Mound (No 2)')

FACTS: The defendant had negligently discharged oil into Sydney Harbour. It eventually ignited, causing a large and damaging fire, when rubbish floating on the oil was ignited by sparks from a welding operation.

HELD: In balancing the risks, the Privy Council held there had been a small but real risk of fire and given that there was no positive benefit in discharging the oil and the cost of avoiding the spillage was non-existent, the defendant had failed to meet the standard of the reasonable person. In *Wagon Mound (No 1)* (see later in the chapter) the Privy Council dealt with the issue of *remoteness* in relation to these facts.

In *Watt v Hertfordshire CC* (1954) the dominant element in the equation was the social utility of the defendant's purpose. A rescue vehicle was rushing to the scene of an accident in which a woman was trapped under a car. An unsecured jack in a rescue vehicle fell, while being transported a short distance, injuring a fireman. Given the urgent, life-saving objective of the defendant rescuers, they had behaved reasonably in not taking the time to secure the equipment.

See also *Latimer v AEC* (1953), in Chapter 9 ('The duty to provide a safe place of work', p 104), which provides another illustration of balancing, this time in the industrial setting.

✔ *Looking for extra marks?*

The above balancing exercise was derived from an 'equation' designed by an American judge, Learned Hand, in 1947. It is indicative of the 'economic' approach to **tort** law, which essentially bases tort liabilities upon financial efficiency.

The Compensation Act 2006

Section 1 suggests that courts, in considering the standard of care in **negligence**, should have regard to the extent to which the imposition of safety requirements could impact upon 'desirable activities'. This provision is directed at the excesses of the 'compensation culture' (introduced in Chapter 1). You may wish to read judicial consideration of s 1 in *Hopps v Mott MacDonald and the Ministry of Defence* (2009) and *The Scout Association v Barnes* (2010), where Jackson LJ remarked that the taking into account of costs of prevention had long been a part of the existing common law.

Revision tip

In answering a problem question, beware of the temptation to assume that the defendant has been negligent. For example, in a **negligent misstatement** problem you will be concerned to establish whether or not there is a **duty of care**, and having done so may then jump to the conclusion of liability without establishing that this duty has in fact been breached.

How is breach established?

The basic rule is that the burden is on the claimant to establish that there has been a breach of duty. The standard of proof is civil: the balance of probabilities.

In some cases, such as road traffic accidents, the defendant may already have been convicted of a criminal offence in respect of the same set of facts. The **Civil Evidence Act 1968, s 11** provides that in such circumstances the criminal conviction can be used to provide strong, although not conclusive, evidence that the defendant has been negligent.

Res ipsa loquitur ('the thing speaks for itself')

In some cases the court will effectively give the claimant the benefit of the doubt by inferring **negligence** from what is known, in the absence of convincing evidence to the contrary.

Three elements must be present before the case is an appropriate one in which to apply *res ipsa loquitur*:

1. The accident must be of the kind which does not normally happen in the absence of **negligence**.

An early illustration is *Scott v London and St Katherine's Dock Co* (1865), where the plaintiff was hit by some bags of sugar which fell out of the window of a warehouse onto his head!

2. The cause of the accident must have been under the defendant's control.

In *Gee v Metropolitan Railway Co* (1873), *res ipsa loquitur* was applied to an accident in which the door of a train flew open a few minutes after leaving the station, causing the plaintiff to fall out. The train doors were presumed to have been the sole responsibility of the train company at the relevant time.

However, in *Easson v London & North Eastern Railway Co* (1944), a similar accident happened near the end of a journey from London to Edinburgh. In this instance, the court held that there would have been too many opportunities for others to tamper with the doors, so the 'control' condition was not met.

3.   There must be no explanation of the cause of the accident.

Res ipsa loquitur is not relevant when there are sufficient facts known in order to prove **negligence**.

This was the case in *Barkway v South Wales Transport Co Ltd* (1950). The plaintiff was injured when a bus in which he was a passenger crashed. It was established that the cause of the crash was a burst tyre and that this would not have occurred had the defendant adopted a proper system of tyre inspection.

Revision tip

Res ipsa loquitur is particularly important in the fields of common law product liability and medical negligence, when the claimant is less likely to possess all the necessary evidence to support his claim.

What is the effect of imposing res ipsa?

This has been a matter of some debate, with some claiming that it places the burden on the defendant to disprove **negligence**. It has been confirmed by the Privy Council in *Ng Chun Pui v Lee Chuen Tat* (1988) that the legal burden of proof remains with the plaintiff. That is, if the defendant raises a plausible explanation for the accident which gives an innocent cause, then the claimant will lose the case.

Res ipsa loquitur was held, by the Privy Council, to be applicable to an air crash in *George v Eagle Air Services*.

George v Eagle Air Services [2009] 1 WLR 2133

The three requirements were fulfilled: planes do not normally crash, the defendant had control over the aircraft, its flight and pilot, and he had failed to give any explanation which was at least consistent with the absence of **fault** on his part. The defendant having failed to displace the inference of **negligence**, the claimant was successful.

✔ Looking for extra marks?

You may have noticed the frequent appearance, throughout the law of **negligence**, of the term '**foreseeability**'. It is used, in slightly different senses, in all three stages of the negligence equation. In relation to duty it is used to establish the required relationship between the claimant and the defendant; here, as part of the process of 'risk assessment' in determining breach, and in **causation** (Chapter 7), in relation to the question of whether an outcome is too remote.

Conclusion
****

(!) Conclusion

This is a highly fact-specific aspect of **negligence** and to some extent each case will turn on its own particular circumstances. However the value of using case law as precedent lies in developing a sense of the way the courts have applied policy in reaching decisions in different categories, for example, comparing the rather strict attitudes towards drivers (**Nettleship**) to the more deferential one towards doctors and other professionals (**Bolam**). Applying the law will usually involve you in a cost–benefit analysis, as seen in **Bolton** and **Wagon Mound**.

(*) Key cases

Case	Facts	Principle
Bolam v Friern Hospital Management Committee [1957] 1 WLR 582	The plaintiff was injured in hospital during ECT treatment. It was held that the relevant standard of care here was that of 'the ordinary, skilled man exercising and professing to have that special skill'.	The **Bolam** test, to be applied when there is a difference of opinion in a professional field, is that an action will not be negligent if it would be approved by a 'responsible body of medical men skilled in that particular art'.
Bolton v Stone [1951] 1 All ER 1078	The plaintiff was hit by a cricket ball hit over a fence and into the road where she was standing. The cricket club was held not to have breached the duty of care owed to her owing to the unforeseeability of such an accident combined with the high cost of avoiding it.	This 'borderline' decision, by the House of Lords, illustrates the way that courts expect the reasonable person to assess the risk of a given situation.
Glasgow Corporation v Muir [1943] AC 448	An urn spilled while being carried down a corridor and several children were scalded, who sued the occupier in negligence. It was held that the accident would not have been foreseeable by the ordinary reasonable person and therefore the duty of care had not been breached.	The objective standard of care, the foresight of the reasonable man, must be applied according to the circumstances pertaining at the relevant time.
Mullin v Richards [1998] 1 WLR 1304	Two 15-year-old girls were fencing with plastic rulers at school. One of the rulers cracked and a piece of plastic entered the eye of one of the girls, causing her to lose sight in that eye. The Court of Appeal dismissed the negligence claim.	'The standard by which [his] conduct is to be measured is not that to be expected of a reasonable adult but that reasonably to be expected of a child of the same age, intelligence and experience.' This principle follows that of the Australian case of **McHale v Watson (1966)**.

Case	Facts	Principle
Nettleship v Weston [1971] 2 QB 691	A driving instructor successfully claimed in negligence against a pupil when he was injured in an accident she caused on her third lesson.	The duty of care to be expected of a learner driver is that of the reasonably competent and experienced driver.
Overseas Tankship (UK) v The Miller Steamship Co [1966] 2 All ER 709, PC (**'The Wagon Mound (No 2)'**)	A negligence action was brought by the owners of two ships which were damaged in a large fire in Sydney Harbour. The fire had occurred after the unlawful discharge of oil by the defendant. The Privy Council held that although such a fire was unlikely it was nevertheless foreseeable.	Lack of any worthwhile purpose in the defendant's discharge of the oil and the low cost of avoidance was weighed against the great extent of potential damage in finding that in the circumstances there had been a breach of duty. This event also gave rise to a very important case on the subject of causation in negligence.
Wilsher v Essex Area Health Authority [1987] QB 730, CA	The negligent act in question had been a junior doctor's administration of excess oxygen to a premature baby in a neonatal special care unit. The issue relating to breach was to what extent the inexperience of the doctor could be taken into account.	The applicable standard of care related not to the person, nor to the task, but to the post occupied within the medical care team. Within the ambit of the post, no further account would be taken of relative inexperience.
Wooldridge v Sumner [1963] 2 QB 43	A photographer at a horse show was seriously injured when a horse and rider breached the perimeter of the ring where he was standing. The standard of care at a sporting event was described in terms of the expectations of the 'reasonable spectator'. It was recognized that in sporting situations it was more difficult to exercise 'reasonable care'.	Here there would be no breach of duty unless the sportsman had shown 'a reckless disregard of the spectator's safety'. This standard has also been applied between participants in sport.

⑨ Key debates

Topic:	**'Medical Negligence and the *Bolam* Test'**
Author:	M. Brazier and J. Miola
Viewpoint:	Questions both the nature and application of the *Bolam* test and argues that, contrary to perceptions, it should not permit a great degree of autonomy to the medical profession.
Source:	'Bye-bye *Bolam*: a Medical Litigation Revolution?' (2000) 8 MLR 85

Exam questions

✳✳✳✳✳✳✳✳✳✳✳✳

Topic:	'The Compensation Culture'
Author:	K. Williams
Viewpoint:	Examines the extent to which perceptions about law and legal decision-making have contributed to what may be a misplaced 'moral panic' about the existence of a 'compensation culture' in Britain.
Source:	'State of Fear: Britain's "Compensation Culture" Reviewed' (2005) 25 LS 499

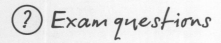 ② Exam questions

Problem questions

1. Martin is leaving work late one evening when he hears an alarm bell ringing in the office of his manager, Raj. He does nothing about this until he returns home and then decides to ring the emergency services. Linda, who takes the call, does not give it priority status and when the police arrive to investigate two hours later, it is discovered that thieves have escaped with most of the contents of Raj's office.

   Advise Raj.

   See the Outline Answers section in the end matter for help with this question.

2. Ted is on his second day working as driver for Ace Medical Supplies. Although he recently acquired an HGV licence, he has been employed to drive small vans only. A call comes into the depot that there has been a serious rail crash and a delivery of blood products is urgently required at the nearby hospital. Greg, the usual HGV driver is ill, and so Angie, the manager, asks Ted to do the delivery because she is anxious not to lose the contract to a competitor. Ted loses control of his lorry on a bend in the road and crashes into Maya, who is running across the road in the dark.

   Advise Maya.

 ⓐ Online Resource Centre

To see an outline answer to this question visit www.oup.com/lawrevision/

#7

Causation in fact

Key facts

- Causation, the third part of the 'negligence equation' (see Figure 7.1), is both fact-based and policy-based.

- Causation is divided into: 'causation in fact' and 'causation in law' (or 'remoteness').

- Causation in fact can be addressed by the 'but-for' test.

- Causation must be established on the balance of probabilities.

- This area of the law involves some conceptual issues which can prove challenging for students.

- The but-for test is inadequate to establish causation in a number of different situations: unknown causes, cumulative causes, and consecutive causes.

- This chapter must be studied in conjunction with Chapter 8.

Figure 7.1 Negligence equation

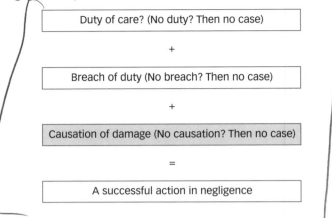

Duty of care? (No duty? Then no case)

+

Breach of duty (No breach? Then no case)

+

Causation of damage (No causation? Then no case)

=

A successful action in negligence

Assessment

Causation may arise in an exam question either as an essay question or as a key component in a problem question. It is an area in which the law has seen some significant shifts in direction in recent years and you should be aware of these, and the policy issues underlying them.

The 'but-for' test

Causation in fact has been described by Winfield as 'primarily a matter of historical mechanics'. As its name states, it involves establishing the facts of how something came about at a given time. Causation in fact may not establish all or even the main causes, but it permits exclusion of certain factors or persons from having contributed to a particular outcome.

The hypothetical 'but-for' test is traditionally used to begin the process of establishing causation in fact. It involves asking the question: 'But for the defendant's breach of duty, would the claimant's damage still have occurred?' If the answer is 'yes', then the defendant's breach generally can be eliminated as a factual cause of the damage. If the answer is 'no', then we know that the defendant's breach is at least one of the contributing causes of the damage (see Figure 7.2).

> **Barnett v Kensington & Chelsea Health Management Committee [1968] 2 WLR 422**
>
> **FACTS:** This case demonstrates the application of the but-for test. The plaintiffs became ill after drinking tea. When they went to hospital, the doctor did not examine them but recommended that they return home and contact their own doctors. Some hours later, one of the men died. It turned out that he had died of arsenical poisoning and that, on the balance of probabilities, the treatment which the doctor would have given him could not have saved him.

> **HELD:** The court accepted that although there had been **negligence** in failing to examine the patients, but for his breach, the death would still have occurred. Therefore it was to be eliminated as a cause of the death.

The burden lies upon the claimant to prove **causation** on the balance of probabilities, as illustrated by _Pickford v ICI (1998)_. This requirement, which can be referred to as the 'all or nothing' approach, has led to significant problems for claimants in areas such as _loss of a chance_, which will be reviewed later in the chapter.

When the 'but-for' test is insufficient

Problems in the application of the but-for test arise in two particular circumstances:

1. When the answer to the question leads to an unjust or contradictory result.
2. When it is impossible to answer the but-for question.

A hypothetical example of the first is as follows. Two people, X and Y, simultaneously light a match in a gas-filled room and an explosion occurs. If we ask: 'But for the negligence of X would the explosion have happened?' the answer would be yes. Then if we ask: 'But for the negligence of Y would the explosion have happened?' the answer would again be yes. Applying the but-for test to the gas-filled room scenario would result in neither X nor Y being regarded as a cause and thus neither would be liable. A more appropriate outcome, to ensure

Figure 7.2 The 'but-for' test

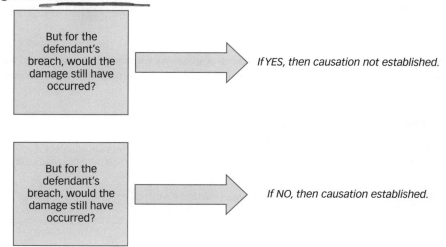

But for the defendant's breach, would the damage still have occurred? → *If YES, then causation not established.*

But for the defendant's breach, would the damage still have occurred? → *If NO, then causation established.*

The 'but-for' test
****

a **remedy** in respect of the explosion, would be to regard both their actions as causes and to make X and Y **jointly and severally liable**.

Several liability

Two or more parties act independently to cause the same damage to a claimant. Each party is separately liable for the whole of the damage (but compensation can only be recovered once).

Joint and several liability

Two or more parties act together to cause the same damage to a claimant. Any or all can be sued, each party being separately liable for the whole of the damage, and in a case when only one is able to pay, he will be liable for the whole of the damage. An example is vicarious liability.

Contribution

Where there is joint and several liability, one party who pays compensation may wish to claim a portion of this from other wrongdoers. The **Civil Liability (Contribution) Act 1978, ss 1 and 2** enable the party who has paid the compensation to bring an action to recover contribution from one or more of the other parties.

Situations in which it is not possible to answer the but-for question accurately vary from the simple to the complicated.

Cook v Lewis [1952] 1 DLR 1

FACTS: This was a Canadian case in which two hunters negligently fired their guns in the direction of the plaintiff. One bullet hit him, but it was not established which gun had fired that bullet.

HELD: In the absence of the required proof, it was held that the hunters would be **jointly and severally liable**. In order to achieve a just result for the victim it was necessary to adapt the normal rules on **causation**.

The but-for test usually involves an element of guesswork concerning what *would have* happened in a given circumstance. Sometimes the guessing focuses on what someone *might*, or *might not*, have done.

McWilliams v Sir William Arrol & Co [1962] 1 WLR 295

FACTS: The deceased's employer had been negligent in failing to provide a safety harness for a steel-worker, who fell to his death. It was clearly established that had the defendant provided a safety harness, the worker would not have worn it.

HELD: But for the defendant's breach, the damage would still have occurred and so there was no liability on the part of the employer.

Allied Maples Group v Simmons (1995) illustrates this point in respect of economic loss.

Loss of a chance

In some cases, the argument will be made that the defendant's **negligence** increased the likelihood of a poor outcome for the claimant or deprived him of the possibility of avoiding such an outcome. The courts have been reluctant to allow 'loss of a chance' to substitute for the 'all or nothing' requirement that causation be proved on a balance of probabilities (ie 51% or more).

Hotson v Berkshire AHA **[1987] AC 750**

FACTS: A schoolboy injured his hip in a fall from a tree. When taken to hospital the seriousness of his injuries was not immediately discovered. Five days later, his condition was correctly diagnosed and treated. However, he developed a serious disability of the hip as an adult, which he claimed was caused by the delayed diagnosis. The hospital admitted **negligence** but denied liability on the grounds of lack of **causation**. According to the medical evidence, given proper treatment the boy would only have had a 25% chance of complete recovery.

HELD: The plaintiff lost his case because on the balance of probabilities the disability would have occurred even without the defendant's negligence.

Revision tip

When you see a problem question in the exam which refers to percentages of chance in relation to damage, it will often be appropriate to apply *Hotson* in your answer.

In another medical negligence case, *Gregg v Scott* (2005), the strict *Hotson* 'balance of probabilities' approach was applied. The claimant had complained of a lump under his arm and Dr Scott concluded that it was benign and did not order any further investigation or tests. A year later it was discovered that the lump was a symptom of cancer. The claimant was given a 25% chance of ten years' survival. That chance would have been as high as 42% at the time he visited Dr Scott.

By a narrow majority, the House of Lords found in favour of the defendant:

- The claimant's loss had been described in terms of the potential for ten years' survival.
- He could not prove that he had a likelihood of survival higher than 50%, even at the time of his first medical consultation.
- The relative diminution in his chances of survival was not a type of **loss** recognized in **negligence** claims, because he had never had a chance of a positive outcome, on the balance of probabilities (see Figure 7.3).

A very different type of causation problem arises when a doctor or other medical professional has been negligent in failing adequately to explain to a patient the risks of a possible course of treatment. Essential to success is the claimant's ability to establish that had

Loss of a chance
✶✶✶✶✶✶✶✶✶✶

Figure 7.3 *Hotson v E Berkshire AHA* and *Gregg v Scott*

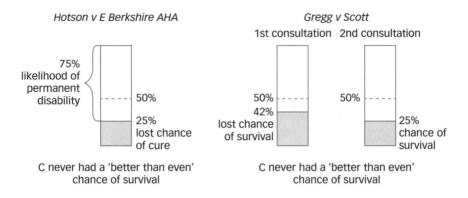

those risks been explained he would not have given consent and the adverse outcome would thereby have been avoided.

Chester v Afshar [2004] UKHL 41

FACTS: A patient consulted a neurosurgeon about her back pain and was advised to undergo surgery. The surgery carried with it a risk of 1–2% of serious nerve damage, even if performed without **negligence**. The claimant was not informed by the surgeon of this risk and following the operation she was found to have suffered the nerve damage.

HELD: The but-for test had not been satisfied. This was because even though, had she been properly informed, the claimant would not have agreed to the operation *at that time*, she might well have gone on to have the surgery in the future when the risk would still have existed.

Despite this, a majority of Law Lords ruled in favour of the claimant. They based their conclusion on the policy grounds of upholding patient autonomy, which justified 'a narrow and modest departure from traditional causation principles'.

✅ *Looking for extra marks?*

You may wish to examine *Gregg* in more depth and compare the positions of the different Law Lords. Baroness Hale, for the majority, stressed how complicated it would be to calculate loss of a chance and then compensate on a proportional basis. Lord Nicholls, on the other hand, favoured imposing liability on the basis of what he regarded as 'medical reality'.

In some cases, the claimant is unable to establish which one of separate unconnected factors caused his damage or, alternatively, to what extent connected causes may have accumulated to bring about his illness or injury.

Material contribution

This particular approach to solving claimants' difficulties in proving **causation** has been used in cases in which the process has been cumulative and the resultant damage can be viewed as indivisible, that is, it cannot be broken down into different parts which can separately be attributed to different causes. The cause is a significant one of many and as such supports liability.

Bonnington Castings v Wardlaw [1956] AC 613

FACTS: The plaintiff developed an industrial lung disease after working in the defendant's workshop. This was caused by the cumulative inhaling of dust, some of which occurred owing to the employer's **negligence** but some of which was unavoidable.

HELD: Although he was unable to establish that but for the employer's negligence he would not have suffered the disease, the plaintiff nevertheless recovered his full **loss**. This was because the House of Lords was satisfied that the negligence had made a 'material contribution' to the damage.

A more recent example of this approach was seen in *Bailey v Ministry of Defence* (2008). The claimant sustained brain damage while under the care of the defendant's hospital. She suffered a cardiac arrest due to the aspiration of vomit and it was claimed that this would not have happened had she not been in a weakened state due to the defendant's earlier failures in her post-operative care. **Negligence** was not disputed; however, the appeal turned on the question of **causation**: had this breach caused her damage?

The Court of Appeal found in favour of the claimant. Her **loss** had cumulative causes (her physical vulnerability combined with the defendant's **negligence**). Although it was not possible to establish the proportion of **causation** to be attributed to the defendant, it was found that but for his inadequate care the claimant would have been less weak and so his breach had *materially contributed* to her damage.

Material contribution to damage was again held by the Court of Appeal to be the issue in *Dickins v O2 plc* (2008), where the claimant was successful in her claim, due to the fact that the defendant's **negligence** had made a *material contribution* to her psychiatric injury.

Material increase in risk

The abovementioned approach can also be applied in cases in which there is no process of accumulation but rather only one, but unidentifiable, cause. Here it may be described as causing '*a material increase in risk*'.

McGhee v National Coal Board [1973] 1 WLR 1

FACTS: A worker sustained a skin disease caused by contact with brick dust, after years of working in a brick kiln. His employer admitted **negligence** in failing to provide adequate washing facilities at the end of the working day. McGhee alleged, but was unable to prove, that it was this extended exposure

---

at the end of the day which had caused his disease. The case for the defendant was that, because his job involved exposure to brick dust all day long, it was more likely than not that the plaintiff's disease had been caused by 'innocent' rather than wrongful exposure.

HELD: A unanimous House of Lords found for the plaintiff, despite recognition that an 'evidential gap' existed, on the basis that when proof was impossible, justice was best served if the party at **fault** bore the **loss** which had been incurred. Lord Wilberforce said, 'the default here consisted not in adding a material quantity to the accumulation of injurious particles but by failure to take a step which materially increased the risk'.

One out of many?

In *Bonnington* and *Bailey* different factors combined cumulatively and in *McGhee* one single factor was involved in the plaintiff's **injury**. However, in *Wilsher v Essex Area Health Authority*, there were five separate possible factors, only one of which actually caused the damage, and no process of accumulation.

Wilsher v Essex AHA [1988] AC 1074, HL

FACTS: Shortly after birth, the plaintiff had been given excess oxygen owing to the **negligence** of the hospital where he had been born prematurely. He later was found to be blind. One cause of blindness in premature babies is excess oxygen; however, there are four other potential causes, all of which could have applied in his case. At the trial, the plaintiff was unable to prove on a balance of probabilities that the excess oxygen had been the cause of his blindness.

HELD: The House of Lords distinguished the 'material contribution' approach of *McGhee*. In *Wilsher*, the defendant had merely added one additional possible cause to four other discrete (non-negligent) causes. Without conclusive evidence that the hospital's **negligence** had been the operative cause, liability could not be imposed.

Current issues in causation: asbestos

The widespread industrial use of asbestos in the first half of the 20th century has led to a growing number of **negligence** claims based upon diseases developed by workers who were exposed to this toxic substance.

Fairchild v Glenhaven Funeral Services [2002] UKHL 22

FACTS: Here, the House of Lords had to deal with a complex **causation** issue which arose in a number of asbestos compensation claims. The claimants were suffering from mesothelioma, a fatal disease caused by exposure to asbestos dust. It was not known scientifically whether the disease was initiated by one fibre of asbestos or by many, or exactly how the cumulative development of the disease occurred. The causation problem arose because the claimants had negligently been exposed to asbestos while working for several different employers, some of whom had gone out of business and could not now be sued. It was impossible to establish which exposure had caused their current disease. Applying the but-for test, the Court of Appeal had rejected all three claims.

> **HELD:** The House of Lords, however, took a novel and controversial approach to **causation**. Following the decision in **McGhee**, each of the defendants was treated as having created a 'material increase of risk' of damage to the claimants. In a decision strongly driven by policy, which was claimed to be a departure from the 'normal but-for' legal principle, the court unanimously allowed the appeals and held all the employers jointly liable.

Barker v Corus UK (2006) also concerned asbestos-related disease and the evidential gap.

The majority in *Barker* described the damage caused by the defendants as *material increase in the risk* of contracting the disease.

Contrary to the decision in *Fairchild*, on the issue of apportionment of **damages**, the Law Lords held that the liability of each defendant would be *apportioned*, that is, each would only be liable in proportion to the amount of risk they had created.

The effect of *Barker* on **apportionment** was quickly reversed by the **Compensation Act 2006, s 3** of which restored the *Fairchild* position of joint and several liability in cases of asbestos-related mesothelioma. This means that any one negligent defendant could, if necessary, be ordered to bear 100% liability, regardless of the extent of his involvement with the claimant. In *Sienkiewicz v Grief* (2011), the Supreme Court held that the '*Fairchild* exception' would apply even when the mesothelioma was attributable to only one negligent source, providing the claimant could satisfy the court that the increase in risk caused was 'material'.

How far will Fairchild apply?

Chester v Afshar, discussed earlier, is an example of the way in which the courts, on occasion, have been prepared to extend the principles of **causation** in order to obtain what is seen as a fair outcome. These cases will be limited, but the future is as yet unpredictable. While in *Gregg v Scott* the '*Fairchild* exception' was not applied, *Bailey v Ministry of Defence* (2008) is a recent example in which the benefit of the doubt on **causation** was extended to the claimant in a clinical negligence case.

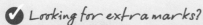 ✔ *Looking for extra marks?*

You might want to find out more about the key policy issues at play in the asbestos litigation. *Barker* was, in part, a challenge by the insurance industry, which was hit very hard by the decision in *Fairchild*. There was, however, strong resistance to the outcome in *Barker* from unions and others. The insurance (and contractual) implications of *Fairchild*, *Barker,* and *Sienkiewicz* were discussed by the Supreme Court in *Durham v BAI* (2012).

Consecutive causes

By this we mean later unconnected events causing the same or greater harm as the first **tort**. In some cases involving two torts, the second wrongdoer may find that his breach of duty caused no additional damage to a victim and that he is therefore not liable to pay compensation.

Consecutive causes

✳✳✳✳✳✳✳✳✳✳✳✳

Performance Cars v Abraham (1962) involved a Rolls Royce which was damaged in a collision due to the **fault** of A and, as a result, the bottom half of the car required a respray. Two weeks later, before the damage could be repaired, B collided with the same car. The damage done required a respray of the bottom half of the car. Because B had created no additional damage, the total liability remained with A.

There may be a situation in which a second event overtakes or wipes out the effect of the damage done by a first **tort**. In *Baker v Willoughby* (1970), the plaintiff suffered a leg injury in a car accident attributable to the **negligence** of the defendant. Some three years later and before the trial regarding the accident, the plaintiff was the victim of a shooting during an attempted robbery, which resulted in the amputation of the same leg. At trial the defendant claimed that his liability for the leg injury should cease at the time of the second injury because the injured leg no longer existed. The House of Lords held that the second event would not be treated as wiping out the original **injury**, which was effectively a concurrent cause of the plaintiff's eventual disability.

The decision in *Baker* is usually contrasted with *Jobling v Associated Dairies* (1981). There, a work injury to his back resulted in a permanent disability to the plaintiff. Three years later, and before the trial, he developed a spinal disease which put an end to his employment completely. On the basis of the decision in *Baker*, the plaintiff expected that the defendant's liability for the first event would be unaffected by the succeeding disease.

In *Jobling*, however, a unanimous House of Lords held in favour of the defendant. The reasoning was that the disease was one of the 'vicissitudes' of life, the possible future occurrence of which is routinely taken into account by judges in calculating **damages** awards. When the eventuality was known to have occurred before the trial it would be irrational to ignore it (see Figure 7.4).

Figure 7.4 Comparing *Baker* and *Jobling*

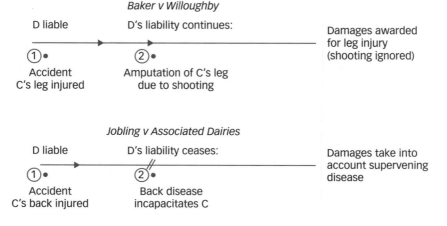

Baker v Willoughby

D liable — D's liability continues:

①• Accident C's leg injured   ②• Amputation of C's leg due to shooting

Damages awarded for leg injury (shooting ignored)

Jobling v Associated Dairies

D liable — D's liability ceases:

①• Accident C's back injured   ②• Back disease incapacitates C

Damages take into account supervening disease

The cases are often distinguished as follows:

- *Baker* concerned two torts; *Jobling*, one tort followed by a natural occurrence.
- The outcome in *Baker* was designed to avoid under-compensation of the plaintiff.

Revision tip

This aspect of **causation** can be confused with ***novus actus interveniens***. The best way of distinguishing them is by timescale. The *novus actus* situation characteristically involves a short period, minutes to weeks. In the *Baker–Jobling* version (which does not arise frequently in exam questions), the second injury is completely unconnected to the first and may occur years later.

(!) Conclusion

Remember that 'causation in fact' is only the first of two aspects of **causation** and that, even when that is proved, the claimant's case may still fail owing to the issue of 'remoteness' (to be explained in Chapter 8). Causation in fact includes some of the more complex conceptual problems in **negligence** and, it can be argued, is currently in a state of flux in which considerations of policy are threatening established legal principle.

(✱) Key cases

Case	Facts	Principle
Bailey v Ministry of Defence [2008] EWCA Civ 883	The claimant suffered brain damage in the defendant's hospital. Two factors combined to create this damage: one negligent and the other not. The claimant was unable to attribute a proportion of her damage to the defendant's negligence.	The court applied the **Bonnington** approach to cumulative damage and held the defendant liable in negligence because he had *materially contributed* to the claimant's loss. In both cases, the damage was treated as indivisible and that is why the principle of material contribution was applicable.
Baker v Willoughby [1970] AC 467	The plaintiff suffered an injury to his leg due to the defendant employer's negligence. Some time later, but before compensation had been paid, the same leg was injured in a shooting and had to be amputated and the defendant argued that his liability should cease at that point.	The House of Lords held that, despite the second damage, the defendant's liability should be regarded as continuing and the original damages award was upheld. This decision was called into some doubt by that in *Jobling*, below.

Key cases

✱✱✱✱✱✱✱✱✱✱

Case	Facts	Principle
Barnett v Kensington & Chelsea HMC [1968] 2 WLR 422	The deceased died following negligent treatment by the defendant hospital. It was established that the cause of death was arsenic poisoning and, regardless of what treatment he received, death was inevitable.	According to the but-for approach to causation, the defendant's negligence had not caused the death. This case is a classic example of the but-for test in operation.
Bonnington Casting v Wardlaw [1956] AC 613	The plaintiff had contracted an industrial disease due to two causes, one of which was his employer's negligence. He was not able to satisfy the but-for requirement.	This case was treated as one of cumulative damage and therefore it need only be proved that the negligence had made a *material contribution* to the damage. The plaintiff was successful.
Chester v Afshar [2004] UKHL 41	The claimant's back surgery carried a 1–2% risk of causing permanent damage, but she was not warned of this in advance. She sustained this damage and sued for negligent failure to warn. On the issue of causation, she was unable to prove that, had she known, she would never have consented to an operation.	The House of Lords relaxed the but-for approach on the basis that it is important to compensate patients damaged following medical negligence. This, like *Fairchild*, was a policy decision.
Fairchild v Glenhaven Funeral Services [2002] UKHL 22	A number of claimants had contracted asbestos-related disease, having been negligently exposed to it at various points in their working lives. However, they were unable to link their exposure to any particular employer.	A majority of the House of Lords departed from the 'all or nothing rule' and held each employer jointly and severally liable and followed the *McGhee* 'increase of risk' approach. There was a strong policy element in this departure and it is expected to be confined to exceptional cases.
Gregg v Scott [2005] 2 AC 176	Owing to the negligence of a doctor, an early diagnosis of the claimant's cancer was missed and treatment was delayed. At this time his chance of medium-term survival was 42%. When the disease was finally diagnosed, his chances of medium-term survival had fallen to 25%.	*Fairchild* was not followed. The claimant's chances of survival had never been 51% or more and compensation would not be based upon mere 'loss of a chance'. According to the 'all or nothing' approach, the claimant had not proved causation and his claim failed.
Hotson v East Berkshire AHA [1987] AC 750	A schoolboy injured his hip in a fall from a tree. The hospital was negligent in diagnosing and treating his injury. He was left with a permanent disability. Even had he been properly treated he only had, at best, a 25% chance of avoiding the disability.	Because the claimant was not able to show, on a balance of probabilities, that but for the defendant he would have recovered, he had not established causation in fact and there was no liability on the part of the hospital.

Case	Facts	Principle
Jobling v Associated Dairies [1982] AC 794	The plaintiff suffered a back injury for which his employer was liable in negligence. Before the trial, however, he developed an unconnected disease which affected his back making him unfit for work.	The House of Lords held that the disease should be treated as a 'vicissitude of life' which, since it was known, had to be taken into account in the calculation of damages. The defendant's liability thus ceased at the time the claimant suffered the disease. It is difficult to reconcile this approach with that in *Baker* and that case is now regarded as of doubtful authority.
McGhee v National Coal Board [1973] 1 WLR 1	The plaintiff developed a skin disease due to exposure to brick dust, which occurred while he worked for the defendant who had negligently failed to provide adequate washing facilities at the workplace. He was unable to link his disease to the time period in which he had been unable to wash.	In this case the proof required was impossible to provide, and only one possible substance, the defendant's brick dust, had caused the damage. Causation, and therefore liability, was established because the defendant's negligence had 'materially increased the risk' of the damage.
McWilliams v Sir William Arrol & Co [1962] 1 WLR 295	The deceased fell while working, his employer having negligently failed to supply him with a safety harness. Evidence was accepted that he regularly refused to wear a harness.	But for the employer's failure to supply a harness (ie if he *had* done so), the accident still would have occurred owing to the expectation that the deceased would not have worn one. Causation in fact was not established and the plaintiff lost their case.
Performance Cars v Abraham [1962] 3 WLR 749	The plaintiff's car was damaged twice within several weeks. In the first accident, defendant A negligently hit the car, requiring the respray of a wing. In the second, defendant B negligently hit the car again, damaging the same wing.	The successive accident did not obliterate or significantly worsen the original damage, therefore the liability to compensate the plaintiff remained solely with defendant A.
Wilsher v Essex AHA [1988] AC 1074, HL	The claimant had been given too much oxygen as a baby owing to the defendant hospital's negligence, but was unable to prove that this negligence was the cause of his blindness.	The *McGhee* approach of increase of risk was not applied to this case, because there were five different and distinct possible causes of blindness, and the claimant failed to establish causation on the balance of probabilities.

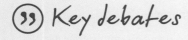 **Key debates**

Topic:	'Unnecessary Causes'
Author:	J. Stapleton
Viewpoint:	An attempt to reconcile 'material contribution' with the 'but-for test' as determinants of factual causation.
Source:	(2013) 129 LQR 39

Topic:	'Loss of a Chance and Causation'
Author:	Lord Neuberger of Abbotsbury
Viewpoint:	A practical examination of the problems of calculating **damages** for **loss** of a chance in both **tort** and contract. Provides a helpful insight into the overlap of the issues between the two areas.
Source:	(2008) 24 PN 206

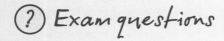 **Exam questions**

Problem question

Martin is leaving work late one evening when he hears an alarm bell ringing in the office of his manager, Raj. He does nothing about this until he returns home and then decides to ring the emergency services. Linda, who takes the call, does not give it priority status and when the police arrive to investigate two hours later, it is discovered that thieves have escaped with most of the contents of Raj's office.

Advise Raj.

See the Outline Answers section in the end matter for help with this question.

Essay question

Analyse the strengths and weaknesses of the but-for test for factual causation.

 **Online Resource Centre**

To see an outline answer to this question visit www.oup.com/lawrevision/

#8

Causation: intervening acts and remoteness

Key facts

- Intervening acts, or ***novus actus interveniens***, may operate to break the chain of causation between a defendant's act and the final outcome.

- The legal impact of an intervening act will depend on the extent to which it is reasonable, when it is committed by the claimant.

- The legal impact of an intervening act will depend on the extent to which it is reasonable or highly foreseeable, when it is committed by a third party.

- This chapter must be studied in conjunction with Chapter 7, 'Causation in fact'.

Assessment

- Intervening acts will arise when the original **negligence** of the defendant has been combined with an additional factor to bring about the damage. You may see this in a problem question which includes contested **causation** in fact.

- Remoteness will be an issue in a problem question when the defendant's negligence results in an unanticipated outcome, or an outcome which is more extensive than would be expected or which occurs in an unusual way.

Intervening acts

One way of portraying **causation** in **negligence** is to speak of a chain of events. There will be a range of situations in which the defendant's act can be said to be a cause of the claimant's loss because it satisfies the 'but-for' test; however, it is followed by one or more events which contributes to the eventual damage in such a way that it can be said that the chain of causation is broken. This is sometimes referred to by the Latin phrase *novus actus interveniens*, or new intervening act.

It will help if you divide these into three categories:

1. Actions by the claimant himself.
2. Actions by a third party.
3. Natural events.

The criteria by which the courts decide whether or not an event has indeed broken the chain of causation differ slightly in each category.

Actions by the claimant

Two cases can be contrasted to illustrate the first category. You will see that the unreasonableness of the claimant's action is a key criterion in determining that it breaks the chain of **causation** (see Figure 8.1).

McKew v Holland [1969] 3 All ER 1621

FACTS: The plaintiff had been injured in a work-related accident for which his employer was liable. Knowing that his leg was weak, McKew descended a steep staircase with no handrail. His leg gave way and he fell down the stairs, breaking his ankle.

HELD: The plaintiff's own unreasonable behaviour, in putting himself in a dangerous situation, broke the chain of **causation**. His employer was not liable for the effects of the second accident.

Figure 8.1 Intervening causes

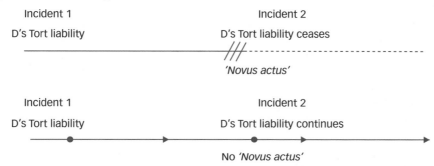

A convenient comparison can be made with the case of *Wieland v Cyril Lord Carpets*:

Wieland v Cyril Lord Carpets [1968] 3 All ER 1006

FACTS: As a result of the defendant's **negligence** the plaintiff had to wear a neck brace, which restricted her ability to use her bifocal glasses. This caused her to miss her step on a staircase and fall down some steps, sustaining further injuries.

HELD: The plaintiff's conduct in walking down the steps had not been unreasonable and therefore the defendant was liable for the additional injuries caused by her fall.

In cases where the level of unreasonableness by the claimant is relatively low, the court may approach it in terms of the defence of **contributory negligence** rather than *novus actus*.

Spencer v Wincanton **(2009)** involved facts very similar to those of *McKew*. The Court of Appeal stated that the level of unreasonableness which will break the chain of **causation** must be very high. Here, the claimant's action in attempting to fill his car with petrol, despite the fact that he was handicapped, had not reached this level. However, one-third contributory negligence was applied.

✅ *Looking for extra marks?*

In *Reeves v Commissioner of Police of the Metropolis* (2000), the claimant's partner had committed suicide in a police cell in a situation in which the police had breached their **duty of care** to supervise him. It was held that this had not broken the chain of **causation**, because it was the precise risk against which the police had a duty to guard. **Damages** were reduced, however, on the grounds of **contributory negligence**.

Other cases in which suicide is considered are *Kirkham v Chief Constable of Greater Manchester* **(1990)** and *Corr v IBC* **(2007)**.

Actions by third parties

A third party, the last actor before the damage, is likely to be either responding to a situation created by the defendant's act (reacting to danger or emergency, possibly as a rescuer) or he is a deliberate wrongdoer, in some cases committing a criminal act.

Regarding the first situation, you will recall that rescuers are a category of claimant who are traditionally regarded favourably in the law of **negligence**, particularly in relation to the question of **duty of care**, as illustrated by *Haynes v Harwood* (1935). However, it may be argued that a rescuer who negligently causes further damage has broken the chain of **causation**.

The Oropesa [1943] 1 All ER 211

FACTS: A collision between two ships was partially due to the **fault** of the defendant. In attempting to rescue his crew, the master took action which resulted in the drowning of nine men.

HELD: The chain was not broken; the emergency situation had been created by the defendant and, for his liability to cease, a completely 'new cause' would have been necessary.

An example of behaviour sufficiently unreasonable to break the chain of **causation** arose in *Knightley v Johns* (1982).

Knightley v Johns [1982] 1 All ER 851

FACTS: A road accident occurred in a tunnel, due to the **negligence** of Johns. Then a police officer on the scene ordered one of his motorcyclists to ride through the tunnel against the flow of traffic. This led to a second accident which injured Knightley.

HELD: The police officer's order broke the chain of **causation** from the first accident and emphasis was placed on the following:

- The fact that his was a positive act rather than a mere omission.
- The second accident could not be seen as a 'natural and probable consequence' of the **negligence** of Johns.
- It was said to be a matter of 'common sense' that the officer's **negligence** was a new cause disturbing the sequence of events.

Wright v Lodge (1993), later in the chapter, provides another example of the same point.

Revision tip

When the defendant's **negligence** has created a situation of danger, the courts will allow him to escape liability for the ultimate outcome only in extreme situations.

Home Office v Dorset Yacht Co (1970) is a key case, discussed in Chapter 2 ('Developments in the duty of care', p 14), on **duty of care**. The deliberate wrongful acts of the Borstal trainees in colliding with the plaintiff's yacht could have broken the chain of **causation** from the guards' negligent supervision but this was not accepted by the court. An act which is 'very likely to happen' will not break the chain of causation, and this was held to be the case with the vandalism of the boys.

In *Lamb v Camden LBC* (1981), an even higher degree of **foreseeability** was said to be required before it would be held that deliberate wrongful acts did not break the chain. Here, it was said that foreseeability nearing inevitability would be required, if liability were to be supported.

You will recall *Stansbie v Troman* (1948) (discussed in Chapter 3 ('Omissions', p 24)). The action of the thief did not break the chain of **causation**. Although this could not be said to have been inevitable, the promise by the decorator to lock the door reinforced liability, both in terms of duty and causation.

In *Wright v Cambridge Medical Group Ltd* (2011) the negligent diagnosis of the claimant's condition by a hospital did not break the chain of **causation** created by a medical professional who first negligently delayed the claimant's referral to that hospital.

✅ *Looking for extra marks?*

You may want to consider the extent to which policy considerations may influence a judge's findings concerning the effect of an intervening act. For instance, in *Lamb* Lord Denning said that one reason for his conclusion in favour of the defendant was that he believed that the **loss** should be paid for by the householder's insurers. See Jane Stapleton's article (Key debates).

Natural events

An unanticipated intervention might come from wind, lightning, storms, or even chemical reactions. In some cases, these are unlikely to be within the risk of the original **negligence**, but on the other hand, should they be held to break the chain of **causation** they would leave the injured party without any source of redress.

Carslogie Steamship Co Ltd v Royal Norwegian Government [1952] AC 292

FACTS: The defendant caused damage to the plaintiff's ship, requiring repairs which would take approximately ten days. Some temporary work was done in England but then, while sailing to the United States, where further repairs were to be undertaken, it was caught in a storm at sea, necessitating an extra 30 days' repair when it reached America.

HELD: Despite the plaintiff's argument that it was owing to the defendant that the ship was caught in the storm, this event was held to have broken the chain of **causation**. Therefore the defendant was only liable for the repair costs of the first collision and not for the loss of profits during the days in which it was being repaired for both the collision and storm damage concurrently.

Remoteness

Revision tip

You will find that natural events are the type of intervention which arises least frequently in exams.

Remoteness

Remoteness is a simpler way of describing what is also known as *causation in law*. It is concerned with the extent of a defendant's duty. Even when there is a factual link between the defendant's act and the claimant's **loss** (causation in fact), the outcome may be either

- so removed from the original **negligence**, or
- of a type which is outside the risk created so that the law would regard it as unjust to make the defendant liable for it.

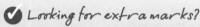 **Looking for extra marks?**

The **tort** scholar Winfield defined remoteness this way: a defendant cannot be made responsible infinitely for all the consequences of his wrongful conduct so 'the law must draw a line somewhere . . . for practical reasons'.

For many years remoteness was dealt with according to the test of *direct consequences*. In *Re Polemis* (1921), cargo was being unloaded from a ship docked in Casablanca. A plank was negligently dropped into the hold by the defendant's employee, which caused a spark, igniting gases in the hold and resulting in an explosion which destroyed the ship. The defendant was held liable for damage caused by this unexpected event on the basis that there should be liability for all the 'direct consequences' of a defendant's **negligence**.

The 'direct consequences' test for remoteness prevailed until *Overseas Tankship (UK) Ltd v Morts Docks and Engineering Co Ltd ('The Wagon Mound (No 1)')* (1961). The facts of this case were set out in Chapter 6, when *The Wagon Mound* (No 2) (1967) was discussed in relation to breach of duty and balancing of risks.

The remoteness issue in *Wagon Mound* was that the fire which caused the damage in Sydney Harbour would not have been easily predicted as the result of the defendant's oil spillage. The Privy Council felt that although some physical damage would have been foreseeable as a result of the **negligence**, ie contamination of the wharf with oil, it was not *reasonably foreseeable* that the oil would spread into the vicinity of the welding. The fire was therefore too remote and there would be no liability for it.

Revision tip

You may want to consider when the use of the *Wagon Mound* test will bring about a different outcome than would that from *Re Polemis*. Both are flexible and open to judicial manipulation.

✅ Looking for extra marks?

Reasonable foreseeability is a concept which you have already seen to be important in establishing **duty of care**: it is set out in *Donoghue v Stevenson* and is one of the three parts of the **Caparo** test for duty.

It has been suggested by Lunney and Oliphant that in these two instances the uses of **foreseeability** are slightly different:

- When *duty* is the issue, we look ahead from an activity and consider a wide range of risks which might, if foreseeable, lead to the imposition of a **duty of care**.
- When *remoteness* is the issue, it is a case of looking back after the event, to assess whether the damage that actually occurred was within the risk set up by the activity in question.

The second use of **foreseeability** is thus narrower than the first.

The decision in *The Wagon Mound* (No 1) was accepted in subsequent cases as having replaced the 'direct results' test with that of 'reasonable foreseeability'. An important early case which applied the *Wagon Mound* test was *Hughes v Lord Advocate* (1963).

Hughes v Lord Advocate [1963] AC 837

FACTS: Workmen left an open manhole, guarded by paraffin lamps. Some children began playing with the lamps and dropped one of them into the manhole where there was an explosion. This resulted in one of the children being knocked into the manhole and badly burned. The defendant's case was that this outcome was not reasonably foreseeable.

HELD: The House of Lords did not agree. The leaving of the paraffin lamps created a risk of reasonably foreseeable injury due to burns and the fact that the plaintiff's burns came about in an unlikely way did not prevent liability.

Revision tip

According to *Hughes*, and subsequent cases, it is only the *type* of damage which must be reasonably foreseeable and not the manner in which it occurs or its extent.

One of the most important aspects of applying the test lies in how to describe the *damage* which has occurred: in a wide or narrow sense? In *Wagon Mound* itself, we have seen that if the relevant outcome had been described as 'physical damage', it would not have been too remote because pollution and fouling of the wharf were reasonably foreseeable. Alternatively, describing it more narrowly as damage by fire led to it being held to be too remote.

> **Tremain v Pike [1969] 3 All ER 1303**
>
> **FACTS:** The claimant worked on the defendant's farm, which had, owing to **negligence**, been allowed to become infested with rats. As a result Tremain contracted Weil's disease (which at the time was relatively rare) from contact with the rats.
>
> **HELD:** His case against his employer failed on the grounds that the disease was not reasonably foreseeable, although injury due to rat bites or contamination of food might have been.

This provides a good example of what can happen when the 'type of damage' question is set too narrowly. It is generally accepted that a fairer result in *Tremain* would have been obtained by describing the **injury** in a wider sense of rat-related disease, thus leading to reasonable **foreseeability** and a finding of liability. A more recent case applying the *Wagon Mound* test is *Jolley v Sutton LBC*.

> **Jolley v Sutton LBC [2000] 1 WLR 1082**
>
> **FACTS:** The defendant was sued under the **Occupiers' Liability Act 1957** for **negligence** in allowing an abandoned boat to be left on its land adjacent to a block of flats. The defendant knew of the boat but had failed to remove it for two years. Some teenage boys were attempting to repair it and one was seriously injured when a jack slipped. According to the defence, although some minor injuries were reasonably foreseeable owing, perhaps, to small children falling through the rotten planks on the boat, the **injury** and the way that it occurred were not foreseeable.
>
> **HELD:** The House of Lords did not accept this. The findings of fact by the trial judge were considered in the context of the precedents of **The Wagon Mound** and **Hughes v Lord Advocate**. These supported the claimant's case.

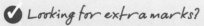 **Looking for extra marks?**

Note the observation in *Jolley* by Lord Hoffmann:

> [I]t has been repeatedly said in cases about children that their ingenuity in finding unexpected ways of doing mischief to themselves and others should never be underestimated.

The 'thin skull' rule

There is one situation in which the defendant will be liable for outcomes which are not reasonably foreseeable. When the **loss** suffered by the claimant is at least partly due to his own pre-existing vulnerability, whether physical, psychological, or financial, its unforeseeability will not affect the defendant's ultimate liability. It is the defendant's bad luck if his victim turns out to have a thin or 'eggshell' skull—he must take his victim as he finds him!

Smith v Leech Brain [1962] 2 QB 405

FACTS: The plaintiff was splashed on the lip by molten metal, due to his employer's **negligence**. The burn he suffered activated a pre-cancerous condition of which he eventually died.

HELD: Despite the fact that the death from cancer incited by the splash would not have been foreseeable at the time of the **injury**, the employer was liable for its full extent. The case provides a clear example of the thin skull rule.

Revision tip

Generally speaking, if a defendant has injured someone who consequently requires medical attention, he is likely to be liable for the consequences of that treatment, even if unforeseeable. *Robinson v Post Office* (1974) provides a good example.

What if the claimant, in mitigating his loss, has to incur extra expenditure solely because of his poor financial situation? In the past, the claimant's 'cash-flow' problems have not been given the benefit of the 'thin skull' rule. This changed with *Lagden v O'Connor* (2003). The claimant was able to recover the full costs of a delayed credit card hire scheme to replace his damaged car because he had not been able to pay out for the lower normal car hire charges.

✔️ *Looking for extra marks?*

You may wish to read the judgment of Laws LJ in *Rahman v Arearose* (2001) on the current state of the law of **causation**. It can be summarized as follows:

- There is a very strong link to the issue of *duty*, as both are concerned with the same question: for what kind of harm should this defendant be held responsible?
- The law uses 'tools' in order to allocate responsibility for the claimant's damage, for example *novus actus interveniens*, the eggshell (thin) skull rule, and the concept of concurrent **tortfeasors**.
- The objective of the law remains that of compensation, but the problems around **causation** can now be described as 'kaleidoscopic'.
- The common law has on the whole achieved just results, but the approach has been heavily pragmatic.

✳ *Key cases*

Case	Facts	Principle
Hughes v Lord Advocate [1963] AC 837	A young boy was badly burned by an explosion and fire when he dropped a lantern, which the defendants had left to guard a manhole. The defendants were liable.	The accident was caused by a known source of danger and, despite the fact the damage came about in an unexpected way and was very serious, it was not too remote from the original negligence.

Key cases

✳✳✳✳✳✳✳✳✳✳✳✳

Case	Facts	Principle
Jolley v Sutton LBC [2000] 1 WLR 1082	The claimant was injured while attempting to repair a boat left abandoned on the defendant's land. The accident came about when the boat was raised on a jack and then slipped. The defendant was liable for the claimant's paralysis.	The risk foreseeable from the defendant's negligence in relation to the boat was categorized as physical injury. The defendant was a local authority; the claimant was a child and benefited from a widely framed concept of damage in this case.
Knightley v Johns [1982] 1 All ER 851	Following a motor accident in a tunnel caused by the defendant's negligence, a police officer gave an order which resulted in a second accident which injured the plaintiff. The defendant was held not to be liable for the second accident.	The action of the police officer constituted such an unreasonable departure from correct practice that it would be treated as a new act and the sole cause of the second accident.
Lagden v O'Connor [2003] UKHL 64	Owing to lack of funds, the claimant was not able to mitigate his loss in the most financially efficient way. The defendant was still held to be liable for the relatively higher costs of car hire.	*Lagden* illustrates what has been described as the 'financial thin skull rule'. That is, if rather than a physical weakness the claimant has financial difficulties, the defendant cannot limit his liability for the full extent of the claimant's loss. He must take his victim as he finds him.
McKew v Holland [1969] 3 All ER 1621	The plaintiff had been injured owing to the defendant's negligence. Some weeks later he put himself in a situation dangerous to someone with his injury. He fell and suffered further damage. The defendant was not liable for the second injury.	The plaintiff's behaviour, because it was unreasonable, was treated as an intervening act which broke the chain of causation between the defendant's negligence and the ultimate damage.
Overseas Tankship (UK) Ltd v Morts Docks and Engineering Co ('The Wagon Mound (No 1)') [1961] AC 388, PC	A careless oil spill in a harbour led debris floating on the water to be ignited by sparks from welding. The resulting fire was held to be too remote and not actionable in negligence.	The new test was to be applied for remoteness of causation: that of reasonable foreseeability. In this case oil pollution was foreseeable, but fire was not.
Reeves v Commissioner of Police [2000] 1 AC 360	A prisoner committed suicide in a police cell owing to the failure of the police to properly supervise him. The police were held liable in negligence.	Despite the fact that the prisoner had committed a voluntary and direct act, it had not broken the chain of causation. The defendant was liable because the damage that occurred was precisely that which his duty of care required him to prevent.

Case	Facts	Principle
Smith v Leech Brain [1962] 2 QB 405	The plaintiff suffered a work-related injury when his lip was burned by molten metal. It interacted with a pre-existing condition and he developed cancer. The employer was held to be liable not only for the burn, which was foreseeable, but for the unforeseeable cancer because it was due to an inherent weakness in the plaintiff.	An illustration of the way that the thin skull or eggshell skull principle operates in favour of a plaintiff whose injury is worse than that which was foreseeable owing to some inherent physical condition or weakness.
Wieland v Cyril Lord Carpets [1968] 3 All ER 1006	The plaintiff fell while walking down a step, due to wearing a surgical collar necessitated by an injury caused by the defendant's negligence. The defendant was held liable for both the first and second injuries.	Unlike that of *McKew*, the plaintiff's action was not unreasonable and so did not break the chain of causation.

⟨᠉⟩ Key debate

Topic:	'Scope of Duty'
Author:	J. Stapleton
Viewpoint:	Both Stapleton and Stauch (below) are searching for a way to conceptualize remoteness which is preferable to that described by Lord Hoffmann in *Banque Bruxelles* (1997) as 'scope of duty'. Stapleton believes that it is often a matter of 'circumstances' which make it necessary to 'draw a line' in the chain of **causation**.
Source:	(1997) 113 LQR 1

Topic:	'Risk and Remoteness of Damage in Negligence'
Author:	M. Stauch
Viewpoint:	Stauch believes that the question of remoteness is inherently principle-based and is best dealt with by focusing on the nature of the risk created by the defendant and the chain of events rather than the specifics of the damage itself.
Source:	(2001) 64 MLR 191

Exam questions

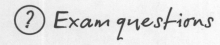

Problem question

Ann asked her husband, Ben, to use her car to fetch her dress from the dry cleaners. While at the cleaners Ben met his friend Colin and they agreed they both needed a drink. They went to the pub where, after drinking a considerable amount of beer, Ben offered Colin a lift home. On the journey home, Ben collided with Diana, a pedestrian trying to cross the street. The collision caused Colin, who had not fastened his seatbelt, to fly through the windscreen. It threw Diana into the path of an oncoming car being driven by Ernie, aged 82. Diana sustained serious internal injuries. At the hospital, Diana's injuries were misdiagnosed by Mary, a junior doctor. Had the nature of her injuries been correctly assessed in A&E, Diana would have had a 40% chance of full recovery. Diana is now paraplegic and Colin has suffered serious facial injuries.

Advise as to the tort liabilities which arise in this scenario.

See the Outline Answers section in the end matter for help with this question.

Essay question

'It is true that the duty of care expected in cases of this sort is confined to reasonably foreseeable danger, but it does not necessarily follow that liability is escaped because the danger actually materializing is not identical with the danger reasonably foreseen and guarded against.' (Lord Jenkins in *Hughes v Lord Advocate*)

Analyse this statement in terms of case law.

To see an outline answer to this question visit www.oup.com/lawrevision/

#9
Employers' liability and vicarious liability

Key facts

- Employers' liability has both a common law and a statutory aspect.

- Employers' liability is concerned with the employer's personal duty in respect of the physical safety of his employees.

- Vicarious liability involves the employer being liable to a third party for the tort of his employee.

- There are three conditions which must be satisfied in vicarious liability: a *relationship of employment* between the tortfeasor and the defendant, the commission of a *tort* and that it occur *in the course of employment*.

- Vicarious liability is not dependent on any fault of the employer and may be imposed even in the case of an express prohibition or a criminal act.

- Vicarious liability does not remove the employee's personal liability and it is possible, but unusual, for the employee to be called upon to indemnify his employer.

Assessment

It is important that you distinguish *employers' liability* from *vicarious liability* (see Figure 9.1). Exam questions are often designed to test this.

Vicarious liability often arises as one aspect of a wider problem question on another topic, such as **negligence**. Do not make the mistake of assuming either that a **tort** has taken place, or that there is an employment relationship.

Figure 9.1 Comparing employers' liability and vicarious liability

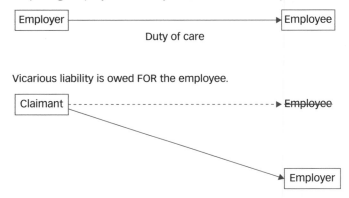

Employers' liability

The history of employers' liability

The law on employers' liability has an interesting history, which begins when a low level of duty was owed in the early days of the Industrial Revolution, but which increased with changes in insurance and social attitudes ultimately leading to the **Workmen's Compensation Act 1897** and the **Employers' Liability (Compulsory Insurance) Act 1969**, as well as the abolition of the doctrine of common employment.

The common law

> **Wilsons and Clyde Coal v English [1938] AC 57**
>
> **FACTS:** A miner had been killed in a mining accident. The defendant employer claimed that he had discharged his duty by entrusting mine safety to a manager.
>
> **HELD:** It was held that the employer remained liable because his duty was both personal and non-delegable.

Here, Lord Wright set out the employer's personal non-delegable obligation to provide:

- a competent workforce;
- adequate plant and equipment (and a safe place of work); and
- an effective system of work.

It is essential to learn this case in order to understand common law employers' liability. This important principle was further illustrated in *McDermid v Nash Dredging & Reclamation*.

McDermid v Nash Dredging & Reclamation [1987] 2 All ER 878

FACTS: The defendant's employee, a deckhand, was injured working abroad on a boat owned and controlled by the parent company.

HELD: Despite the somewhat remote nature of the accident, it was held that the responsibility to ensure the deckhand's safety remained with the defendant.

The four components of the common law duty will be considered in turn; however, some claims may reflect an overlapping between them.

The duty to provide a competent workforce

This is not as important as it would have been when the doctrine of common employment applied. In *Hudson v Ridge Manufacturing* (1957), however, an employer was held liable for failing to deal with an employee whose known tendency of practical joking resulted in **injury** to a colleague.

The duty to provide adequate plant and equipment

In *Davie v New Merton Board Mills* (1959) the plaintiff lost the sight in his eye when a tool supplied by his employer split and a chip flew into his eye. The employer's successful defence was that he had fulfilled his **duty of care** by purchasing the tool from a reputable supplier and there was no means of discovering the defect by inspection.

However, it is important to note that the effect of *Davie* was reversed by the **Employer's Liability (Defective Equipment) Act 1969**.

The Employer's Liability (Defective Equipment) Act 1969, s 1

According to **s 1(1)**:

- where an employee suffers personal injury in the course of employment,
- in consequence of a defect in equipment provided by the employer for the purposes of the employer's business,

---

Employers' liability
✳✳✳✳✳✳✳✳✳✳✳✳

- and the defect is due wholly or partly to the **fault** of a third party,
- then the liability will be attributed to the employer.

Note that this presumption will apply regardless of whether the third party is identified or not.

What comes within the meaning of 'equipment'?

The concept is generously interpreted. In *Coltman v Bibby Tankers* (1988) it included a ship and in *Knowles v Liverpool City Council* (1993) a flagstone being laid by the worker was 'equipment' because it had been provided by the employer for the purposes of work.

The duty to provide a safe place of work

In *Latimer v AEC* (1953), the defendant's factory flooded. He took various steps to dry out the floor, including the laying of sawdust, and it was held that he had discharged his **duty of care**, despite the fact that one of his employees slipped and was injured.

Revision tip

Latimer provides a useful illustration of the fact that this is not a **strict liability** duty; rather it only requires taking the steps that an ordinary, prudent employer would take.

The duty to provide a safe system of working

This includes instructions from the employer, as well as training and warnings.

In *General Cleaning Contractors v Christmas* (1953) it was held that the employer had been in breach of this duty by failing to instruct, train, and supervise its workers adequately in safe methods of cleaning windows.

✔️ *Looking for extra marks?*

See *Mulcahy v Ministry of Defence* (1996), where it was held that it would not be 'fair, just and reasonable' to impose a **duty of care** upon one soldier for the safety of another on the battlefield. Further, the employer's duty to provide a safe system of working would not apply in that situation.

What type of loss is covered?

Financial loss

The fundamental position has been that the employer's duty covers physical safety but does not extend to the employee's financial security. In *Reid v Rush & Tompkins Group* (1990) the plaintiff was injured in a motor accident while working abroad and sued his employer for failing to advise him of the importance of obtaining private medical insurance. It was held that the employer had not been under a duty in **tort** to provide that type of advice.

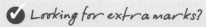

See *Spring v Guardian Insurance* (1995) (Chapter 4) and *Scally v Southern Health and Social Services Board* (1992), which demonstrate alternative ways in which an employer may indirectly protect the financial interests of his employees.

Psychiatric injury

You will recall from Chapter 5 that psychiatric injury is generally actionable in its own right only when it results from shock and fulfils the requirements necessary for claims by either primary or secondary victims. A different approach will be evident in the field of employers' liability.

Walker v Northumberland County Council [1995] 1 All ER 737

FACTS: A social services manager suffered a nervous breakdown due to his heavy workload. After some time off for recovery, he returned to work and his employer knowingly failed to reduce his workload, whereupon he suffered a second breakdown and had to cease working.

HELD: The employer was held to be liable, on the basis that he was in breach of his employer's common law **duty of care**. There was no reason that psychiatric injury should not be within the scope of the employer's duty; the claimant's second breakdown was foreseeable and **causation** had been established. *Walker* is a key case because it marked the first successful claim by an employee for psychiatric injury resulting in a cumulative process of work-induced stress.

Questions about the nature and extent of this duty were addressed in *Hatton v Sutherland*.

Hatton v Sutherland [2002] EWCA Civ 276

FACTS: This was a combined claim by a number of teachers who suffered from psychological conditions brought about by work-induced stress.

HELD: The Court of Appeal set out guidelines to be applied in approaching future such claims. The main points are:

- No jobs are inherently stressful.
- Stress is a subjective concept.
- What is 'reasonably foreseeable' must be determined in relation to the individual worker, rather than in a general sense.
- Issues to be considered in relation to **foreseeability** include the nature of the work, the workload, and any signs from the employee.
- Unless there is evidence to the contrary, the employer is entitled to assume that the employee can cope with the normal stresses of the job.
- The precautions to be expected from the employer depend on the size of the operation, his resources, whether it is the public or private sector, and the interests of other employees.

Employers' liability
✱✱✱✱✱✱✱✱✱✱

In *Barber v Somerset County Council* (2004) the House of Lords implicitly approved the *Hatton* guidelines while stressing that they were, in effect, elaborations on what was fundamentally required of the 'reasonable and prudent employer'.

> **Revision Tip**
>
> This is a developing and topical aspect of employers' liability and therefore one which may be focused on by examiners. Case law shows that such claims will each turn on their own particular facts.

In *Hartman v South Essex Mental Health NHS Trust* (2005) the first of the *Hatton* guidelines was confirmed in denying liability to a nurse who worked with children who had learning disabilities.

There had been a breach of duty, however, in *Melville v Home Office* (2005) when a prison health care worker had not been offered support and counselling following distressing involvement in suicides. It has been argued that, due to the factor of shocking events, *Melville* has more in common with the *Alcock* line of cases than with *Walker* and *Hatton*.

Daw v Intel (2007) confirms that merely offering an employee counselling services is not a panacea which would discharge **duty of care** in all cases. See also *French v Chief Constable of Sussex* (2006) on the need for **foreseeability**.

Statutory regulation of employers' liability

There is also a significant body of statutory regulation of employers' duties to employees and this operates in a complementary manner to the common law, sometimes described as a 'dual liability system'.

Background

Traditionally this was accomplished by a multitude of statutes pertaining to different industries such as the **Mines and Quarries Act 1954** and **Offices Shops and Railway Premises Act 1963**. One of the most comprehensive statutes, often cited in cases, was the **Factories Act 1961**.

The Health and Safety at Work etc. Act

This was passed in 1974, with the objective of providing a unified and comprehensive framework, obliging employers to ensure, as far as is reasonably practicable, the health, safety, and welfare at work of all employees. In accordance with EU directives, the majority of pre-existing statutes have now been repealed and replaced by many different regulations, under the scheme of the **Management of Health and Safety at Work Regulations 1999**.

These regulations cover all aspects of employment and are actionable by individuals, subject to establishing

- that a duty is owed to the claimant,
- that the duty was broken, and
- that damage was caused by the breach of duty.

The standard of care is frequently stated in the regulations and resulting case law as the duty to act according to what is 'reasonably practicable' or 'so far as practicable'.

In many cases this will result in a higher standard than that of the common law: to act 'reasonably'. In *Fytche*, the House of Lords considered the question of statutory breach.

Fytche v Wincanton Logistics Ltd [2004] UKHL 34

FACTS: A driver of a milk tanker sustained frostbite due to a tiny hole in the steel-toed boots issued to him by his employer. He sued his employer, claiming that he had breached his duty to him under the **Personal Protective Equipment at Work Regulations 1992**.

HELD: The statutory duty to maintain protective equipment in good working order only pertained to its primary function, that of protecting the claimant's toes from heavy objects. The damage suffered fell outside of the risks of normal working conditions and so would not be compensated.

✅ *Looking for extra marks?*

Although *Fytche* was pursued only on the basis of breach of statutory duty, Lady Justice Hale in her dissenting speech used comparisons with the standard of duty under the common law to argue that the employer's statutory duty should be approached in the spirit of **strict liability**. Depending on the facts, you must be prepared to consider these two forms of liability as alternatives.

Vicarious liability

Justifications for vicarious liability

Making one party (here, the employer) liable for the wrong of another requires justification. The most common reasons for the legal device of vicarious liability are as follows:

- That the employer is taken to have control over his employee. He determines who he employs, what work is done, and how, and is thus assumed to be best able to ensure that care is taken.

- It is also seen as a means of loss-spreading. Owing to the legal obligation to insure and to defray costs by charging higher prices, the employer will have the 'deepest pocket' when it comes to compensation.

- Because the employer stands to profit from the enterprise, it is fair that he should also bear the risks.

- Identifiability. For example, for a wrong occurring in an NHS hospital setting, an injured patient need not identify the precise medical professional responsible but may claim against the hospital or health authority.

The three ingredients of vicarious liability

Vicarious liability makes the employer liable for

- a **tort**,
- committed by his employee,
- in the course of employment.

1. A tort

This will most commonly be a common law tort such as **negligence** or **battery**; however, *Majrowski v Guys and St Thomas's NHS Trust* (2007) held that vicarious liability can also apply to breach of statutory duty in the employment context.

2. The employment relationship

It must be established that the wrongdoer was actually an employee. Older cases often make the distinction between a contract 'of service' (or employment) and a contract 'for services'. It is clearer now to use the terms 'employee' and 'independent contractor'. A private chauffeur would be an example of the former and a taxi driver of the latter.

Vicarious liability does not apply to the torts of an independent contractor, although there can be personal liability in the case of ultra-hazardous tasks or when the employer is at **fault** for the way a job has been done. See, for instance, *Ellis v Sheffield Gas Consumers* (1853).

Tests

The law relies on the reality of the relationship, rather than the terms of the contract or what is the understanding of the parties. Historically, case law has developed successive tests for determining a person's employment status.

The 'control test'

The 'control test' was based upon the idea that an identifiable characteristic of an employer would be the ability to control the way a job was done. The culture of work has changed and now 'control' is merely one of the criteria that will be taken into account.

Revision tip

An exam question may state: 'X works for Y'. That does *not* automatically imply that he is an employee. Additionally, students are sometimes wrongly tempted to cite the control test, which is no longer sufficient in itself.

The 'integration test'

The 'integration test' of *Stevenson Jordan & Harrison Ltd v McDonald & Evans* (1952) focused on the extent to which the worker was integrated into the enterprise as a whole. This has now been assimilated into a list of many factors that the court will take into account in the 'composite test'.

The 'composite test'

The 'composite test', as set out in *Market Investigations Ltd v Minister of Social Security* (1969), involves taking an overview of a number of different aspects of the relationship. The facts concerned a market research interviewer who was employed on a series of short-term contracts, where the defendant had a large degree of control over how she did the job, but she did not receive holiday pay. Here, in applying a 'composite test', no provisions of her contract were inconsistent with contracts of service.

In *JGE v The Trustees of the Portsmouth Roman Catholic Diocesan Trust* (2012), the Court of Appeal confirmed that vicarious liability could be imposed on the Roman Catholic bishop who had appointed a parish priest who then went on to sexually abuse children living in a children's home administered by his diocese. Despite the absence of a contract of employment, direct control, and payment of wages, two out of three Appeal Court judges held that the relationship was 'sufficiently akin to employment' to found vicarious liability in the case of this complex social ill (see Table 9.1). See *Woodland v Swimming Teachers' Association* (2013) for examples in which a 'non-delegable duty' arises, creating liability for the acts of independent contractors.

✅ Looking for extra marks?

It is interesting to note that many of the cases on this aspect are not, in fact, vicarious liability cases, but instead concern the issue of employment in relation to tax or benefit matters. It may be the case that there should be different determinants for employment, depending on the context.

Table 9.1 Comparing the employee and the independent contractor

Employee	Independent contractor
Is integrated into the business, with the possibility of profit sharing.	Has no interest in the 'employer's business'.
Is paid a regular wage.	Is paid by the job done.
Has tax and benefits provision from employer.	Does not have tax or benefit provision.
Is supplied with tools, uniform, or vehicle.	Supplies his own tools, uniform, or vehicle.
Works at a regular time and place.	Determines his own hours and methods.

Vicarious liability

✱✱✱✱✱✱✱✱✱✱✱✱

Borrowed, or 'hired-out' employees

In some situations, when a worker is lent or hired-out, the question may arise as to which of two (or more) organizations is the employer for purposes of vicarious liability.

Mersey Docks and Harbour Board v Coggins & Griffiths [1947] AC 1

FACTS: The Board employed the **tortfeasor** as crane driver and lent both him and his crane to a firm of stevedores, C&G. The contract between the Board and C&G provided that the driver should be the employee of C&G. The driver continued to be paid by the Board, which also had the power to dismiss him. When a third party was injured as a result of the driver's **negligence**, the question arose of who was to be treated as his employer for the purposes of vicarious liability.

HELD: The House of Lords held that, despite the terms of the contract, the Board had failed to rebut the presumption that it remained the employer for the purposes of vicarious liability. The fact that, additionally, the crane was lent at the same time strengthened the presumption.

Viasystems Ltd v Thermal Transfer Ltd (2006) establishes that dual vicarious liability may be possible in cases where the negligent employee was working under supervision and control of employees of two different companies. This will not be a common solution and does not displace the presumption of *Mersey Docks*.

3. *In the course of employment*

The rationale for vicarious liability requires that it be restricted to torts committed in the course of employment, rather than, say, when the employee is engaged in private activities. This requirement is the one that has generated the most case law and has been the subject of recent significant legal developments.

Carelessness and motive of employee

Century Insurance v Northern Ireland Transport Board [1942] AC 509

FACTS: A petrol tanker driver threw down a lighted match causing a fire while delivering petrol to a garage. Unsurprisingly, this caused an explosion and extensive damage.

HELD: He had remained in the course of employment, while performing the task he was employed to do, despite the high degree of **negligence**.

See also *General Engineering Services Ltd v Kingston and St Andrew Corporation* (1989), a case concerning industrial action by a fire brigade, illustrating the fact that despite appearing to be in the course of employment the motive of the employee plus its influence on how the task is performed, which can take it outside the course of employment.

Acting contrary to instructions

It may be surprising to learn that an employee may be held to be acting within the course of employment, even when deliberately acting in a way that was expressly prohibited by his employer.

Two cases can be contrasted to illustrate the boundaries of this principle:

In *Rose v Plenty* (1976) a 13-year-old boy was injured while riding with a milkman on his float to help him deliver milk. Such giving of lifts on the float was contrary to the employer's express prohibition. It was held to be within the course of employment because it was an improper way of doing exactly what the milkman was employed to do, and thereby furthered the employer's business.

On the other hand, in *Twine v Beans Express* (1946) a driver giving a lift in his delivery van to someone, contrary to instructions, was held to be outside the course of employment. The passenger was a trespasser and in no way contributing to the purpose of the employment.

See also *Limpus v London General Omnibus Company* (1862) and *Conway v George Wimpey* (1951).

Revision tip

Although it is sometimes difficult to find consistency in the course of employment decisions, a useful question is: 'What exactly was the worker employed to do?'

Diversions and detours

How is 'course of employment' applied when the wrongdoer has gone on what *Joel v Morrison* (1834) called 'a frolic of one's own'?

The answer is that it is treated as a matter of degree—to be determined by looking at a range of factors with each case turning on its own facts.

In *Storey v Ashton* wine delivery drivers returning to base after delivery took a detour to visit relatives after hours. The horse and cart ran over and killed a small child. This was not in the course of employment but a new and independent journey, entirely on their own business.

See *Harvey v O'Dell* (1958) and *Hilton v Thomas Burton (Rhodes) Ltd* (1961) regarding meal breaks.

Travelling to and from work is usually outside the course of employment. Travelling between workplaces was the issue in *Smith v Stages*.

Smith v Stages [1989] AC 928

FACTS: Peripatetic laggers working at a power station in the Midlands were sent by their employer to an urgent job in Wales. They were paid for eight-hour journeys to Wales and back. They finished

> the job early and, while driving back to the Midlands, the driver hit a brick wall and the plaintiff was seriously injured.
>
> **HELD:** The driver was acting within the course of employment. It was not an ordinary case of travelling to work; and the fact that the plaintiffs had left early was immaterial.

Intentional and criminal acts

This category of wrongs predictably has brought some rigorous challenges regarding the extent of course of employment and has been the focus of the most recent development of legal principle.

The mere fact that an act is illegal does not take it outside the course of employment.In *Lloyd v Grace Smith & Co* (1912) a managing clerk for a solicitor who embezzled a client's property was held to be acting within the course of employment. He used his ostensible authority to commit fraud while performing a task for which he was paid.

The employee went too far in *Warren v Henleys* (1948) to be acting in the course of employment. A petrol station worker who wrongly thought that the plaintiff had been attempting to drive away without paying ended up assaulting him. This had become personal vengeance.

See also *Morris v Martin & Sons* (1966) and *Keppel Bus Co Ltd v Ahmad* (1974).

'Close connection'

> **Lister v Hesley Hall [2002] 1 AC 215**
>
> **FACTS:** The warden of a boarding house at a school for emotionally disturbed children sexually abused children in his care, which constituted the **tort** of **battery**. Following his conviction and imprisonment, his victims sued the owners of the school in vicarious liability.
>
> **HELD:** The defendants were vicariously liable. *Lister* provided the House of Lords with an opportunity to reformulate the test for course of employment in terms of 'close connection'.

Since the early 20th century, the courts have applied a test described by the author of *Salmond on Torts* as: 'was it a wrongful act authorised by the employer or was it an unauthorised *mode* of doing something which was authorised by the employer?'

A strict application of the '*Salmond* test' would not have supported vicarious liability, but a further reading of *Salmond* revealed that a master, 'is liable even for acts which he has not authorised, provided they are *so connected* with acts which he has authorised, that they rightly be regarded as modes—though improper modes—of doing them'.

In *Lister*, the torts had been so *closely connected* with the employment that it was fair and just to impose vicarious liability. The responsibility the warden had over the boys gave him the opportunity to commit the crimes. A gardener, however, would not have been within the course of employment.

The way in which the application of the *'close connection'* test indicates an extension of vicarious liability is illustrated by *Mattis v Pollock* (2003). A bouncer assaulted a patron of a nightclub, after first returning home for a knife, following a row outside the club. Despite the suggestion of personal vengeance, the act was held to be closely connected to his role of keeping order in the club. The employer was vicariously liable. There was evidence that he had colluded with, and encouraged, bouncers' violence. In the commercial case of *Dubai Aluminium Co Ltd v Salaam* (2002) the House of Lords used the following test: 'The master ought to be liable for all those torts which can fairly be regarded as reasonably incidental to the risks to the type of business he carries on.'

See also *Attorney General v Hartwell* (2004) and *Bernard v Attorney General of Jamaica* (2005).

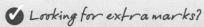 **Looking for extra marks?**

The *Lister 'close connection'* test was applied in *Maga v Archbishop of Birmingham* (2010) to vicarious liability of an archdiocese for sexual abuse committed by a Catholic priest. The complicating factor here was that the priest did not encounter his victim in the context of his immediate church responsibilities, but rather out in the extended community. The Court of Appeal was persuaded that he was still acting in the course of his employment as his employers had encouraged and given him the authority for this community role.

Various Claimants v Catholic Child Welfare Society (2013)

FACTS: Brothers in a monastic teaching order had abused students in a school which was managed by several diocesan bodies and a lay Roman Catholic order ('the Institute'). The Supreme Court had to decide who bore vicarious liability, and whether the wrongful acts had satisfied the 'close' connection' test.

HELD: Despite the fact that the brothers were bound to the defendant by vows rather than a contract of employment, their relationship bore enough features to make it equivalent to contract. The Institute had put the abusers in a position which 'created or significantly increased the risk' of the abuse and for that reason close connection was established.

Indemnity

In *Lister v Romford Ice and Cold Storage* (1957), the employer was held to be entitled to reimbursement from the negligent employee for **damages** paid out to the injured party. Generally, this indemnity will be pursued only in exceptional cases of wilful misconduct or collusion between the employer and employee.

See also **Civil Liability (Contribution) Act 1978** discussed in Chapter 16, 'Defences and limitation'.

Key cases

Employers' liability cases		
Case	**Facts**	**Principle**
General Cleaning Contractors v Christmas [1953] AC 180	A window cleaner fell and was injured when cleaning while standing on a sash window.	The employer had breached his duty of care to instruct in a safe system of working and to ensure that it would be carried out.
Hatton v Sutherland [2002] EWCA Civ 276	A group of appeals by teachers who had been suffering from work-induced stress.	The Court of Appeal set out key guidelines for employers' duty of care in cases of stress at work.
McDermid v Nash Dredging & Reclamation [1987] 2 All ER 878	A deckhand employed by the defendant was injured while working abroad under the supervision of the parent company.	The duty of care to provide a safe system of work was non-delegable and so the employer was liable.
Reid v Rush & Tompkins Group [1990] 1 WLR 212	The plaintiff was injured in a car accident while working for the defendant in Ethiopia. His employer had not warned him about the importance of obtaining adequate insurance.	The employer had no contractual or tortious duty of care to protect the employee's financial position by advising about insurance cover.
Walker v Northumberland County Council [1995] 1 All ER 737	A social work manager had a second nervous breakdown, after returning to work following a breakdown due to overwork.	The employer's duty of care extended to prevention of psychological harm caused by stress. In this case it had been foreseeable and inadequate precautions had been taken.
Wilsons and Clyde Coal v English [1938] AC 57	A miner was crushed by machinery while working under the supervision of an agent of his employer.	The non-delegable duty of the employer for the safety of his workers was set out in three parts: safe workforce, safe tools, and safe system.
Vicarious liability		
Century Insurance v Northern Ireland Transport Board [1942] AC 509	The defendant's petrol tanker driver dropped a match while he was delivering petrol to a garage.	Despite the extremely careless nature of the employee's act, he was within the course of employment for the purposes of vicarious liability.

Case	Facts	Principle
Lister v Hesley Hall [2002] 1 AC 215	A boarding house warden had sexually abused children in his care and his employer was sued in vicarious liability.	The owners of the school were vicariously liable for these torts of battery. The *Salmond test* for course of employment was adapted to include acts 'closely connected' to the employment.
Lloyd v Grace Smith & Co [1912] AC 716	A solicitor's managing clerk embezzled funds from a client of the firm.	His employer was vicariously liable. These criminal acts were in the course of employment because this position gave him the ostensible authority to commit the frauds.
Market Investigations Ltd v Minister of Social Security [1969] 2 QB 173	A woman was an intermittent interviewer for a market research company, under their instruction and control but not receiving holiday or sick pay.	A composite test was applied that took into account all aspects of the relationship, including the amount of control the defendant had. She was an employee rather than an independent contractor.
Mersey Docks and Harbour Board v Coggins & Griffiths [1947] AC 1	A crane driver was loaned by his main employer, along with a crane. They continued to pay him and had the power of dismissal but the contract stipulated that his employment would shift to the company to whom he was lent.	In such situations it will be difficult for the main employer to show that liability has shifted from them, and they remained his employer for the purposes of vicarious liability.
Rose v Plenty [1976] 1 WLR 141	A young boy was injured while helping a milkman deliver milk, despite the fact that the milkman was forbidden from employing help of this sort.	The milkman was within the course of employment because the obtaining of assistance from the boy had been in pursuance of his employer's business.
Smith v Stages [1989] AC 928	The workers, who had been sent away from their usual base for a period of days, were involved in an accident on their return journey, which was earlier than had been planned.	They were within the course of employment. Here the House of Lords laid down five key factors which would determine the question of 'course of employment' in similar situations.
Storey v Ashton (1869) LR 4 QB 476	A wine delivery driver, after hours, diverted his horse and cart from the usual route and went off on an independent errand, when he ran down and killed the plaintiff.	This new and independent journey had nothing to do with his employment and so the defendant was not vicariously liable.

Key debates

✳✳✳✳✳✳✳✳✳✳ ✳

Case	Facts	Principle
Twine v Beans Express [1946] 1 All ER 202	A van driver had given a lift to a hitchhiker, which was contrary to his employer's instructions.	In contrast to ***Rose***, this act had not been within the course of employment as it did not further the employer's enterprise in any way.
Viasystems Ltd v Thermal Transfer Ltd [2006] QB 510	A flood was caused in the claimant's factory due to the negligence of a fitter of an air conditioning unit.	The fitter was under the supervision and control of the employees of two companies and for that reason dual vicarious liability was applicable.

🗩 Key debates

Topic:	**'Employment Law and Tort Law: the Borrowed Servant'**
Author:	M. Jefferson
Viewpoint:	Highlights the complexity of the relationship between employment law and vicarious liability in the light of recent developments in legal culture.
Source:	(2009) 25 PN 215

Topic:	**'Vicarious Liability on the Move'**
Author:	P. Morgan
Viewpoint:	A recognition that the law of vicarious liability must adapt to the changes in work relationships.
Source:	(2013) 129 LQR 139

Topic:	**'Stress at Work: Law and Practice since** Hatton v Sutherland**'**
Author:	A. Buchan
Viewpoint:	An overview of the legal and practical consequences of ***Hatton v Sutherland***, including parallel statutory duties and the guidance of the Health and Safety Executive.
Source:	(2007) JPIL 49

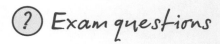
Exam questions

Problem questions

1. June had been a nurse for Thameside NHS Trust for six years. Deepak was a fellow nurse, recently employed, who had not yet attended a training course for using the lifting hoist. One day, Deepak offered to help June in bathing Victor, a patient at Brookside, who weighed 16 stone and had recently had a hip operation. June reminded Deepak that he had not yet done the required training course but he insisted, saying 'There's nothing to it—let me at him!' June protested but Deepak began to fit the hoist onto Victor. He started to raise the hoist but suddenly it let Victor slip and he began to fall off the bed. June tried to catch Victor and in the process sustained a serious back injury. Statutory regulations stipulated that a lifting hoist had to be used when turning patients who weighed more than 11 stone, and that two people were required to operate it.

    Advise June.

    See the Outline Answers section in the end matter for help with this question.

2. Brian works for Altamont plc as a delivery driver. He drives his own van but wears a uniform supplied by Altamont, who pay his monthly salary. On Monday afternoon he is on his way to do his last delivery when he gets a call from his daughter Patti and agrees to collect her from school. As they leave the school and drive in the direction of the delivery destination, Brian's van skids and hits Keith's car.

    Advise Keith.

Online Resource Centre

To see an outline answer to this question visit www.oup.com/lawrevision/

#10
Product liability

- Common law product liability is based upon the law of negligence.
- Statutory product liability is strict liability.
- The relevant statute is the **Consumer Protection Act 1987 (CPA 1987)**.
- When damage relates to quality or value, the only remedy will be in contract.

Assessment

- The foundation for answering questions is a sound understanding of the principles of **negligence**.

- Possible common law and statutory liability must both be considered in each case (see Table 10.1).

- You will find relatively little case law illustrating the application of the **CPA 1987**.

The common law

Donoghue v Stevenson (1932), which had as its 'wide *ratio*' the '**neighbour principle**', also had a 'narrow *ratio*'. In the absence of a contractual **remedy**, it established for the first time the liability in **negligence** of a manufacturer for damage caused by his product—here, a bottle of ginger beer allegedly containing a snail.

It was not necessary that the plaintiff should be the ultimate consumer of the product; for instance in *Stennett v Hancock and Peters* (1939) there was negligent liability to a pedestrian who was struck when a wheel flew off a lorry.

The common law **duty of care** is owed by manufacturers, as in *Donoghue*, but also by repairers, fitters, makers of component parts, and even those selling products after inspection or repair. You should note that the **tort** duty is in relation to the safety of the product, rather than its value or quality, which would be protected only by the law of contract.

Intermediate examination

> ### *Grant v Australian Knitting Mills* [1936] AC 85
>
> **FACTS:** The plaintiff developed a skin disease due to a chemical that was left in his underwear following production by the defendant, but he was not able to point to the exact nature of the **negligence** in the manufacturing process.
>
> **HELD:** The plaintiff's success rested on the presence of the harmful substance in the underwear which was intended to be worn, as supplied, without inspection or washing. The burden was placed on the defendant to provide a non-negligent explanation, which it was unable to do.

Evans v Triplex Safety Glass (1936), however, was a case in which there was no liability because the flaw in the car's windscreen could have occurred at a later stage, after it left the defendant manufacturer's control. In *Kubach v Hollands* (1937) the manufacturer of a chemical for use in school experiments had stipulated that it be tested before use. When an accident occurred in the absence of testing, he was not liable in **negligence**.

> *Revision tip*
>
> Remember that from a different perspective, *Evans* and *Kubach* are examples in which a *causal link* was not established between the defendant and the damage.

Under the common law the injured party often had problems proving the defendant's **negligence**. This and other procedural problems were exemplified in the Thalidomide tragedy of the 1960s.

The Consumer Protection Act 1987 (Part I)

Strict liability

This statute was passed in response to a European Union directive of 1985, which had the objective of achieving a harmonized, EU-wide regime of **strict liability** for defective products. Liability does not depend on proof of **fault** by the defendant. Liability is not absolute, however: there must be a *defect* in the product and there are a number of statutory defences. You must keep in mind that the statute does not replace, but rather is complementary to, the common law. It will be shown that differences in scope may lead to some cases being suitable for action under one regime but not the other.

'Products' covered by the Act

Section 1(2) defines products as goods, electricity, and those products which may be comprised in another product, ie a component part. Also included are substances, growing crops and things attached to land, any ship, aircraft, or vehicle, but buildings are exempted. *A v National Blood Authority* (2001) establishes that blood products are covered by the Act.

The Directive permitted some derogations for member states. In the UK, primary agricultural produce and game were excluded from the ambit of the regime until the **Consumer Protection Act 1987 (Product Liability) (Modification) Order 2000**.

Who can be sued?

In s 2(2) the Act provides an expanded hierarchy of possible defendants:

- Primary liability lies with the producer, which includes the manufacturer.

Also liable may be the following:

- The importer of the product into the EU.
- The 'own brander', who holds himself out as the producer.

- Lastly, liability may fall upon a 'supplier' (retailer) of the product in the course of a business who cannot identify for the consumer, in a reasonable time, the producer, own brander, or importer.

What must be proved by the claimant?

According to s 3, the claimant must establish that

> there is a *defect* in the product [meaning that] the safety of the product is not such as persons generally are entitled to expect.

The **objective standard** which is applied to the question of defect is sometimes called '*the consumer expectation test*'. You will note that, as in the common law, the concern is with safety rather than quality or value.

In determining defectiveness, the following must be taken into account:

- the manner and purpose of marketing, the use of any mark (such as a 'kitemark'), instructions, and warnings;
- what might reasonably be expected to be done with the product; and
- the time at which the product was supplied.

A v National Blood Authority [2001] 3 All ER 289

FACTS: The claimants had received blood transfusions, which were infected with Hepatitis C. This virus was discovered in 1988 and a screening test was developed and made available in 1989 but was not purchased by the NHS until 1991. The claims related to infections between 1988 (when the Act came into force) and 1991 (liability for infections after that date having been accepted).

HELD: Burton J found in favour of the claimants. The question of defect should not depend on what consumers expect but rather what they are legitimately entitled to expect. Even if the test for the virus was too difficult or expensive (or even impossible), the public was entitled to expect that blood used in transfusions be 100% safe. This is an important case on how the courts should interpret and apply the Act and it gives a vivid illustration of the meaning of **strict liability**.

Abouzaid v Mothercare [2001] EWCA Civ 348

FACTS: An older child was helping to strap a baby into a sleeping bag in a pushchair when a metal buckle on an elastic strap hit him in the eye, causing serious injury.

HELD: The accident was not foreseeable enough to constitute a breach of duty to support a claim under common law **negligence**. However, the manufacturer had failed the 'consumer expectation test' as it should have done more to prevent accidents, either by improving the design or by warning customers, and was therefore liable under the **CPA 1987**.

The consumer expectation standard was achieved, however, in *Pollard v Tesco Stores* (2006), which concerned the 'child-resistant' nature of a lid on a container of dishwasher soap powder. It was held that the lid did not quite reach the British Standard for safety; however, the product had been packaged or labelled as having reached that standard. Consumers were entitled to expect that the lid would be more difficult to open than a normal lid, and that had been achieved. There had been no breach of the Act.

The question of defect often involves balancing risk and benefit. In *Bogle v McDonald's Restaurants* (2002) it was held that coffee must be served in a safe cup but must also be hot! Here, the standards of safety of both the common law and the Act had been met.

Revision Tip

You should be aware that proving a defect is not enough to establish liability. The claimant must also establish a causal link between the defect and his damage, and failure to do so will mean that he cannot recover under the Act. Subject to the defence in **s 4(1)(d)** discussed later in the chapter, this could have caused problems for the claimant in *Evans v Triplex*.

For what kinds of damage is compensation *not* available?

According to s 5, compensation is not available for

- **loss** or damage to the product itself (this would be **pure economic loss**);
- loss or damage to property not ordinarily intended for private use, occupation, or consumption and intended by the claimant for that purpose;
- loss or damage to property totalling less than £275.

What are the defences under the Act?

These are set out in s 4 and are as follows:

1. That the defect is attributable to compliance with any requirement imposed by or under any enactment or with any EU obligation.
2. That the person proceeded against did not at any time supply the product to another.
3. That the supply was not in the course of a business and otherwise than with a view to profit.
4. That the defect did not exist in the product at the relevant time (of supply).

See *Piper v JRI (Manufacturing) Ltd* (2006). An 'artificial hip' fractured two years after implantation. Evidence about the thoroughness of the manufacturing process and inspection established that the defect could not have existed in the product at the time of supply.

5. That the state of scientific and technical knowledge at the relevant time was not such that a producer of products of the same description as the product in question might be *expected* to have discovered the defect if it had existed in his products while they were under his control.

This is the 'development risks' or 'state of the art' defence and is intended to protect the process of scientific and technical innovation.

6. That the defect

    (a) constituted a defect in a product in which the product in question had been comprised, and

    (b) was wholly attributable to the design of the subsequent product or to compliance by the producer of the product in question with instructions given by the producer of the subsequent product.

Revision tip

You will find that the development risks defence has been controversial and it is the defence which is most likely to come up in either an essay or a problem question.

✓ *Looking for extra marks?*

The **1985 EU Directive art** 7(e) described the development risks defence using the stricter test: 'was not such as to *enable* the existence of the defect to be discovered', but left discretion over the exact wording to the member state.

Table 10.1 Comparisons of the two types of product liability in tort

Common law	CPA 1987
Duty not owed by suppliers.	Duty owed by suppliers in some cases: wider list of defendants.
Breach of duty to be proved.	'Defective product' must be proved.
Causation must be proved.	Causation must be proved.
No minimum compensation for property damage.	Compensation only for property damage over £275.
Type of property damage unrestricted.	No liability for damage to 'business property'.
Damage to product itself is pure economic loss.	No liability for damage to defective product itself.
Usual common law defences.	Statutory defences include 'development risks'.
Normal limitation period.	10-year 'long-stop'.

Key cases

Commission of the European Communities v United Kingdom (1997) saw a challenge that the wording of s 4(1)(e) was insufficiently consistent with the Directive. The European Court rejected the challenge, holding that the burden of proof of the defence remained on the producer, as intended, and there was no evidence that UK courts would not apply the defence in the spirit of art 7(e).

In *A v National Blood Authority* (2001), it was held that the defendant had known of the defect in the blood product and so did not come within the s 4(1)(e) defence, despite the fact that precautions were difficult or even impossible.

What are the time limits?

According to the **Limitation Act 1980, s 11A(4)** the action must be brought three years from the date of damage (or the date on which it reasonably could have been discovered).

There is a ten-year 'long-stop' from the date on which the product was first put into circulation.

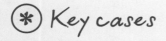 (✱) Key cases

Case	Facts	Principle
A v National Blood Authority [2001] 3 All ER 289	Blood products had been supplied by the defendant, some of which were contaminated by the Hepatitis C virus.	Despite the defendant's claim that testing for the virus was difficult or even impossible, this had been a defective product under the **1987 Act**. The development risks defence was not available.
Abouzaid v Mothercare [2001] EWCA Civ 348	A boy lost the sight in one eye after he was hit by the metal buckle on the elastic strap of his brother's push chair sleeping bag.	There would not have been a breach of duty under the common law; however, the product was held to be defective under the **CPA 1987**, establishing liability by the producer.
Commission of the European Communities v United Kingdom Case C-300/95 [1997] All ER (EC) 391	The wording of the 'development risks defence' (**s 4(1)(e) CPA 1987**) was challenged in the European Court of Justice.	The wording of **s 4(1)(e)**, when considered in the context of British courts' interpretation, was not inconsistent with **art 7(e)** of the **EU Directive**.

Case	Facts	Principle
Donoghue v Stevenson [1932] AC 562	A woman who became sick after drinking ginger beer from a bottle containing a snail was not able to sue in contract because she had not made the purchase.	A manufacturer owes a duty of care for damage caused to the ultimate consumer of his product.
Evans v Triplex Safety Glass [1936] 1 All ER 283	Injuries were caused when a car windscreen broke. The manufacturers were sued in negligence.	Although there would have been a duty of care owed, the fact that the accident occurred a year after manufacture meant that causation was doubtful. The negligence could have been attributed to a fitter, or other cause.
Grant v Australian Knitting Mills [1936] AC 85	The plaintiff developed a skin rash due to chemicals left in his underwear by the manufacturer.	The presence of the chemicals was presumed to be due to the negligence of someone. The manufacturers were unable to discharge the heavy burden of proving that the fault had not been theirs.
Pollard v Tesco Stores [2006] EWCA Civ 393	A young child was injured by dishwasher soap powder, which had been consumed after prying off the 'childproof' lid.	There was no liability under either the common law or the **1987 Act**. Consumers were entitled to expect that the lid would be difficult to remove, and it had been so.

 **Key debate**

Topic:	**'Development Risks: Unanswered Questions'**
Author:	C. Hodges
Viewpoint:	Criticizes the decision of the European Court of Justice on the validity of the 'state of the art' defence, arguing that the decision does not really solve the problem of how to clearly implement the **strict liability** objective of the original Directive.
Source:	(1998) 61 MLR 560

Topic:	**'A v National Blood Authority'**
Author:	G. Howells and M. Mildred
Viewpoint:	A detailed analysis of Burton J's judgment in **A**, which argues that while it appears to be a pro-claimant decision, it may not be. The concept of 'defect' requires further clarification.
Source:	(2005) 65 MLR 95

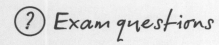
(?) Exam questions

Problem question

Luke employs Barbara and Clive in his nursery business, which produces hanging baskets for municipal displays. He has recently purchased a new insecticide, Buzz-Off!, which is manufactured by 'Bugs R Us'. After a week of decanting Buzz-Off! into spray canisters, Luke develops a serious respiratory illness.

Luke has recommended that protective visors and gloves be worn when insecticide is being sprayed. Clive is keen to develop a good tan, so removes his visor. He sustains serious sunburn while spraying during a heat wave. Barbara is wearing her visor and gloves but when the spray canister bursts she is splattered with Buzz-Off! and due to her sensitive skin, she now has severe scarring to her arms.

Advise L, B, and C.

See the Outline Answers section in the end matter for help with this question.

Essay question

'The objective of strict liability has not been realized in the Consumer Protection Act 1987.'
Discuss.

Online Resource Centre

To see an outline answer to this question visit www.oup.com/lawrevision/

#11

Intentional torts

- Torts of *trespass* (in respect of the person, land and goods) are the oldest torts.

- The torts of *trespass to the person* are

  - battery,

  - assault, and

  - false imprisonment.

- These torts are united by three characteristics. They are

  - committed *intentionally*;

  - take the form of *direct* harm; and

  - are actionable *per se*, that is, without proof of damage.

- The tort of *trespass to land* should be understood in outline.

- An additional intentional tort is derived from *Wilkinson v Downton* (1897).

- More recently, this category of harm has been augmented by the **Protection from Harassment Act 1997**.

- Trespass to the person involves a significant overlap with the criminal law.

Assessment

It is important that you be able to distinguish actions in **trespass** to the person from those in **negligence**. Many problem questions will require you to demonstrate your understanding of more than one trespass **tort** and apply this to a scenario containing a number of different actionable events.

Background to trespass to the person

Direct

To distinguish 'direct' from 'indirect', the illustration is often given that if a log was thrown onto the highway and hit someone it would be **trespass**, but that if someone stumbled over it then it would be actionable in 'case' (or **negligence**).

As regards the **tort** of **battery**, you will see that the application of some degree of force must occur, but in respect of **assault** and false imprisonment, directness is less clear. The requirement of directness has become diluted over the years and is no longer of great importance.

Intentional

The requirement of 'intention' means that the act which caused the harm must be intentional, or voluntary. It is not necessary that the outcome, or harm, be intended.

Letang v Cooper [1965] 1 QB 232

FACTS: The plaintiff's legs were run over by the defendant while she was sunbathing in a car park. Due to a problem with the limitation period, she sued in trespass to the person.

HELD: There was no action in negligent trespass. If the running over had been done intentionally the action would be in **trespass**, but if unintentionally, then the appropriate form of action was **negligence**.

'Actionable *per se*'

The **tort** does not require proof of damage in order to be actionable. In the case of false imprisonment, for example, deprivation of liberty, for however short a time, is a wrong in itself. The amount of damage will, however, be taken into account when **damages** are quantified.

Revision tip

You will recall that **defamation** is another **tort** which is **actionable per se**.

Battery

Battery consists of the:

- intentional and
- direct
- application of force to another
- without his consent.

Intentional

This is the principle discussed above in relation to all **trespass** torts.

Williams v Humphrey (1975) illustrates intention in **battery**. The defendant pushed the plaintiff into a swimming pool, causing injury which was not intended. This was still action-able in battery as the original pushing was intentional, even if the outcome was unforeseen.

It would appear that 'transferred intent' applies to this **tort**, ie when the defendant has intended to hit A but instead hits B, he thereby becomes liable for **battery** to B. (See *Bici and Bici v Ministry of Defence* (2004).)

Direct

This is interpreted widely, so that in *Haystead v Chief Constable of Derbyshire* (2000), when the defendant struck someone in the face causing her to drop the baby she was holding, this was held to constitute **battery** in relation to the baby.

A schoolboy who put a harmful chemical into a hairdryer was also held to have inflicted force directly and was thereby liable in **battery**: *DPP v K* (1990).

Application of force to another

Some physical contact with the claimant (or his clothes) is required. In *Kaye v Robertson* (1991) it was doubted whether shining light into the plaintiff's eyes would suffice; similarly the blowing of smoke at someone is thought not to be tangible enough to constitute **battery**.

Revision tip

Thinking more widely, you will see that if the smoke or light had caused some damage, then it is likely to be actionable in **negligence**, subject to **duty of care** and **foreseeability**.

Without his consent

There are two senses in which this requirement is important.

First, it addresses the question of ordinary social touching, such as brushing against people in a crowd, to which there is presumed consent. The requirement from *Wilson v Pringle* (1987) of evidence of 'hostile intent' from the defendant has generally been disapproved.

Instead the more accepted standard is derived from *Collins v Wilcock* (1984), which is that touching will not be treated as **battery** if it is 'contact acceptable in the ordinary conduct of everyday life'.

Second, even when the touching is outside the boundaries of ordinary social life, consent can negative **battery**. The obvious example is in the medical context where, subject to issues about capacity, explicit or even presumed consent will justify painful or invasive procedures.

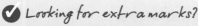 ✔ **Looking for extra marks?**

In *F v West Berkshire HA* (1989) the House of Lords gave extensive consideration to the **tort** of **battery** in a case of medically-imposed sterilization for a mentally subnormal patient. Although this could not be described as 'hostile', in the absence of meaningful consent it would constitute **battery**, unless a different source of authority could be found. A declaration was given that the procedure was necessary in the *best interests* of the patient.

Assault

An **assault** is committed when the defendant has caused another to:

- reasonably apprehend
- the direct and immediate application of force.

Reasonably apprehend

This is determined objectively and an unfounded apprehension will not found an action in **assault**. In *Thomas v National Union of Mineworkers* (1986), those being transported past picket lines on buses were being threatened by those on strike, but this did not constitute **assault** as it would have been impossible for the threats to be carried out.

However, in *Stephens v Myers* (1830), the defendant went to strike the plaintiff but someone intervened and prevented him. Here, an **assault** was committed as it had been reasonable for the plaintiff to anticipate a hit.

The direct and immediate application of force

There has been an evolution in the case law concerning the impact of speech. According to *R v Meade* (1823), words cannot constitute assault; however, this was doubted in *R v Ireland* (1998). It seems that in the age of telephone and cyber-stalking if words caused a reasonable apprehension in the recipient, an actionable **assault** would have taken place. (**The Protection from Harassment Act 1997** may provide a more appropriate **remedy**, however.) An example of a case where words negated **assault** was *Tuberville v Savage* (1669), where the defendant said, 'If it were not assize time, I would not take such language from you.'

In many cases, an anticipation of force (**assault**) will be followed by the impact itself (**battery**), and any compensation for the first will be included within that for the second.

Revision tip

There is a cross-over between criminal and **tort** case law in this area. The criminal cases are indicative but not authority for tort law.

False imprisonment

False imprisonment is:

- the complete restraint of bodily movement
- which is not expressly or impliedly authorized by law.

In this definition, 'false' indicates wrongfulness and 'imprisonment' indicates any restraint of movement.

There must be a detention in which restraint is complete

A detention takes place when freedom of movement is restricted. This could take place in an area as small as a prison cell or as big as Oxford Circus.

R v Bournewood etc NHS Trust, ex p L [1999] 1 AC 458

FACTS: It was held that a voluntary mental patient who was kept sedated in an unlocked ward had not been under detention, despite the fact that he was incapable of leaving and was likely to be compulsorily detained if he attempted to do so.

HELD: This case was taken to the European Court of Human Rights (ECHR), where it was held that the patient had been denied his **art 5(1)** right to liberty. (See *HL v United Kingdom* (2005).)

There is no false imprisonment if the claimant has a reasonable means of escape.

Bird v Jones (1845) 7 QB 742

FACTS: The plaintiff climbed into a portion of a footpath on Hammersmith Bridge which had been blocked off by the defendant and then claimed that he had been detained, in not being permitted to proceed along that path.

HELD: His action for false imprisonment was unsuccessful because it had been open to him to proceed in the same direction down the footpath on the other side of the bridge. The restraint was not complete.

The imposition of reasonable or lawful conditions by the defendant again negates the **tort**.

In *Robinson v Balmain Ferry Co Ltd* (1910), the plaintiff was caught on the wrong side of the defendant's turnstile and could have passed through by paying one penny. For this reason, it was not accepted that he had been falsely imprisoned.

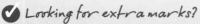 ✅ *Looking for extra marks?*

Herd v Weardale Steel Coal and Coke Co (1915) posed more complicated issues. Owing to the fact that his shift had not yet ended, a coal miner was refused his request for a lift to take him up to the surface. His false imprisonment action failed for two reasons: first, he had contractually agreed to a defined period of deprivation of liberty for the duration of his shift, and therefore the detention was deemed to be consensual. Second, the situation was the result of an omission rather than a positive act by the defendant. (But see cases such as *ex p Evans*, later in the chapter, which raise doubts as to the requirement for a positive act by the defendant.)

The claimant need not have been aware of imprisonment

It is an indication of the great value which is placed on liberty that false imprisonment has occurred even if the claimant did not know that he was being detained. This is consistent with the fact that the **trespass** torts are **actionable** per se.

> **Meering v Grahame-White Aviation (1919) 122 LT 44**
>
> **FACTS:** The plaintiff had been detained in a room while being investigated for suspected theft from his employer. He did not know that two police officers had been stationed outside the door, who would have prevented him from leaving if he had tried.
>
> **HELD:** Liability for false imprisonment was imposed, despite the fact that the plaintiff had been unaware at the time that he was detained.

See also *Murray v Ministry of Defence* (1988).

Of course factors such as the immediate effect on the claimant and the length of the detention are relevant to the **quantum** of compensation to which the claimant may be entitled.

Defences

Lawful authority

Many actions for false imprisonment are against the police or prison authorities. A detention, such as an arrest, will not constitute false imprisonment if it is authorized by law. Common law and statutory powers of arrest are an area of law which is beyond the scope of this **tort** text, and are detailed in the **Police and Criminal Evidence Act 1984**, ss 24, 24A, and 28 and the **Public Order Act 1986**.

In *Hague v Deputy Governor of Parkhurst Prison* [1992] the House of Lords rejected an action in false imprisonment by a prisoner kept in solitary confinement contrary to the Prison Rules on the grounds that a lawfully detained prisoner has no residual liberty to be deprived of.

When the unlawfulness is based, not upon the conditions of detention but rather the fact of detention itself, the case of *R v Governor of Brockhill Prison, ex p Evans* (2001) is important. A prisoner who was kept some two months extra in custody owing to a mistaken calculation of her term obtained compensation for false imprisonment by the prison authorities.

Necessity

This defence has increasingly been used as an answer to claims brought under art 5. In *Austin v Metropolitan Police Commissioner* (2005), the House of Lords interpreted art 5 as permitting reasonable measures for crowd control in 'extreme and exceptional circumstances'. This rejection of the action by protestors who had been 'kettled' in Oxford Circus was upheld by the ECtHR in *Austin v United Kingdom* (2012).

Revision tip

You may have observed that the authorities are inconsistent regarding whether elements such as consent or lawful authority are defences or whether their absence is in fact a component of the **tort** itself. It will be simpler for your revision if you learn them as defences.

The tort in *Wilkinson v Downton*

In the case itself, in 1897, the defendant told the plaintiff (falsely) that her husband had been involved in a serious accident. As a result of this unfortunate joke, the plaintiff suffered nervous shock. The type of damage suffered was not, at the time, actionable in **negligence** and no action in **trespass** could be brought because there had been no application of force upon her. A **remedy** was provided in **tort**, on the grounds that the defendant had:

- wilfully
- committed an act
- calculated to cause physical damage to the plaintiff
- by indirect means.

In the past, even when the potential for actions in **negligence** was more limited, the rule in *Wilkinson v Downton* was rarely applied. See, for instance, *Janvier v Sweeney* (1919).

Later developments have been restrictive. In *Wong v Parkside Health NHS Trust* (2003) it was held that 'mere distress' would not be enough. Psychological injury would only be actionable if it constituted recognized psychiatric illness.

✶✶✶✶✶✶✶✶✶✶✶✶

Wainwright v Home Office [2004] 2 AC 406

FACTS: An action was brought by a mother and son in respect of humiliation and distress they suffered due to the manner in which they were strip-searched on a prison visit.

HELD: The son, who suffered from learning difficulties, succeeded in the **tort** of **battery**. *Wilkinson v Downton* did not apply, on the ground of insufficient proof of intention by the defendant to cause harm to the plaintiffs.

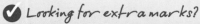 **Looking for extra marks?**

You should revise *Wainwright* in conjunction with Chapter 15, 'Privacy', where an attempt in *Wainwright* to invoke a **tort** claim based on invasion of privacy also failed.

Trespass to land

Unlawful interference with land, which is *direct*, *intentional* and **actionable per se**.

- **What is land?** The surface of and anything permanently attached to the land (eg trees, crops); including the subsoil below and airspace above to a reasonable height and depth (*Bernstein v Skyviews* (1978)).

- **What intention is required?** That to do the physical act of entering or coming into contact with the land. Mistake about the legal rights over the land does not negate trespass.

- **Defences to trespass to land:** Consent of the person in possession of the land, although this can be withdrawn; necessity.

- **Remedies:** Damages (compensatory or nominal), an injunction, or a declaration of legal rights over the land.

The Protection from Harassment Act 1997

In cases which might have led to claims under the **trespass** torts considered earlier, a new form of action is available under the **Protection from Harassment Act 1997**.

An action in **tort** is possible in respect of:

- a course of conduct (on at least two occasions)

- pursued against the claimant

- which alarmed the claimant or caused distress.

For an application of this statutory **tort**, see *Majrowski v Guys and St Thomas's NHS Trust* (2007), which was discussed in Chapter 9 (The three ingredients of vicarious liability, p 108).

Defences to trespass to the person

For the five defences listed below, the defendant will have the burden of proving the necessary elements of his defence, on a balance of probabilities.

Consent

As we have seen, it is a defence to an action in **trespass** to the person for the defendant to prove that the claimant had consented, or led the defendant to believe that he was consenting.

This defence often arises in medical cases (see *Chatterton v Gerson* (1981)), and such claims may overlap with those in **negligence**.

Lawful authority

This will be based upon a common law or statutory power, for instance, to detain or arrest. Like consent, the burden will be on the defendant to prove this defence.

Self-defence

As in the criminal law, it will be a defence to prove that the action in question was reasonable and in proportion to the perceived force.

> **Lane v Holloway [1968] 1 QB 379, CA**
>
> The plaintiff had called the defendant's wife a 'monkey-faced tart'. He then hit the defendant on the shoulder, who retaliated with a blow to the face which required 19 stitches. This was disproportionate to the threat posed, in part due to the plaintiff's age, and the self-defence was not accepted in response to the **battery** claim.

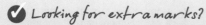 **Looking for extra marks?**

You might compare the cases of *Ashley v Chief Constable of Sussex Police* (2008) and *Bici v Ministry of Defence* (2008) where the House of Lords considered whether the ingredients of self-defence should be the same in **tort** and criminal law, as well as the implications of the 'vindicatory' nature of the **trespass** torts.

Necessity

This strictly construed defence is applicable in cases in which the action in question was in response to threat of a greater harm.

It may be applied in the medical context, as in the case of *F v West Berkshire Health Authority* (1989), considere earlier in the chapter, where the best interests of the patient require action to be taken in the absence of consent.

Protection of public safety formed the basis of the defence of necessity in *Austin v Commissioner of Police for the Metropolis* (2009).

Contributory negligence

Co-operative Group (CWS) Ltd v Pritchard (2011) confirms that **contributory negligence** will not be a defence in cases of **assault** or **battery**.

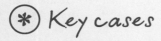 (✳) Key cases

Case	Facts	Principle
Austin v Commissioner of Police for the Metropolis [2009] 1 AC 564	A group of demonstrators were detained in the street for seven hours by the police. They sued in false imprisonment and for breach of their **art 5** rights.	The police were entitled to use the defence of necessity in this extreme case, because a breach of the peace was anticipated, although there was no specific concern about the behaviour of the claimants.
Collins v Wilcock [1984] 1 WLR 1172	A police officer took hold of the plaintiff's arm in an attempt to stop her from walking away.	This was held to constitute battery, as it was unwanted and went beyond normal social touching.
F v West Berkshire HA [1989] 2 WLR 1025	A declaration was sought by the health authority on the legality of the sterilization of a young woman who was mentally incompetent to consent.	A declaration was given that the procedure would be legal as it was necessary in the best interests of the patient. Without such necessity, it would constitute battery.
Hague v Deputy Governor of Parkhurst Prison [1992] 1 AC 58	The plaintiff claimed that he had been detained in solitary confinement contrary to the Prison Rules and sued in false imprisonment.	The prisoner had no liberty capable of being taken away, therefore the tort of false imprisonment had not occurred.
Lane v Holloway [1968] 1 QB 379	Following an insult to the defendant's wife, the plaintiff struck the defendant who then retaliated with a severe blow causing serious injury.	In the battery action, the defendant could not use self-defence as his response had been disproportionate to the threat.
Letang v Cooper [1965] 1 QB 232	The defendant ran over the plaintiff's legs, while she was sunbathing in a car park. For limitation reasons, she sued in the tort of battery.	The claim was unsuccessful. Because the act had been unintentional, the only possible action was in negligence. There is no tort of negligent trespass.

Case	Facts	Principle
Meering v Grahame-White Aviation (1919) 122 LT 44	The plaintiff was taken to his employer's office, under suspicion of theft. Unknown to him, police were outside the door to prevent him leaving. He brought an action for false imprisonment.	The unlawful imprisonment had taken place, despite the fact that at the time he was not aware of it. The tort is actionable *per se*.
R v Governor of Brockhill Prison, ex p Evans [2001] 2 AC 19	A prison governor had failed to calculate correctly the length of term of a prisoner who was detained for two months beyond his proper release date.	This constituted false imprisonment because it did not have lawful authority.
Robinson v Balmain Ferry Co Ltd [1910] AC 295	The plaintiff had turned back from a ferry boarding station but was unable to pass through the turnstile without paying one penny.	This was a reasonable condition; and therefore his detention had not been complete and the action for false imprisonment failed.
Stephens v Myers (1830) 4 C&P 349	The defendant attempted to strike the plaintiff but was prevented by a third party.	The tort of assault had been committed because the plaintiff had reasonably anticipated an immediate battery.
Thomas v National Union of Mineworkers [1986] Ch 20	The plaintiffs were in a bus passing a picket line and were threatened by the gestures from the picketers.	The tort of assault had not taken place because there had not been a reasonable apprehension of immediate battery.
Wainwright v Home Office [2004] 2 AC 406	A mother and son were subjected to a strip search when they visited a prison, resulting in psychiatric injury. They sued the Home Office in the rule in **Wilkinson v Downton**, battery, and for breach of privacy.	Only the battery action was (partially) successful. **Wilkinson** depended on an intention to cause harm, which was not established. **Wainwright** indicates the extremely limited scope of **Wilkinson**.
Wilkinson v Downton [1897] 2 QB 57	The plaintiff suffered nervous shock as a result of the defendant telling her, falsely, that her husband had been seriously injured in an accident.	A tort occurs when the defendant wilfully acts in a way intending to cause harm to the claimant by indirect means, and this results in physical or psychiatric injury.
Williams v Humphrey The Times, 12 February 1975	The defendant child pushed another, the plaintiff, into a swimming pool, resulting in serious injury.	The battery action was successful. The act of pushing was intentional, but the injury was not required to be intended.
Wilson v Pringle [1987] QB 237	While involved in horseplay, one boy grabbed another's satchel, causing him injury.	The intentional application of force was sufficient to constitute battery, despite the fact that the injury was unintentional.

Key debates

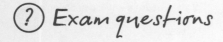

Key debates

Topic:	'Human Rights: Art 5, its Application to Measures of Crowd Control by Police'
Author:	A. Ashworth
Viewpoint:	An analysis of the decision of the Grand Chamber of the European Court of Human Rights in the case of *Austin v United Kingdom*.
Source:	(2012) Crim LR 544–8

Topic:	'Police Shootings and the Role of Tort'
Author:	P. Palmer and J. Steele
Viewpoint:	A case commentary analysing the significance of the decision in *Ashley v Chief Constable of Sussex*, including the relationship between the **trespass** torts and the criminal law, as well as self-defence.
Source:	(2008) 71 MLR 801

Exam questions

Problem question

Eddie was disturbed by a knock on his front door late in the evening. The caller was Grant, a neighbour, who was complaining about the noise from Eddie's TV. Eddie refused to turn it down and then shoved Grant, who retaliated by striking Eddie several vicious blows on the head.

Hearing the fight, Grant's wife Ruby ran to stop it and accidentally knocked Eddie and Grant through a plate glass window. She then administered first aid to Grant, who was unconscious, and rang the police to report the incident. In addition, she locked the doors and windows so that Eddie would be prevented from attempting to leave the house before the police arrived.

Advise Eddie, Grant, and Ruby of their rights and liabilities.

See the Outline Answers section in the end matter for help with this question.

Essay question

'The role of intention in the torts of trespass to the person is a complex one.'
Discuss.

 Online Resource Centre

To see an outline answer to this question visit www.oup.com/lawrevision/

#12

Nuisance and *Rylands v Fletcher*

Key facts

- The term 'nuisance' relates to three very different actions: private nuisance, public nuisance, and statutory nuisance. The same event may be actionable under more than one of these.

- All three are land-related torts, occurring indirectly.

- Unlike negligence, in nuisance the law is concerned less with the nature of the defendant's conduct than with its *effect*.

- *Rylands v Fletcher* is a variety of nuisance which carries strict liability.

Assessment

There are overlaps in the different causes of action that can apply to the same factual situation. When considering an answer involving **nuisance**, you must also be able to consider possibilities in private nuisance, public nuisance, statutory nuisance, **strict liability,** and **negligence.** Nuisance is likely to arise as a problem question. See Figures 12.1 and 12.2 for comparisons.

Private nuisance

According to Winfield:

> Private nuisance consists of a continuous, unlawful and indirect interference with the use or enjoyment of land, or of some right over or in connection with it.

Unlawful

An 'unlawful' interference is one which is *unreasonable.* The rightness or wrongness of the defendant's actions will be determined by their effect on the claimant's ability *to enjoy and use his land*. The court makes a decision on what is unreasonable by balancing the rights and needs of landowners, in all the circumstances. The key factors are outlined below.

Continuous

The duration of the defendant's activity is one factor which may determine unreasonableness. In *De Keyser's Royal Hotel Ltd v Spicer Bros Ltd* (1914) an injunction was granted to prevent pile-driving at night, even though it was a relatively short-lived activity.

When a 'one-off' incident is treated as **nuisance** this is often on the basis that the situation which gave rise to the incident was a continuing state of affairs.

This was the reasoning in *Spicer v Smee* (1946), where faulty wiring caused a fire.

Revision tip

Isolated events are more likely to be actionable in **negligence** or *Rylands v Fletcher*.

'Interference with use and enjoyment of land'

This is the type of *damage* to which the **tort** of private nuisance is directed. Proof of damage is necessary; it is not **actionable** *per se*.

In *St Helen's Smelting Co v Tipping* (1865), noxious fumes from a nearby smelting factory damaged trees and shrubs on the plaintiff's land. In holding the defendant factory liable in **nuisance**, the court divided actionable damage into two categories:

1. material physical damage, as in *St Helen's*; and

2. loss of amenity, such as smell and noise. These do not cause tangible damage but detract from enjoyment (and value) of the land.

In *Bone v Seal* (1975), **damages** were awarded for the effect of smells emanating from a pig farm.

Personal injury, as such, will not be compensated in private nuisance, but it may be taken into account in establishing the above elements.

Who can sue in private nuisance?

Because it is a land-based **tort**, only someone who has a *possessory* or *proprietary interest in land* can sue in private nuisance. This means that the claimant will usually be an owner or tenant, but not a guest or employee.

This was established in *Malone v Laskey* (1907) and confirmed by the House of Lords in *Hunter v Canary Wharf*.

Hunter v Canary Wharf [1996] 1 All ER 482

FACTS: A private nuisance action was brought against the developers of the Canary Wharf development by a large number of the local community who were affected by construction dust and by interruption of their television signals by the erection of the Canary Wharf Tower.

HELD: The House of Lords' decision was significant for two reasons:

1. It confirmed that only those plaintiffs who had an interest in land could sue in private nuisance. (This had been doubted by the Court of Appeal in *Khorasandjian v Bush* (1993).) To hold otherwise would be to convert it from a 'tort to land into a tort to the person' (and potentially pose a threat to the **tort** of **negligence**).
2. It was held that television interference could constitute an actionable nuisance, but it would not be actionable in tort when caused by the building of a fixed structure.

Who can be sued in private nuisance?

There are three main categories of potential defendants in an action in private nuisance.

- The *creator* of the nuisance, even when the defendant is no longer occupying the land which is the source of the **nuisance**.
- The *occupier* of the land which is the source of the nuisance.

In *Sedleigh-Denfield v O'Callaghan* [1939] The occupiers of land which contained a drain, which had been blocked by someone unknown years earlier, were held liable for the flooding it caused. Because they had taken no steps to repair the blockage, they were treated as having adopted it.

There are situations in which an occupier may have a positive duty to address a **nuisance** which has arisen on his property.

A *landlord*, in some cases, will be liable if his land is the source of a nuisance.

In *Tetley v Chitty* (1986), land was let for the purpose of holding go-cart racing. The landlord was liable for the noise caused because it was the natural consequence of the letting.

In *Lippiatt v South Gloucestershire County Council* (1999) the defendant Council was held liable for the anti-social activities of travellers, having allowed them to occupy a site, and not having taken action to evict them.

This case is usually contrasted with *Hussain v Lancaster City Council* (1999), where a **nuisance** action against a Council landlord for the racist activities of a tenant failed.

Specific factors

The locality

It was famously stated in *Sturges v Bridgman* (1879) that '[w]hat would be a nuisance in Belgravia would not necessarily be so in Bermondsey'. In Victorian London Belgravia was a fashionable residential district while Bermondsey was the home of the notoriously smelly leather industry. The law required residents of the latter to be more tolerant than those of the former.

In *St Helen's Smelting Co v Tipping* (discussed earlier) it was held that locality would only be taken into account when the **nuisance** alleged was loss of amenity (smell, noise, etc.). If there were material damage to property, then the nature of the locality would not be a factor against finding nuisance.

Planning permission

In some cases, planning permission was taken to change the nature of the locality. In *Gillingham BC v Medway (Chatham) Dock Co* (1993), the grant of planning permission to convert land to become a commercial dock meant that the area around it could no longer be regarded as residential, but industrial. This case was often contrasted with *Wheeler v Saunders* (1996), where permission to extend a pig breeding operation did not alter the nature of the locality.

The decision in *Gillingham* has now been disapproved by the Supreme Court in *Coventry v Lawrence (No 1)* (2014) where Lord Neuberger's speech concluded that planning permission cannot in itself legalize a nuisance, although in some cases the existence of planning permission will be one relevant factor for the court to take into account in examining the overall picture.

Deciding if and when planning permission has changed the nature of the locality, for the purposes of the law of **nuisance**, is not simple and includes a strong element of policy. This must be done on a case-by-case basis; see *Barr v Biffa Waste Services Ltd* (2012) where the mere fact that waste tipping was being conducted with the benefit of a permit did not mean it did not still constitute a nuisance.

Private nuisance

******** ** ***

The sensitivity of the claimant

A claimant may feel that his neighbour is committing a **nuisance**, but this may be due to his own unreasonably high standards or peculiar requirements.

In *Robinson v Kilvert* (1889) the plaintiff's storage of delicate paper constituted special sensitivity. However, in *McKinnon Industries v Walker* (1953), where the **loss** was caused to orchids, this was held not to be special sensitivity because any ordinary plants would also have been affected by the defendant's activity.

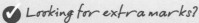
The utility of the defendant's conduct

The fact that the defendant's activity is providing employment or an amenity will not mean that it cannot still be held to be a **nuisance**. This was the outcome in an action against a popular (but smelly) local fish and chip shop in *Adams v Ursell* (1913). See also *Bellew v Cement Co* (1948).

Social utility may, however, affect the **remedy** which the court prescribes. In *Miller v Jackson* (1977) the Court of Appeal refused an injunction against a nuisance-causing village cricket club; whereas one was granted in respect of the less respectable sport of motor boat racing in *Kennaway v Thompson* (1981).

The defendant's motive

If the activity is done deliberately or with malice then this may convert what would otherwise be lawful into a **nuisance**. In *Hollywood Silver Fox Farm Ltd v Emmett* (1936) the defendant repeatedly fired his gun to disrupt the breeding season of the neighbouring silver foxes. What might otherwise have been lawful became a nuisance owing to the malicious motive. See also *Christie v Davey* (1893).

Positive duties arising from acts of nature

If a **nuisance** arises due to the effect of nature on the defendant's land, then he may be liable if he fails to take action to correct it.

Goldman v Hargrave [1967] 1 AC 645

FACTS: A tree on the defendant's land was struck by lightning. He did not take adequate steps to put the fire out and it spread and damaged the plaintiff's property.

HELD: He was liable in **nuisance** for the damage because he had not taken the steps which a landowner in his position ought reasonably to have taken.

Similar liability arose in *Leakey v National Trust* (1980), where, despite warnings, the defendant did not take preventative action in respect of a natural mound, which eventually toppled onto the plaintiff's property.

Holbeck Hall Hotel Ltd v Scarborough Borough Council [2000] 2 All ER 705

FACTS: The claimant owned a cliff-top hotel which was destroyed owing to loss of support from the land on which it stood, which was owned by the defendant. Although the defendant had been generally aware of the danger of landslips, that which occurred would only have been predictable following an extensive geological survey.

HELD: Given the resources of the defendant, it would not have been reasonable to expect him to undertake such a survey. He was therefore not liable in **nuisance** for failing to take steps to avert the damage, on the grounds of unforeseeability.

The outcome was different in *Delaware Mansions Ltd v Westminster City Council* (2001), where the defendant was liable for the damage caused by encroaching tree roots, because he 'knew or ought to have known' that they constituted a continuing **nuisance**.

See also *Bybrook Barn Garden Centre v Kent County Council* (2001).

Revision tip

In considering these cases, you should note the difference in the way that **fault** is treated in **nuisance**, compared to breach of duty in **negligence**. In nuisance, the test is subjective because the resources of the defendant are taken into account. In negligence, the standard is objective.

The human rights implications of the law of nuisance

The 'balancing' between the needs of the parties involved in determining **nuisance** can now have significant human rights implications when public authorities have resource constraints and wider public obligations to take into account in their activities.

Marcic v Thames Water Utilities [2002] 2 All ER 55
FACTS: The defendant water authority had failed to repair and update sewers to cope with increased demand, and this resulted in periodic flooding to a large number of local homes. The claim was brought in private nuisance and under the **Human Rights Act 1998** for breaches of **art 8** (right to private and family life) and **art 1** of **Protocol 1** (peaceful enjoyment of possessions).
HELD: The private nuisance claim was successful in the Court of Appeal, although it was reversed by the House of Lords owing to the existence of a statutory scheme regulating the activities of the water authority. No final decision was made on the human rights aspects of the case, although both the judge at first instance and the Court of Appeal suggested that they could be persuaded that the claimant's **art 8** rights had been breached.

Marcic does not, then, provide a sound precedent in this area but it laid a foundation which was built upon in *Dennis v Ministry of Defence*.

Dennis v Ministry of Defence [2003] EWHC 793
FACTS: This was an action by a large private landowner in respect of the noise from low-flying military training flights.
HELD: It succeeded, both in private nuisance and in establishing a breach of **art 8** and **art 1** of **Protocol 1**. There was, however, recognition of a strong public interest in continuing the training flights and so **damages** were awarded in lieu of an **injunction** in respect of the **loss** of enjoyment in the property as well as its diminution in value.

Defences to private nuisance

Before defences are considered, it is important to emphasize the key principle: '*coming to the nuisance is not a defence*'. It is not open to the defendant to argue that the claimant is barred from complaining about a situation of which he should have been aware.

In *Miller v Jackson*, discussed earlier, the plaintiffs brought a successful claim in **nuisance**, despite having built their house next to an existing cricket pitch. See also *Sturges v Bridgman*.

Revision Tip

It is helpful to be aware that, in some cases of 'amenity damage', the taking into account of the factor of *locality* will have the same effect as the unacceptable defence of *coming to the nuisance*.

Prescription

If the defendant's activity has been causing a **nuisance** for 20 years or more, then he has acquired a legal right which acts as a defence to a nuisance claim. This does not apply to public nuisance, considered later in the chapter.

> **Sturges v Bridgman (1879) 11 Ch D 892**
>
> This provides an example of the courts' strict interpretation of this defence. Here, the neighbour's long-standing confectionery business did not cause a **nuisance** until the plaintiff moved his consulting rooms to the end of the garden. The defence of prescription could not be used.

Statutory authority

The defendant may be a public body acting under statutory powers. This will serve as a defence to any **nuisance** action, if the nuisance is the unavoidable outcome of authorized activity.

> **Allen v Gulf Oil Refining Ltd [1981] AC 1001**
>
> Local inhabitants brought a **nuisance** action in respect of smell, noise, and vibrations coming from a refinery, whose construction was authorized by statute. The House of Lords decided, after careful interpretation of the statute, that it had effectively authorized the nuisance.

Remedies

Injunction

The continuing nature of most nuisances means that the biggest concern of the claimant is likely to be bringing about its end, or reduction, by means of an **injunction**. For example in *De Keyser's Royal Hotel Ltd v Spicer Bros Ltd*, discussed previously, an injunction was granted limiting the noisy work to hours when neighbours would not want to sleep.

Damages

Damages were granted in lieu of an **injunction**, according to the principles set out in *Shelfer v City of London Electric Lighting Co* (1895), where:

- injury to the claimant's legal rights is small, and
- it is one which is capable of being estimated in money, and
- it is one which can be adequately compensated
- by a small money payment, and
- the case is one in which an injunction would be oppressive to the defendant.

Both *Miller v Jackson* and *Dennis v Ministry of Defence*, considered earlier, were regarded as exceptional cases in which the award of **damages** was made outside of the requirements set by *Shelfer*. In *Coventry v Lawrence (No 2)* (2014), however, the Supreme Court signalled a distinct shift away from a strict application of the *Shelfer* criteria, to a situation in which damages would no longer be an exceptional remedy in nuisance cases. The rights of the public as well as those of other parties, and those of the claimant and defendant, are to be taken into account in determining the appropriate remedy.

Abatement

Abatement of the **nuisance**, or 'self-help'. In a small number of cases, the injured party takes appropriate steps to stop the nuisance.

In *Delaware Mansions Ltd v Westminster City Council* (2001) it was appropriate for the council to pay to have encroaching roots removed. A party who wrongly exercises abatement can be criminally liable, as in *Burton v Winters* (1993).

Public nuisance

According to *Attorney General v PYA Quarries* (1957), public nuisance is an act

> which materially affects the reasonable comfort and convenience of life of a class of Her Majesty's subjects.

Despite its name, public nuisance does not have a lot in common with private nuisance. It is a *crime as well as a* **tort** and covers many sorts of situations: from holding a rave to allowing pigeon droppings to foul a pavement.

Who can sue in public nuisance?

Public nuisance covers situations in which it is not realistic for one individual to bring an action. Because *a class* or cross-section of the public is affected, an action will be brought by a local authority on behalf of the community under s 222 of the **Local Government Act 1972** (or, exceptionally, in an Attorney General's 'relator action').

An action in **tort** by an individual is only available when the claimant has suffered special damage (direct and substantial) over and above that of other members of the public.

Tate & Lyle Industries v GLC [1983] 2 AC 509

The defendant's construction works caused general silting of the Thames. However, the plaintiffs brought a successful individual action because the silting blocked access to their industrial jetties, causing special damage.

Unlike private nuisance, the public nuisance claim need not be connected to an interest in land. See, for example, *Castle v St Augustine's Links* (1922), where the plaintiff was hit by a golf ball while driving on the highway.

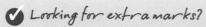

☑️ *Looking for extra marks?*

In *R v Rimmington* (2006) the House of Lords held that it is not possible to add together a number of essentially individual events (racist letters sent to over 500 people) to comprise the crime of public nuisance.

Who can be sued in public nuisance?

The creator of the **nuisance**.

What kind of damage is covered?

Damages can be recovered for:

- property damage: *Halsey v Esso Petroleum* (1961);
- obstruction of, or damage to, the public highway: *Rose v Miles* (1815); *Wandsworth LBC v Network Rail* (2001);
- personal injury: *Claimants in Corby Group Litigation v Corby BC* (2008); and
- economic loss: *Benjamin v Storr* (1874), where the entrance to the plaintiff's coffee house was blocked, causing him loss of profits.

Revision tip

Reading *Halsey v Esso Petroleum* (1961) will give a helpful illustration of the way that the defendant's failure to control emissions from and traffic to its oil refinery in a residential area gave rise to claims in both public and private nuisance. It also illustrates the use of remedies in such cases.

Figure 12.1 Nuisance: Public and Private

Public nuisance	Private nuisance
Is a crime as well as a tort	Only a tort
The claimant does not need an interest in land to sue	Only those with an interest in land can sue
Damages are recoverable for personal injury	Damages are not recoverable for personal injury
An isolated incident may give rise to a Tclaim	An isolated incident will not give rise to a claim; there must be an ongoing state of affairs
The claimant must be one of a class of Her Majesty's subjects who suffered damage over and above the rest of the class affected	An individual may sue, not as a part of a class
Remember: The same wrong may be both public and private nuisance	

Public nuisance

✴✴✴✴✴✴✴✴✴✴✴✴

> ### Rylands v Fletcher
>
> In the case of **Rylands v Fletcher (1868)**, a new **tort** was established which provided for **strict liability** of defendants in certain nuisance-related situations.
> The required elements of the tort are as follows:
>
> - in the course of 'non-natural use' of the land,
> - the defendant brings onto his land and collects and keeps there,
> - something likely to do mischief if it escapes,
> - it does escape,
> - and causes damage of a foreseeable kind.

Non-natural use

The most problematic aspect of the **tort** is what was described as *non-natural user* (see Table 12.1).

This was defined in **Rickards v Lothian (1913)** as: 'Some special use bringing with it increased danger to others and [which] must not merely be the ordinary use of the land.'

What is regarded as non-natural is subjective and changes over time, in line with developments in technology and society. You will see that the quantity in which the item is collected can contribute towards a finding of non-natural use.

The current definition was provided in **Transco plc v Stockport MBC (2003)**: 'non-natural use' must involve 'an exceptionally dangerous or mischievous thing in extraordinary or unusual circumstances'.

Revision tip

Non-natural use is the element which is likely to be the most difficult to establish in a potential *Rylands v Fletcher* action.

Table 12.1 Comparing non-natural and natural use

Non-natural use	Natural use
Mason v Levy Autoparts (1967) Large quantities of inflammable auto parts	**Read v Lyons (1947)** A munitions factory in war time
Cambridge Water Co v Eastern Counties Leather (1994) Large quantities of industrial chemicals	**Stockport MBC (2003)** A domestic water supply to a block of flats

Accumulation

This must be artificial, rather than something naturally present. In *Giles v Walker* (1890) there was held to have been no accumulation owing to failure to cut thistles naturally growing on the defendant's land.

Things likely to do mischief if they escape

The substance need not be intrinsically dangerous, but can be seen as capable of causing mischief if it escapes. The case of *Rylands* itself concerned the storage of a large quantity of water in an artificial reservoir on the defendant's land.

Escape

In *Rylands*, the risk materialized when the water flooded off the defendant's property into the plaintiff's mine.

However, in *Read v Lyons & Co* (1947), an explosion in a munitions factory did not involve an *escape*, rather it stayed within the defendant's factory and so no action in the **tort** in *Rylands* was possible.

Rigby v Chief Constable of Northamptonshire (1985) involved a release of tear gas which was deliberate, and so only the **tort** of **trespass** rather than *Rylands* was applicable.

Damage of a foreseeable type

The type of damage which is recoverable under this **tort** is limited to damage to land or to property on land. There are older cases, such as *Read v Lyons* (earlier) and *Perry v Kendrick* (1956), which (*obiter*) assumed that personal injury damage was included. However, in *Cambridge Water v Eastern Counties Leather* (1994) and *Transco* it was finally clarified that *Rylands* is closely related to **nuisance** and, as such, only pertains to land-based damage. Personal injury would only be recoverable, if at all, under the **tort** of **negligence**.

A recent and important development, deriving from the decision in *Cambridge Water*, is that the **tort** is only complete when the relevant damage is of a *reasonably foreseeable* type.

Revision Tip

The question must be asked, 'Given the escape (for which there is **strict liability**), would this damage have been reasonably foreseeable?'

Defences to *Rylands v Fletcher*

Consent of the claimant or common benefit

This defence operates like that of **volenti**. In *Carstairs v Taylor* (1871) rainwater was collected and stored on the roof of a block of flats. There was no liability in *Rylands* when a rat gnawed through the container and caused flooding, as the collection and storage had been for the benefit of all the inhabitants. In *Colour Quest v Total Downstream UK Ltd* (2009) it was held that consent will not operate in cases where the defendant has been negligent.

Act of a stranger

When the **tort** is caused by the act of an unknown third party over whom the defendant has no control, he will not be liable in *Rylands*.

This defence operated in *Perry v Kendricks* (1956), where a child trespasser threw a lighted match into a petrol tank, causing an explosion.

Act of God

It is thought that this defence would only operate for an exceptional event, such as an earthquake. In *Nichols v Marsland* (1876) a very heavy rainstorm qualified for this defence; however, that would probably not be accepted today.

Statutory authority

As with **nuisance**, where the activity in question takes place in the exercise of a statutory duty, this will provide a good defence in the absence of **negligence**. See *Dunne v North Western Gas Board* (1964).

✔ **Looking for extra marks?**

The future of the **tort** in *Rylands v Fletcher* is by no means clear and is a source of academic debate. In *Burnie Port Authority v General Jones Pty Ltd* (1994) it was assimilated into the tort of **negligence** for the purposes of Australian law.

However, in *Transco plc v Stockport MBC* (earlier) the House of Lords resisted any temptation to do the same. You may wish to read the speech of Lord Bingham for the reasoning behind the decision to maintain the tort in English law.

Liability for fire

Generally in English law, there is no **strict liability** for the spread of fire. According to the **Fires Prevention (Metropolis) Act 1774, s 86**, no action can be brought against an occupier for a fire accidentally started. However, if fire were caused by the **negligence** or **nuisance** of the occupier (or someone he has permitted to be on his land) it would be actionable.

It has generally been difficult to adapt liability for fire to the **tort** in *Rylands v Fletcher*, because it is doubtful that the spread of fire can be described as the 'escape of a dangerous thing which has been collected'. In *Stannard v Gore* (2012), the Court of Appeal

Table 12.2 Comparing private nuisance, public nuisance, and *Rylands v Fletcher*

	Private nuisance	*Rylands v Fletcher*	Public nuisance
Who sues?	One with an interest in land	One with an interest in land	One suffering 'particular damage'
Who is sued?	Creator or adopter	One who collects, in course of non-natural user, etc	Creator or adopter
'Fault' required?	Yes, when continuing or adopting a nuisance	No	No
Damages for personal injury?	No	No	Yes
Time frame?	Continuous	One-off	Continuous

confirmed that escape of fire was not enough to found an action in *Rylands*. The law requires that the dangerous thing itself must escape. See also *LMS v Styrene Packaging and Insulation* (2006).

Statutory nuisance

Many of the situations in which the common law torts of public and private nuisance and *Rylands v Fletcher* would apply are now covered by statute. The **Environmental Protection Act 1990** consolidates many of the previous statutes and imposes duties upon local authorities to take action regarding complaints about many of the situations discussed in this chapter, particularly noise and environmental pollution.

The resultant **remedy** would be an **injunction**, or perhaps a fine; for **damages**, individuals will still be required to pursue a common law **nuisance** action.

 ⊛ *Key cases*

Case	Facts	Principle
***Cambridge Water Co v Eastern Counties Leather* [1994] 1 All ER 53**	The defendant had long been operating a tanning operation which had required the storage and use of chemicals. These spilled onto the floor and seeped down into the aquifer, eventually contaminating the plaintiff's water supply.	This constituted non-natural user for the purposes of the tort in *Rylands v Fletcher*, but the type of damage was unforeseeable and for that reason the defendant was not liable.

Key cases

✳✳✳✳✳✳✳✳✳✳

Case	Facts	Principle
Coventry v Lawrence (No 1) [2014] UKSC 13	Planning permission had long ago been granted for speedway racing, on the basis of which it was claimed constituted noise nuisance.	Planning permission could not change the character of a neighbourhood so as to effectively 'legalize' a nuisance.
Dennis v Ministry of Defence [2003] EWHC 793	A landowner successfully sued the MoD in private nuisance for damage to his enjoyment of his land and diminution in value, citing breach of **art 8** and **art 1** of **Protocol 1 of the ECHR**.	The public benefit of the flights did not prevent them being held to be a nuisance, but it did mean that damages, rather than an injunction, was the remedy.
Gillingham BC v Medway (Chatham) Dock) Co (1993) QB 343	Planning permission had been granted to develop a commercial port in a neighbourhood which had previously been residential. Owing to the effective change in the character of the locality, the nuisance claim failed.	Planning permission can be the basis for a definitive change in the nature of a locality. It is not the same as the defence of statutory authority.
Goldman v Hargrave [1967] 1 AC 645	A tree on the defendant's property was hit by lightning and he neglected to put out the fire adequately, which spread to the plaintiff's property.	The defendant was liable for this naturally occurring source of nuisance which he should have, but failed to, abate.
Halsey v Esso Petroleum [1961] 1 WLR 683	The defendant operated a large oil refinery in a residential area, causing smoke fumes and acid smuts to fall in the neighbourhood. Lorries were noisy all night.	The defendant was liable in both private nuisance to home owners and in public nuisance to those whose cars were damaged.
Hollywood Silver Fox Farm Ltd v Emmett [1936] 2 KB 468	The defendant shot guns on the edge of his property, where it bordered the plaintiff's sliver fox farm. He did it in order to disturb the breeding of the animals.	Although the shooting was not in itself unlawful, the malicious purpose of the defendant made it an actionable nuisance.
Hunter v Canary Wharf [1996] 1 All ER 482	The construction of the Canary Wharf development created a large amount of dust in the neighbourhood, as well as interfering with the TV reception of many of the residents.	Interference with TV could constitute an actionable nuisance, when not caused by a standing structure. Contrary to previous suggestions by the Court of Appeal, only those with an interest in land could bring an action in nuisance.
Marcic v Thames Water Utilities [2002] 2 All ER 55, CA; [2003] UKHL 66	The defendant had failed to repair sewers he had responsibility for and they overflowed causing flooding.	In the first major nuisance case to employ human rights arguments, the defendant was initially held liable in private nuisance but the House of Lords overruled this owing to the existence of a statutory scheme of regulation.

Case	Facts	Principle
Rickards v Lothian [1913] AC 263	A sink became blocked in the defendant's property. It overflowed and caused a flood in the premises below. The claim in *Rylands v Fletcher* failed.	This could not be described as 'non-natural user of land'. The definition was given of a 'special use' bringing with it 'increased danger' to others.
Robinson v Kilvert (1889) LR 41 Ch D 88	The defendant produced warm air in the basement of a building and it reached the second floor where the plaintiff stored delicate brown paper.	The warm air would not have damaged ordinary paper. Owing to the plaintiff's special sensitivity, no nuisance had been committed.
Rylands v Fletcher (1866) LR 1 Ex 265; affd (1868) LR 3 HL 330	The defendant employed independent contractors to build a reservoir on his land. They failed to secure old shafts and the water burst through and flooded the plaintiff's mine.	The defendant was held strictly liable on the basis that he had collected this mischief-causing water on his land and allowed it to escape and damage the plaintiff's land. The tort in *Rylands v Fletcher* was established.
Sedleigh-Denfield v O'Callaghan [1939] 1 All ER 725	A drain had been placed on the defendant's property by a third party without permission. The defendant had allowed it to become blocked and it overflowed onto the plaintiff's land.	The defendant was liable in nuisance, because as the occupier of the land, he had used the drain for his own purposes and had thus adopted it.
St Helen's Smelting Co v Tipping (1865) 11 HL Cas 642	The defendant's copper smelting works produced vapours which damaged trees on the plaintiff's estate and therefore was liable in nuisance.	In cases involving material injury to property, the influence of the locality in which the events took place would not be taken into account in determining nuisance.
Sturges v Bridgman (1879) 11 Ch D 892	For more than 20 years a doctor had property which adjoined a confectionery works. He then built a new consulting room at the end of his property and was then disturbed by noise and vibration from the confectionery works. It was held to be an actionable nuisance.	Coming to the nuisance is not a defence. Nor did the defence of prescription apply because the source of the nuisance was new.
Transco plc v Stockport MBC [2003] UKHL 61	The water pipe installed by the defendant burst, leading to a landslip, which meant that the claimant had to make extensive repairs to protect his gas main. His action under *Rylands* was unsuccessful.	The piping of water to domestic premises was not a non-natural use of land. The tort in *Rylands* still has a place in English law and should not be incorporated into negligence or nuisance.

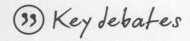 Key debates

Topic:	'What is Private Nuisance?'
Author:	M. Lee
Viewpoint:	A detailed and in-depth analysis of the law of **nuisance** and its relationship to **negligence** and the **tort** in *Rylands v Fletcher*.
Source:	(2003) 119 LQR 298

Topic:	'The Merits of *Rylands v Fletcher*'
Author:	J. Murphy
Viewpoint:	A thorough examination of the nature of the **tort** and a defence of its importance as a tool for environmental protection.
Source:	(2004) 24 OJLS 643

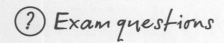 Exam questions

Problem question

Last winter Tony and Cherry moved into a scenic riverside bungalow, which features a jetty where they moor their rowing boat. At the bottom of the long garden is a small group of allotments, provided for the last 30 years by Avonmere District Council, where local residents grow fruit, vegetables, and flowers on small plots.

When spring arrives, they realize that Arthur, the allotment holder nearest to their garden, burns his refuse in a bonfire on the other side of their wall. Smoke and ash frequently blow into their garden. When they put out their garden furniture and sun canopies they often become stained and smelly. When Tony complains to Arthur, he immediately doubles the number of bonfires. Sunbathing is often impossible for Cherry. The situation becomes even worse when Tony realizes that someone on the allotment must be growing marijuana, the seeds of which have blown into his garden and self-seeded.

In 2000 their jetty becomes unusable when it becomes blocked by silt from a small industrial quarry upstream. This was recently established by 'The Rock Shop', which obtained planning permission to do so from the Council.

Advise Tony and Cherry.

See the Outline Answers section in the end matter for help with this question.

Essay question

'In *Hunter v Canary Wharf* the House of Lords refused to extend the categories of those who could benefit from the law of nuisance.'

Discuss.

To see an outline answer to this question visit **www.oup.com/lawrevision/**

#13

Occupiers' liability

- Occupiers' liability is based upon the law of negligence.
- Occupiers' liability is one of the few areas in tort which is now largely regulated by statute.
- The key statutes are the **Occupiers' Liability Act 1957** and the **Occupiers' Liability Act 1984**.
- Liability to lawful entrants is viewed differently from liability to trespassers.
- In determining to whom the duty is owed, it is necessary to identify *the status of the entrant* onto land.
- To determine who owes the duty, the main criterion is *control* of the land.

Assessment

Occupiers' liability typically is examined in a problem question involving various types of liability to different types of entrants onto land. It is essential that you be able to identify the issues particular to occupiers' liability and that you are well acquainted with the two key statutes. Additionally you must know about the operation of the **Unfair Contract Terms Act 1977**.

Introduction

Prior to 1957, the extent of **duty of care** owed in respect of occupation, or control, of land was based on the common law. It was owed, in descending order, to those under contract, invitees, and licensees, with little or no duty owed to trespassers. You will encounter these terms in older case law, but since the **Occupiers' Liability Act 1957** the first three types are united into the category *lawful visitors*, and this is the term you will now use.

Occupiers' Liability Act 1957

The scope of the Act

According to s 1(1), the Act was intended to

> regulate the duty which an occupier of premises owes to his visitors in respect of dangers due to the *state of the premises* or to things done or omitted to be done on them.

This has been interpreted as creating an 'occupancy' rather than 'activity' duty. The source of damage must originate with the premises itself rather than with what someone does on it.

Who owes a duty under the Act?

Section 1(2) refers to 'a duty imposed by law in consequence of a person's occupation or control of premises'.

In the absence of a detailed statutory definition of 'occupier' the common law is of assistance. The key concept is *control*.

Wheat v Lacon [1966] AC 552

FACTS: The defendant brewery owned a pub, which it entrusted to a manager and gave him permission to live with his wife on the first floor and take in paying guests. A paying guest was killed falling down an unlit staircase, which had an inadequate stair rail.

HELD: The House of Lords held that there was nothing in law to prevent there being more than one occupier of a premises. Here, the defendant, along with the manager, was the occupier of this staircase but neither had breached their duty as the light bulb had recently been removed by a stranger.

See also *AMF International Ltd v Magnet Bowling Ltd* (1968), where on a large building project both the owner of the property and the contractors were held to be occupiers of the site.

You should note that occupation does not require any interest in land, although of course it may well overlap with such interest. The party with control is taken to be best able to regulate who is and is not allowed to enter, and also to take necessary steps to prevent accidents. In *Harris v Birkenhead Corp* [1976] the defendant local authority was held to be the occupier of a vacant building due for demolition, even though it had never entered or taken possession of it.

Premises

Section 1(3)(a) defines premises as 'any fixed or moveable structure'. It includes ladders, electricity pylons, grandstands, diving boards, lifts, airplanes, airport runways and, in *Furmedge v Chester-le-Street DC* (2011), an inflatable sculpture.

To whom is a duty owed under the Act?

Section 1(2) refers to 'visitors'. Visitors are those who have express or implied permission to enter the premises, and would have been licensees and invitees under the old common law. This will also include those who enter in the exercise of a right, such as a fireman, but does *not* include those using a right of way.

In *Lowery v Walker* (1911) the court found that a plaintiff who regularly used a short-cut across the defendant's land had an implied permission to be there but in *Edwards v Railway Executive* (1952), where the defendant had repeatedly tried to fence a railway line from children, it was held that 'repeated **trespass**' did not confer a licence.

Limitations

An entrant can be a visitor in one part of a premises but a trespasser in another. It was said in *The Calgarth* (1927), 'When you invite a person into your house to use the stairs, you do not invite him to slide down the banisters.'

In *Ferguson v Welsh* (1987) unauthorized subcontractors on a building site were visitors in relation to their immediate employer but trespassers to the owner of the property.

See also *Glasgow Corporation v Taylor* (1922), later in the chapter.

The standard of care

According to s 2(2) visitors are owed

> a duty to take such care as in all the circumstances of the case is reasonable to see that the visitor will be reasonably safe in using the premises for the purposes for which he is invited or permitted by the occupier to be there.

It is the visitor, not the premises, that must be reasonably safe, and the duty applies to the purpose for which the visitor was allowed entry. Known as the *common duty of care*, it covers negligent omissions in addition to acts and damage to property, as well as personal injury and death.

Specific guidance

You should note that the 1957 Act gives specific guidance in relation to:

- children,
- skilled visitors,
- warnings, and
- independent contractors.

Children

Section 2(3)(a) specifies: 'an occupier must be prepared for children to be less careful than adults.' Though this could be regarded as stating the obvious, children are a vulnerable group in this area of the law and so the duty is more explicit.

Glasgow Corporation v Taylor [1922] 1 AC 44

FACTS: A child playing in a public park was tempted by some berries which were in fact poisonous.

HELD: Although the child was technically a trespasser in relation to the bush, the concept of *allurement* was used by the court, so that he was treated as a 'licensee' (now, visitor) to whom a **duty of care** was owed.

When children are very young, occupiers are entitled to assume that responsibility for their safety lies with the parents. This was illustrated in *Phipps v Rochester Corporation* (1955), where an occupier was held not to be liable for injuries suffered by a five-year-old boy playing on his land with his seven-year-old sister.

Bourne Leisure v Marsdon [2009] EWCA Civ 671

FACTS: A two-year-old child tragically drowned in a pond at a holiday park. There was a fence but it was not high enough to prevent the child climbing in.

HELD: There had been no breach of duty by the occupiers of the park. The danger would have been obvious to adults and it was reasonable to expect such a child to have been under adult supervision.

Occupiers' Liability Act 1957
****

You will recall *Jolley v Sutton LBC* (2000), the case of the abandoned boat studied in Chapter 8 on remoteness. In placing liability on the occupiers, Lord Hoffmann said of children: 'their ingenuity in finding unexpected ways of doing mischief to themselves and others should never be underestimated.'

Revision tip

The concept of 'allurement' enabled children to be treated as visitors in some situations. However, implied permission is no longer so important now that the level of duty owed to trespassers has been raised under the **Occupiers' Liability Act 1984**.

Skilled visitors

According to s 2(3)(b), 'an occupier may expect that a person, in the exercise of his calling, will appreciate and guard against any special risks ordinarily incident to it.' It is important to understand that this provision is concerned with injury to the skilled visitor, rather than that caused by him.

Roles v Nathan [1963] 1 WLR 1264

FACTS: Two chimney sweeps were killed by fumes from a boiler they were cleaning, despite warnings on behalf of the occupier.

HELD: The occupier was not liable.
   This was exactly the sort of special risk arising from their calling which the plaintiffs should have guarded against. If, however, one of them had fallen through a weak floorboard, this would not have been covered by **s 2(3)(b)**.

See also *General Cleaning Contractors v Christmas* (1953).

Warnings

The occupier can use warnings to assist in discharging his **duty of care**, providing they are adequate—that is, that they tell the visitor enough to enable him to be reasonably safe (see Figure 13.1).

Occupiers' Liability Act 1957, s 2(4)(a)

[W]here damage is caused to a visitor by a danger of which he had been warned by the occupier, the warning is not to be treated without more as absolving the occupier from liability, unless in all the circumstances it was enough to enable the visitor to be reasonably safe.

The example given by Lord Denning in *Roles v Nathan* is of a house which has a river in front of it with one bridge. A sign saying the bridge is dangerous is not an adequate warning,

Figure 13.1 Occupiers' liability notices

| CAUTION |
| SLIPPERY |
| WHEN WET |

A warning!
OLA 1957
s 2(4)(a)

Management
accept no
responsibility
for loss or
damage
howsoever
caused

NOT a warning
(attempt to
exclude liability)

DO NOT
ENTER

NOT a warning
(restriction on entry)

since the visitor has no choice as to whether to use the bridge. If there are two bridges with one saying, 'Danger, use other bridge' then a person injured using the dangerous bridge would have no claim.

There is no general duty to warn about obvious risks. In *Darby v National Trust* (2001), where a man drowned while swimming in a deep and murky pond on the defendant's property, it was held that the occupier had not been required to put up a sign warning of the obvious dangers.

See also *Staples v West Dorset DC* (1995).

Revision tip

It is important that you distinguish clearly between the following:

1. A warning: 'Danger Slippery Floor.'
2. An exemption of liability: 'The management accepts no responsibility for loss or damage howsoever caused.'
3. A limitation of entry: 'Only authorized personnel beyond this point.'

Students often mistake **2.** and **3.** for warnings.

Independent contractors

Section 2(4)(b) provides a defence to occupiers in some circumstances when damage is attributable to the work of an independent contractor on their premises.

Contrasting the following two cases provides a good illustration of how this provision operates:

- *Haseldine v Daw* (1941)

A visitor was killed when a lift failed in the defendant's building. The repair of the lift had been entrusted by the occupier to an apparently competent engineer and, owing to the technical nature of the task, it would not have been expected that the occupier could have checked whether it had been performed properly. The occupier was not liable.

- *Woodward v Mayor of Hastings* (1945)

A cleaner was given the task of clearing school steps of ice and snow, but a pupil slipped and was injured on the steps. This was not a technical task and the defendant should have checked and realized that it remained a danger.

In addition to ensuring that the contractor is competent, *Gwilliam v West Herts NHS Trust* (2002) indicated that it also may be expected that the occupier satisfy himself that the contractor is also adequately insured. This has now been doubted by *Glaister v Appleby-in-Westmoreland Town Council* (2009).

The Compensation Act 2006 and occupiers' liability

You will recall that the **Compensation Act 2006, s 1** reminds judges, when considering a **negligence** claim, to take into account its potential impact upon desirable activities. In *The Scout Association v Barnes* (2010) Jackson LJ observed, *obiter*, that this had always been a part of the balancing exercise under the common law. Here, allowing scouts to play a game in the dark had significantly increased risk of **injury**, while not adding to the value of the game, and so a breach of the common **duty of care** had occurred.

Exclusion of liability and defences

The Act, in s 2(1), allows the occupier to restrict, modify, or exclude his liability 'in so far as he is free to do so'. This area is now governed by the **Unfair Contract Terms Act 1977**, which states that in cases of premises used for business purposes an occupier cannot exclude liability for death or personal injury caused by **negligence**. As regards property damage, an attempt to exclude liability will be subject to the 'reasonableness test'. 'Business purposes' does not include those which are educational or recreational.

- s 2(5) preserves the defence of *volenti non fit injuria*, and
- s 2(3) implies that the defence of **contributory negligence** can apply to actions under the Act.

Occupiers' Liability Act 1984

At one time, occupiers could only be liable for deliberately or recklessly causing harm to trespassers, as stated in *Addie v Dumbreck* (1929). Following *Addie* this position was gradually modified (often in cases of child trespassers) until, in *British Railways Board v Herrington* (1972), the House of Lords established that a 'duty of common humanity' was owed by occupiers to trespassers.

Following a report by the Law Commission, the **Occupiers' Liability Act 1984** was passed. Its provisions are deliberately wide and general, thereby affording the courts flexibility in applying the law to the facts of each case.

Scope of occupier's duty

Under s 1(1)(a), the Act applies to 'persons other than visitors': mainly *trespassers*, but also those using *private rights of way*. Those exercising a public right of way may be covered by the Countryside and Rights of Way Act 2000 (see later).

Personal injury and death are within the scope of the duty but property damage is not. As under the 1957 Act, it is an 'occupancy' not an active duty.

Revill v Newberry [1996] QB 567

FACTS: The defendant lay in wait for vandals who had been damaging his allotment shed. He shot at them through a hole in the door, injuring one of them.

HELD: In a **negligence** action against him, it was held that although they were trespassers, the 1984 Act did not apply. This was because the source of the damage was the defendant occupier's action in shooting, rather than the state of the premises. He was, however, liable under common law negligence. The injured vandal was held to be two-thirds contributorily negligent for his injury. The court was concerned to point out that the fact of being a criminal trespasser did not make the claimant 'an outlaw'—beyond the protection of civil law.

Revision tip

Revill holds that even where the occupiers' liability legislation does not apply to a situation, there still can be liability under ordinary common law **negligence**.

See also *Keown v Coventry Healthcare NHS Trust* (2006), where it was held that an 11-year-old trespasser who fell from a fire escape had no duty owed to him, because his accident was due to his climbing onto the fire escape rather than its condition.

The best way to apply the Act is to:

- first, establish whether a **duty of care** to the claimant arises. If it does arise, then
- second, consider whether the standard of care has been achieved.

1. When does a duty arise?

Section 1(3): an occupier owes a duty if:

(a) he is aware of the danger or has reasonable grounds to believe that it exists; *and*

(b) he knows or has reasonable grounds to believe that the trespasser is in the vicinity of the danger concerned or that he may come into the vicinity of the danger; *and*

(c) the risk is one against which, in all the circumstances of the case, the occupier may reasonably be expected to offer the other some protection.

> ### *Tomlinson v Congleton DC* [2003] UKHL 47
>
> **FACTS:** The claimant, aged 18, was injured when diving into a lake on the defendant's property. The claimant, like many others, had ignored a sign: 'Dangerous water: no swimming'. Prior to the accident, the defendant had assessed the risk and decided to take further deterrent steps but had not yet done so.
>
> **HELD:** The House of Lords was not certain that **s 1(3)(a)** had been satisfied, but held that **s 1(3)(b)** had been. However, because the danger arose not from the state of the lake itself but from the claimant's activity in ignoring the sign and diving in the shallow water, **s 1(3)(c)** had not been satisfied and so the defendant was not liable. Additionally, the risk should have been obvious to the claimant.

All three of the requirements must be fulfilled before a duty arises. The occupier must have knowledge of the primary facts leading to appreciation of risk. He is under no duty to enquire and constructive knowledge does not apply.

In *Donoghue v Folkstone Properties* (2003) the accident occurred when the claimant dived off a slipway in midwinter. Although the occupier had knowledge of trespassers in the summer, it had no reason to suspect their presence in the winter and so s 1(3)(b) had not been satisfied.

2. The standard of care

If a duty arises, the nature of that duty is set out in s 1(4): 'the duty is to take such care as is reasonable in all the circumstances of the case to see that [the entrant] does not suffer injury on the premises by reason of the danger concerned.' Note that the duty is to take such care *as is reasonable in all the circumstances*. Unlike the duty under the 1957 Act, here the financial circumstances of the occupier may be taken into account (see *Ratcliff v McConnell* below) (see Figure 13.2).

Warnings

According to s 1(5) a warning may discharge the duty 'in appropriate cases'. Regarding adults, *Tomlinson* implies that almost any notice will be adequate. With children, prevention from entry will be more appropriate.

Volenti

Section 1(6) specifically retains the defence of *volenti* (or consent). This was applied in *Ratcliff v McConnell* (1999), where the claimant was held to have knowingly accepted the risk when, while drunk, he climbed over a high fence into a locked swimming pool after hours. There was also a warning sign and a situation of obvious danger.

Figure 13.2 Duty of care to trespassers under **Occupiers' Liability Act 1984**

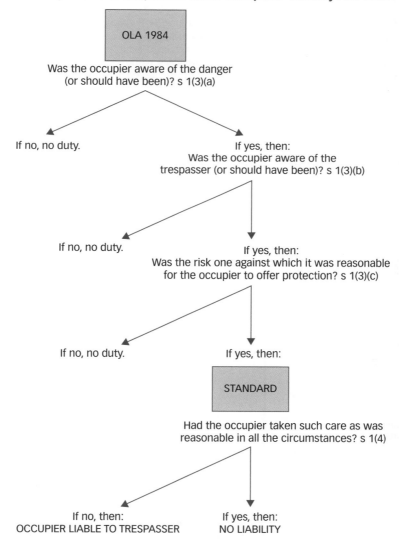

Exclusion of liability

The **1984 Act** does not mention exclusion of liability but it is thought that the statutory duty is excludable; otherwise trespassers would be in a better position than visitors.

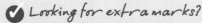

> ✅ *Looking for extra marks?*
>
> Some non-visitors are not trespassers. In *McGeown v Northern Ireland Housing Executive* (1995) it was held that no duty was owed to the plaintiff injured while using a public right of way. Now, following the **Countryside and Rights of Way Act 2000**, a duty is owed under the **1984 Act** to those exercising 'access to land' for 'open-air recreational' purposes, such as ramblers, but excluding risks resulting from natural features of the landscape and by some non-natural features such as climbing over a wall or fence.

Defective Premises Act 1972

This statute was introduced in Chapter 4, following discussion of *Murphy v Brentwood DC* **(1991)**. **Section 4** imposes liability on landlords for damage caused by defects owing to failure to maintain or repair premises.

✳ *Key cases*

Case	Facts	Principle
Glasgow Corporation v Taylor [1922] 1 AC 44	A child playing in a park was poisoned by eating some attractive berries he took from a bush.	Although the child was a trespasser in relation to the bush, the berries were seen as an *allurement* and therefore the child was to be treated as a licensee (or visitor) to whom a duty of care was owed.
Haseldine v Daw [1941] 2 KB 343	A visitor was killed in a lift which had been repaired by a firm of specialist engineers on behalf of the occupier.	Under **s 2(4)(b) of the 1957 Act** the defendant had reasonably entrusted the work of a technical nature to an independent contractor and therefore had not breached his duty of care to the visitor.
Jolley v Sutton LBC [2000] 1 WLR 1082	A boy was injured in an unexpected way when he used a jack to lift an abandoned boat on the defendant's land.	In applying the **Wagon Mound (No 1)** test of reasonable foreseeability, the type of accident was not too remote. The local authority occupier was liable for breach of duty to the child visitor.

Case	Facts	Principle
Phipps v Rochester Corp [1955] 1 QB 450	A five-year-old child, being looked after by an older sibling, was injured falling into a trench on the defendant's land.	The occupier was entitled to expect that a child of tender years would be in the care of a responsible adult, so no duty of care had been owed.
Ratcliff v McConnell [1999] 1 WLR 670	Late one night, while drunk, the claimant was injured when he dived into the defendant's swimming pool, having climbed a wall and entered as a trespasser.	There was no duty of care owed under the **1984 Act**. The main reason for the decision was that, according to **s 1(6)**, the plaintiff had voluntarily accepted the risk.
Revill v Newberry [1996] QB 567	The claimant was a vandal who had been shot through the door of an allotment shed by the occupier who was hiding inside.	The damage resulted from an activity rather than the state of the premises, but even if the **1984 Act** did not apply the common law duty of care could still support liability in negligence. The claimant was two-thirds contributorily negligent.
Roles v Nathan [1963] 1 WLR 1264	Two chimney sweeps were killed by fumes from a boiler they had been sent to clean.	Under **s 2(3)(b) of the 1957 Act** the deceased should have been expected to guard against the dangers inherent in their special calling: the occupier was not liable.
Tomlinson v Congleton DC [2003] UKHL 47	The claimant was seriously injured when he ignored warning signs and dived into the shallow end of a lake on the defendant's property.	The defendant may have been aware of the danger and certainly was aware of the presence of the trespassers, but the risk was not one regarding which it was reasonable to expect protection. No duty arose because the injury stemmed from what the claimant had done, rather than the state of the premises.
Wheat v Lacon [1966] AC 552	A guest fell to his death down the stairs leading to guest rooms above a pub. The handrail was too short and an unknown stranger had recently removed the light bulb.	There was a dispute over whether the occupier was the owner of the brewery or the licensee. It was held that the two were concurrent occupiers. However, there had been no breach of duty in this case owing to the act of the stranger.
Woodward v Mayor of Hastings [1945] KB 174	The steps leading into the defendant's school had been inadequately swept by an independent contractor and the plaintiff was injured when he slipped on them.	**Section 2(4)(b) of the 1957 Act** did not operate to shift liability from the occupier to the contractor, because of the non-technical nature of the task.

Key debates
✳✳✳✳✳✳✳✳✳✳

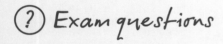 **Key debates**

Topic:	'The OLA '84: Has *Herrington* Survived?'
Author:	R. Buckley
Viewpoint:	A review of the changes in liability to trespassers, considering what aspects of the common law may still apply.
Source:	(1984) Conv 413

Topic:	'Swag for the Injured Burglar'
Author:	T. Weir
Viewpoint:	A critical analysis of the controversial decision in *Revill v Newberry*
Source:	(1996) 55 CLJ 182

(?) **Exam questions**

Problem question

Ambleside District Council has let a portion of Wingfield Park to Oasis Ltd, where they have created 'Summerland Park'. Mrs Bates and her son Norman, three, buy tickets and settle down to spend the afternoon at the Park. By the ticket booth is a large sign, which reads, 'Oasis accepts no liability for loss or damage, howsoever caused'.

There are signs around the children's splash pool reading 'No running'. 'Pools4U' are repairing the filter system and working next to the children's pool. While they are working, the filter releases a toxic gas which causes two of the workers, George and Fred, to pass out. Norman, who has been watching them, begins to vomit. Mrs Bates hears his cries and runs to help. She slips on the wet tiles and falls, breaking her ankle.

That night, Nick and Dave are on their way home from the pub. Acting on a dare from Dave, Nick ignores signs outside the complex stating 'Pools closed between 10 pm and 7 am' and 'No entry' and climbs the fence surrounding the pool. He hits his head while diving into the pool and sustains severe concussion. The iPod in his pocket is ruined.

What issues in tort arise in this scenario?

See the Outline Answers section in the end matter for help with this question.

Essay question

Compare and contrast the duty of care owed to trespassers with that owed to visitors. Do you agree that the distinction is appropriate?

 Online Resource Centre

To see an outline answer to this question visit www.oup.com/lawrevision/

#14
Defamation

- Defamation protects the interest in reputation.
- The tort is divided into libel, which concerns communications in permanent form, and slander, which concerns communications in transitory form.
- Libel has been actionable without proof of damage; but note the impact of the **Defamation Act 2013, s 1**.
- Slander is actionable only with proof of damage except in certain exceptional situations.
- Defamation is one of the few remaining areas of civil law in which, until recently, jury trials have been common. In the past, this had a significant influence on the awarding of compensation. However now the **Defamation Act 2013, s 11** stipulates that trial will be without jury unless the court orders otherwise.
- Learning the defences to defamation is an integral part of studying this tort.
- The primary defence to defamation is truth.
- Law on the tort of defamation is partially found in common law and partially in statute.
- The action in defamation is exceptional in that it does not survive the death of either the claimant or the defendant and the limitation period is one year from the date of publication.
- The action in defamation is subject to a complex procedural regime.
- The study of defamation law requires an understanding of the impact of human rights law, particularly the right to freedom of expression in **art 10** of the **European Convention on Human Rights (ECHR)**.
- Defamation should be studied in conjunction with Chapter 15, 'Privacy'.

Assessment

Defamation is a topic which can lend itself equally well to problem questions (often complex!) or essay questions. A sound understanding of the defences to defamation is essential.

Libel and slander

The **tort** of **defamation** is divided into two causes of action: libel and slander. Libel is a defamatory statement in permanent form. In the past this applied mainly to publications in writing, but it now includes TV and radio broadcasts (**Defamation Act 1952**) and theatre performances (**Theatres Act 1952**). Libel is **actionable *per se***, that is, without proof of damage. However, the **Defamation Act 2013** has stipulated in **s 1(1)** that the claimant must satisfy the court that 'serious harm' has been, or is likely to be, suffered, before a statement is actionable.

Defamation in a transitory form, such as speech or a gesture, is *slander*. It is generally actionable only with proof that the claimant has suffered special damage, usually in a financial sense.

There are two situations in which proof of damage is not required:

1. Imputation of a criminal offence, punishable by imprisonment.

2. Imputation of unfitness or incompetence in an office, profession, or business (**Defamation Act 1952, s 2**).

Revision tip

The exception concerning imputation of unfitness is the one which you are most likely to encounter in a problem question, closely followed by the imputation of a criminal offence.

There are three basic requirements for the action in **defamation**:

1. a defamatory statement which causes or is likely to cause serious harm;

2. the statement refers to the claimant, and

3. that statement is published.

A defamatory statement

Winfield's definition of defamatory meaning is based on *Sim v Stretch* (1936):

> Defamation is the publication of a statement which tends to lower a person in the estimation of right thinking members of society generally; or which tends to make them shun or avoid that person.

According to the **Defamation Act 2013, s 1(1)**, a statement is not defamatory unless its publication has caused or is likely to cause serious harm to the reputation of the claimant. The internet-based action in *Tamiz v Google Inc* (2013) would most likely have been rejected on this basis had the Act been in force.

Procedurally, once the judge decides that a defamatory meaning is arguable, the issue must then be left for the jury to determine. In *Byrne v Dean* (1927) it was held that the implication that a member of a golf club had informed the police about the illegal activities of fellow members would not lower him in the eyes of right-thinking people. In *Thompson v James* (2014) the Court of Appeal accepted that the ordinary meaning of the words 'slush fund' implied that the money had corrupt associations and thus were defamatory.

'Mere abuse' will not be actionable. However, the position of the claimant is relevant, as in *Berkoff v Burchill* (1996).

Context will be taken into consideration. See *Charleston v NGN* (1995), where it was held that a publication (a photo, headline, and text) had to be read as a whole.

Innuendo

At times, the defamatory meaning of the statement may not be self-evident. There are two types of innuendo:

1. The true or legal innuendo applies to a situation in which additional facts must be pleaded by the claimant in order to establish the defamatory meaning for the statement.

Tolley v Fry (1931)

An ostensibly innocent chocolate advert featuring a famous golfer only became defamatory when his amateur status was known, thereby implying that being paid for endorsing a product would jeopardize that status.

---

2. The false or popular innuendo requires knowledge of alternative or slang meanings of words, or 'reading between the lines'. Examples are words such as 'gay' or 'grass', which have double meanings.

In *Allsop v Church of England Newspaper* (1972) it was required that the plaintiff specifically plead the defamatory meaning of the word 'bent'. See also *Lewis v Daily Telegraph* (1964).

Which refers to the claimant

In many cases, this will be absolutely straightforward. Sometimes, however, a claimant will allege that a defendant's description of a real or fictional character might be taken to refer to him.

Hulton v Jones [1910] AC 20

FACTS: Artemus Jones, a barrister, brought a successful **defamation** action against a newspaper for publishing an article which referred to a fictitious churchwarden with the same name.

HELD: The test to be applied was whether reasonable people would believe that the statement referred to the plaintiff. The intention of the defendant was not relevant. Other cases which illustrate this point are **Newstead v London Express Newspapers (1940)**, where the statement was true of someone other than the plaintiff, and **Morgan v Odhams Press (1971)**, where it was held that a picture was capable of impliedly defaming the plaintiff.

Revision tip

These cases of 'mistaken identity' may be appropriate for an 'offer of amends' under the **Defamation Act 1996, ss 2–4**, discussed later in 'Defences to defamation'.

✅ *Looking for extra marks?*

The influence of the **ECHR** was evident in *O'shea v MGN* (2001), where the claimant failed in a **defamation** action based upon her resemblance to a model on a pornographic website. If the **'strict liability'** approach of cases such as *Hulton* had been applied, it would have placed such a heavy burden on publishers as to constitute a significant restriction on the **art 10** right to freedom of expression.

Group or class defamation

This arises when a claimant says that a statement referring to a group, such as 'all law students are lazy', is defamatory of him. According to *Knupffer v London Express Newspapers* **(1944)**, if the words refer to a small enough group that they may be taken to refer to each member, then it may be actionable as such.

The law is somewhat unsatisfactory in this area (ie how small must the group be?) and it has been suggested that the best solution would be to apply the *Hulton* test: would the reasonable person believe that the words referred to the claimant?

Publication

The defamatory statement must be communicated to a third party, that is, other than the claimant. Publication to one's spouse is not treated as being to a third party.

Reasonable foresight

Complications arise when the defendant did not intend a third party to read the statement.

Libel and slander

✷✷✷✷✷✷✷✷✷✷

> ### *Huth v Huth* [1915] 3 KB 42
>
> **FACTS:** The defendant had posted a letter to the plaintiff but it was opened and read by the butler.
>
> **HELD:** The court applied a test of whether this had been reasonably foreseeable, and answered in the negative; therefore, the defendant would not be treated as having published the defamatory words.

Huth is often contrasted with *Theaker v Richardson* (1962) and it is interesting to note that even in relatively recent times, a court held that it was reasonably foreseeable that a husband would open and read his wife's post.

Revision tip

Unintentional defamation is a favourite with examiners, who will often employ it as one aspect of a complex problem question.

Repetition

Every repetition of a **defamation** constitutes a fresh defamation and is thus actionable. This could make not only the author, printer, and publisher liable but also apply to 'secondary publishers' such as newsagents, booksellers, and even libraries. See the **Defamation Act 1952, s 1**, discussed later in the chapter.

See *Slipper v BBC* (1991), where it was held that a repetition was arguably the 'foreseeable' result of the publication and therefore the defendant's possible responsibility for it should be put to a jury.

✔ *Looking for extra marks?*

McManus v Beckham (2002) was a case in which several newspapers reprinted comments made in a shop by Victoria Beckham about the authenticity of souvenirs claiming to have been autographed by her husband. There was some debate in the Court of Appeal about the usefulness of the **foreseeability** test in cases of repetition, although ultimately this appears to have been a difference of opinion over semantics.

Defamation and the Internet

Publication on the Internet raises problems concerning both the attribution of responsibility and the definition of 'publication'. The first major case to confront this was *Godfrey v Demon Internet Ltd* (2001).

The decision in *Godfrey v Demon Internet Ltd* [2001] established that an Internet Service Provider (ISP) could be entitled to the 'distributors' defence' of innocent dissemination under the **Defamation Act 1996, s 1**. However, here the ISP had been notified of the defamatory posting on its bulletin board but had not removed it in two weeks. There was liability because the defendant could not be said to have exercised reasonable care before publishing. *Demon* can be contrasted to *Bunt v Tilley* (2006). Since the implementation of the **Defamation Act 2013**, providers such as those above might be able to use the protection provided by **s 5** or **s 10**.

Repeated access of archived material on the Internet raises the prospect of countless repeat 'publications'. In the United States there has been some use of a 'single publication rule'. This was rejected by the Court of Appeal in *Loutchansky v Times Newspapers (No 2)* (2001) and in *Times Newspapers v United Kingdom* (2009) the ECtHR agreed with the Court of Appeal that this attitude did not threaten the **art 10** right to freedom of expression. **Section 8** of the **Defamation Act 2013** restricts defamation actions on republications (substantially the same) which fall outside the primary limitation period, to one year from the original publication. This is known as the single publication rule.

See *Bunt v Tilley* (2006) and *Metropolitan International Schools Ltd v Designtechnica Corp* (2009), which concern the question of how much involvement is required for a defendant to qualify as a 'publisher'. In *Tamiz v Google Inc* (2013) it was held that in providing a platform for blogs, Google could be regarded as the publisher once it had been notified the defamatory statements had been posted on the platform.

Limits to the action in defamation

Derbyshire CC v Times Newspapers [1993] AC 534

The House of Lords held that to allow local authorities and other governmental bodies to sue for **defamation** would have a 'chilling effect', that is, inhibit free public debate on political matters, which is of the 'highest public importance'.

Derbyshire pre-dated the **Human Rights Act 1998**, under which such questions would now be considered under **art 10 ECHR**.

This principle would also apply to actions by political parties, but individual politicians can, and often do, sue in their personal capacities, as in *Reynolds* (see later).

Companies can and do bring **defamation** actions for injury to their business reputations. See, for example, the infamous 'McLibel trial': *McDonald's Corp v Steel (No 4)* (1995). The **Defamation Act 2013** in **s 1(2)** requires that defamation is actionable by a body trading for profit only if it has caused or is likely to cause *serious financial loss*.

Defences to defamation

At the time of writing, the Defamation Bill has not yet become law. For that reason, what follows is the common law position. If and when the Bill is passed, **s 3** will set out new statutory defences of 'truth', 'honest opinion', and 'publication on a matter of public interest'. See Table 14.1 and the Online Resources for further details on the legislation.

Libel and slander

✱✱✱✱✱✱✱✱✱✱✱✱

Table 14.1 Defences to defamation

Honest opinion	Defeated by lack of honest belief
Privilege	
Absolute	Not defeated by malice
Qualified	Defeated by malice
Defamation Act 1996	
Innocent dissemination **s 1** Offer of amends **ss 2–4**	For mechanical distributors If accepted, ends the proceedings
Defamation Act 2013 **s 4 Publication on a matter of public interest**	Formerly the '**Reynolds** defence' Defeated by lack of reasonable belief
s 5 For operators of websites	Defeated if claimant can prove notice of complaint not addressed.

Revision tip

Having a good grasp of the defences to **defamation** is as important as knowing the constituent elements of the **tort**. This is an area where the law, in both substantive and procedural senses, is undergoing significant development.

Truth (formerly justification)

The first and most frequently applied defence is truth (*formerly justification*) according to the **Defamation Act 2013, s 2**. English law begins with the assumption that a defamatory statement is false, and the burden is on the defendant to prove that it is objectively true, on the balance of probabilities. This is an absolute defence and so is not defeated even if it is made maliciously (an exception to this rule is the **Rehabilitation of Offenders Act 1974, s 8**).

When a statement contains more than one allegation, the defendant is obliged only to prove the truth of the 'sting', or harmful, portion rather than the truth of every word. This is specified by the **Defamation Act 1952, s 5**. A report that the claimant officeholder is dishonest and unpunctual will not be justified by proving that he was late for work every day last week.

When an allegation is specific, it cannot be justified by evidence of a general tendency. See *Bookbinder v Tebbitt* (1989).

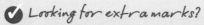

✓ Looking for extra marks?

At times, it is difficult to agree on what exactly the sting of the **defamation** is. An example is *Grobbelaar v News Group Newspapers* (2002), where a footballer successfully sued over corruption allegations but ultimately was awarded only £1.

Honest opinion

Formerly known as 'fair comment' this defence as set out in s 3 of the 2013 Act protects the socially important function of honest and fair criticism and debate, which, because it is based upon opinion, cannot be proved to be true or false.

There are two requirements for this defence:

1. The opinion must be genuine and 'honestly held', rather than an imputation of fact.

2. The statement must implicitly or explicitly indicate the factual basis for the opinion.

Genuine and honestly held

Associated Newspapers v Burstein (2007) arose from an opera about suicide bombers at the Edinburgh Festival. It was reviewed by the defendant, who wrote that it seemed 'anti-American'. In his **defamation** action, the claimant alleged that the review had implied that he sympathized with terrorism. An objective test was applied: could this view honestly be held by someone who had seen the opera? The court answered 'yes', so the defence of fair comment was upheld.

Factual basis

Because it is the maker's opinion, it cannot be proved true or false; however, the facts upon which it is based must be justified. If it is said that '[d]ue to his affair with a parishioner, the vicar should resign his position', it is necessary to prove the affair before the defence of honest opinion can be applied to the opinion about his resignation.

In *Kemsley v Foot* (1952) it was required that the opinion that the plaintiff's newspaper was 'lower than Kemsley' be based upon the true conduct of Kemsley Newspapers.

Detailed consideration of what is required for the factual basis of the opinion was undertaken by the Supreme Court in *Spiller v Joseph* (2010). Here, the defence of fair comment was applied to a statement implying that a performer was unprofessional and untrustworthy. The court upheld the use of the defence, because the defendant had sufficiently indicated in his published statement '. . . in general terms, the facts on which [the opinion] is based'.

✓ Looking for extra marks?

In *Singh v British Chiropractic Association* (2011) the defendant, a journalist, was held to be entitled to rely on the defence of fair comment. He had written that in his opinion the claimant was promoting bogus treatments which had not been verified by scientific evidence. The true facts upon which his opinion was based were the existence of the claimant's claims.

Libel and slander

✳✳✳✳✳✳✳✳✳✳

The **Defamation Act 1952, s 6** provides that, as with the defence of truth, it is not necessary that the truth of every allegation of fact on which the opinion is based be proved, as long as those which are complained of have a basis of truth.

Absolute privilege

This **privilege** is 'absolute' because it is not defeated by proof of malice. Its protection covers situations in which it is very important that participants be able to speak freely and honestly without fear of repercussions.

- *Parliamentary privilege* applies to statements made in Parliament by members of both Houses of Parliament and fully authorized parliamentary reports. It can be waived under the **Defamation Act 1996, s 13**.

- *Judicial privilege* covers all oral and written statements made in the course of judicial proceedings, and fair and contemporaneous reports of such proceedings.

- *Executive privilege* protects certain communications between officers of state.

Qualified privilege

This is 'qualified' because it can be defeated by malice. The meaning of malice is different from that in fair comment, considered earlier. According to *Horrocks v Lowe* (1975) qualified privilege will be lost if the defendant is proved to have held a 'dominant and improper motive' accompanied by lack of honest belief in the truth of the statement, or recklessness regarding its truth.

Statutory

The **Defamation Act 1996**, in s **15** and **Sch 1**, sets out a long list of different types of report which are covered by qualified privilege. **Section 6 of the 2013 Act** adds peer-reviewed statements in scientific and academic journals to this category.

Common law

Common law qualified privilege is accorded to someone who is acting under a legal, moral, or social duty to communicate information to a person who had a corresponding interest in receiving that information.

Watt v Longsdon [1930] 1 KB 130

FACTS: The defendant, a company director, received a letter containing serious allegations about the plaintiff, an employee of the company. The defendant shared this information with other directors, as well as the plaintiff's wife.

HELD: While communication with directors was protected by qualified privilege, that with the wife was not, as there was no duty to her.

Revision tip

You may encounter situations in which a defamatory statement has been dictated to a clerk or secretary. This is likely to attract qualified privilege based either on a common shared interest with the maker and copier or derived from **privilege** between the maker and recipient. See *Bryanston Finance v de Vries* (1975).

Publication on a matter of public interest (formerly 'Reynolds privilege' or responsible journalism)

It has been difficult to fit publications by the press to the public at large into qualified privilege because there is no identifiable reciprocal duty/interest, as there was in cases such as *Watt*. This was addressed by the House of Lords in a landmark case of *Reynolds*, below, and is now embodied in a revised form in s 4 of the **Defamation Act 2013**.

Reynolds v Times Newspapers [2001] 2 AC 127

An accusation was made by *The Times* that the former Prime Minister of Ireland had lied to Parliament. Following a jury verdict in his favour, which awarded him 1p in **damages**, the defendant appealed on the issue of the availability of the defence of qualified privilege.

The House of Lords considered the issue in the context of freedom of expression and the public's 'right to know' under **art 10 ECHR**. This had to be balanced with the important individual interest in protection of reputation.

Factors which should be taken into account in deciding whether a particular report could be protected by qualified privilege were, according to Lord Nicholls in *Reynolds*:

1. the seriousness of the allegation,
2. the nature of the information and the extent to which the subject matter is of public concern,
3. the source of the information,
4. the status of the information,
5. the steps taken to verify the information,
6. the urgency of the matter,
7. whether comment was sought from the claimant,
8. whether the article contained the gist of the claimant's version of the story,
9. the tone of the article, and
10. the circumstances of the publication including the timing.

Times Newspapers lost its appeal in *Reynolds* because it was denied the defence of qualified privilege, having failed to satisfy the expectation that the claimant's version of events should be included in the story.

Libel and slander

✳✳✳✳✳✳✳✳✳✳✳

Reynolds has been applied and interpreted in a number of subsequent cases, for example *Loutchansky v Times Newspapers (No 2)* (2001), where the Court of Appeal described the '*Reynolds* test' as one of responsible journalism.

One early and important interpretation of *Reynolds* was *Jameel v Wall Street Journal Europe (No 3)* (2006).

Jameel v Wall Street Journal Europe (No 3) [2006] UKHL 44

FACTS: The defendant published an article alleging that the claimant's company was suspected by the government of the United States to have connections to terrorism. It was difficult for the defendant to satisfy the test of responsible journalism because there were anonymous sources who had to be protected.

HELD: The Court of Appeal's rejection of the *Reynolds* defence, based at least partly on the defendant's failure to check the story thoroughly with the claimant, was overturned by a majority in the House of Lords. Here, it was indicated that the courts were in danger of applying the *Reynolds* test in too strict a manner. The list of ten factors is not exhaustive, nor will each factor be relevant in each case.

The tone of the article was important. '*Reynolds* privilege' was thought to apply to all types of media and is not confined to political information. The **privilege** attached to the publication itself, rather than to the occasion. It was not necessary to consider malice separately as its absence will be implied if responsible journalism is established.

Flood v Times Newspapers [2012] UKSC 11

FACTS: The judge at first instance accepted the defence of *Reynolds* privilege pleaded by *The Times* in relation to an article concerning bribery investigations against the claimant, a detective. This was overturned in the Court of Appeal, where it was reasoned that, although the article was on a matter of public interest, it included damaging and detailed allegations which had not been thoroughly verified.

HELD: However the Supreme Court gave a more generous interpretation to the defence, in allowing the newspaper's appeal. The court confirmed that the details of a criminal investigation, including factual details of the charge and the suspect's name, could indeed constitute a matter of public interest. In fact the article would probably have been unpublishable without them. More significantly, the court felt that journalists' efforts at verification that the allegations existed had been adequate and consistent with those in *Jameel*. Looking at the publication as a whole, it fulfilled the requirements of responsible journalism.

According to s 4 of the **Defamation Act 2013**, the so-called '**Reynolds** defence' has been abolished and replaced with the category of qualified privilege known as 'publication on a matter of public interest'. It requires the defendant to give affirmative answers to the following two questions:

1. Is the statement complained of on a matter of public interest, or part of such a statement? AND

2. Did the defendant reasonably believe that publishing the statement was in the public interest?

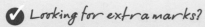

Looking for extra marks?

In the United States, following the landmark case of *Sullivan v New York Times* (1964), it is required that public figures convincingly prove 'actual malice' (in terms of dishonesty) before they can succeed in a **defamation** action regarding 'political speech'. Taking this route was rejected by the House of Lords in *Reynolds*, where, according to Jenny Steele (2010), the stance was more supportive of the 'public right to know', rather than simply freedom of the press.

Offer of amends

This defence applies to unintentional or 'innocent' **defamation**, occurring either because the defendant thought that the statement was true of the claimant or made a statement which was true of someone else but was taken to refer to the claimant. The defence is set out in the **Defamation Act 1996, ss 2–4** requiring the defendant to:

- make an offer in writing to the claimant that he will,
- publish a correction and apology, and
- pay compensation and costs.

If the offer of amends is rejected by the claimant, it may later be relied on as a defence in subsequent proceedings but not in conjunction with any other defence.

Innocent dissemination

The common law defence, which was available to mere mechanical distributors of defamatory material, such as newsagents, libraries, and some broadcasters, has been replaced by the **Defamation Act 1996, s 1**. The defendant must not be an 'author, editor or publisher' of the statement but rather be involved in mechanical processing, copying, or distribution of the material. This defence is not available if the defendant cannot prove on the balance of probabilities that he took reasonable care in relation to its publication. For an example of lack of reasonable care, see *Godfrey v Demon Internet Ltd* (2001). This defence is complemented by ss 5, 10, and 13 of the 2013 Act concerning internet service providers (ISP) and operators of websites.

Remedies

One of the more controversial aspects of the **tort** of **defamation** has been the level of **damages** which have been awarded by juries. You should be aware of cases in which this issue has been addressed by the courts and also understand the statutory and judicial attempts to regulate excessive awards. Injunctions are an additional **remedy** which may be applicable.

Libel and slander

✻✻✻✻✻✻✻✻✻✻✻✻

Damages

The awarding of **damages** in **defamation** is atypical for two reasons:

1. Exceptionally in the civil justice system, juries were tasked with assessing compensation in defamation cases.

2. It is one of the actions in which exemplary (or punitive) damages can be added to those which are **compensatory**.

Problems with disproportionately high **damages** awards for libel became evident in the 1980s (see, for example, *Rantzen v MGM* (1986)). Consequently, in the **Courts and Legal Services Act 1990**, s 8 the Court of Appeal was given the power to review specifically the **quantum** of **damages**, as distinct from the outcome in the case as a whole. The **Defamation Act 2013**, s 11 stipulates that trial will be without a jury unless the court orders otherwise.

John v MGN [1997] QB 586, CA

FACTS: Elton John won a libel action in respect of an article in the *Daily Mirror* which claimed that he had adopted a bizarre weight-loss strategy.

HELD; The jury awarded him **damages** totalling £350,000 but this was reduced to £75,000 on appeal under the 1990 Act. The Court of Appeal endorsed for the first time that the judge may indicate to the jury appropriate guidelines of the range of appropriate damages in the case; furthermore that it may be appropriate for him or her to draw comparisons with levels of damages in personal injuries cases.

Of course it is notoriously difficult to put an accurate price on loss of reputation. The fact that the claimant had a poor reputation can serve to mitigate **damages**, that is, lower the amount which he is awarded. In *Pamplin v Express Newspapers (No 2)* (1988) it was held that the jury could take into account the claimant's general reputation as a 'rascal'. **damages** of one half penny were confirmed. A similar approach to damages was taken in *Grobbelaar* (see earlier).

Exemplary damages may be imposed when the publisher has made a cost–benefit analysis and then knowingly published a libel. In *John* the award comprised £25,000 **compensatory** damages and £50,000 exemplary damages.

In *Cairns v Modi* (2012), a professional cricketer had been accused on Twitter of match-fixing. In his successful **defamation** claim, the judge's **damages** award of £90,000 for injury to his sporting reputation was upheld by the Court of Appeal. This included £15,000 **aggravated damages** for his counsel's 'aggressive assertion of justification at trial'. In general, defamation damages have gradually reduced since *John*.

Injunction

In **defamation** cases, it is highly unlikely that an **interim injunction** will be granted to prevent an initial publication. According to *Bonnard v Perryman* (1891) such a threat to the

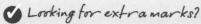
right of free speech would only be justified in the most 'exceptional' case. Injunctions are discussed in more depth in Chapter 17, 'Remedies and principles of compensation'.

✅ **Looking for extra marks?**

Section 12(3) of the **Human Rights Act 1998** provides that when courts are petitioned for relief which could threaten freedom of expression, this is to be granted only where the applicant is 'likely' to succeed in a full trial. This would appear to be a lower threshold than that in *Bonnard*; however, in *Greene v Associated Newspapers* (2005) the Court of Appeal stated that a statutory protection for 'freedom of expression' could not be interpreted so as to make it any easier to obtain an **interim injunction** for **defamation**.

Policy issues

There are a number of policy issues which arise in this area, any of which could form the basis of a challenging essay question:

- The role of the jury both at trial and in calculating **damages** continues to be debated.
- It is not clear that the common law has sufficiently adapted to the particular issues around Internet **defamation**.
- It has been argued that the use of the **conditional fee agreement (CFA)**, sometimes known as 'no-win, no-fee', has been partly responsible for a number of recent trends leading to London being known as the libel capital of the world.
- Costs in libel actions are extremely high and many media defendants are reluctant to defend cases, which are increasingly being settled rather than litigated.
- Concerns about threats to **art 10** rights to freedom of expression, the so-called 'chilling effect', have led to calls for reform of **defamation** law and procedure, and legislation on some of the more controversial aspects is likely.

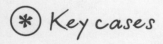 **Key cases**

Case	Facts	Principle
Byrne v Dean [1937] 1 KB 818	A verse posted on a noticeboard at a golf club appeared to condemn one of the members for telling the police about illegal betting machines at the club.	In determining whether a publication had a defamatory meaning, 'right-thinking people' would be presumed to condemn rather than condone informing police of illegal activity.

Key cases

✱✱✱✱✱✱✱✱✱✱✱✱

Case	Facts	Principle
Charleston v NGN [1995] 2 All ER 313	A computer-generated photo appeared to portray television stars in a pornographic scenario, but the text of the attached article contradicted any defamatory implication.	In determining the effect of a publication, it must be assumed that the reasonable reader will read it in context. Here, taking the picture and article as a whole, there was no defamatory meaning.
Flood v Times Newspapers [2012] UKSC 11	The defendant reported that a Metropolitan Police detective was under investigation for allegedly taking bribes from Russian exiles in return for information about extradition proceedings. The *Reynolds* defence was accepted at first instance, but failed in the Court of Appeal, due to concerns about the defendant's efforts at verification.	The Supreme Court unanimously upheld the use of the defence. The clearest statement of the *ratio* can be read in the speech of Lord Mance, who confirmed the importance of the careful balancing exercise, between protection of reputation and freedom of expression, undertaken in such cases. The courts have a role in supporting responsible journalism.
Godfrey v Demon Internet [2001] QB 201	The defendant was an Internet Service Provider (ISP) and the case concerned the application of the defence of innocent dissemination in **s 1 of the Defamation Act 1996**.	An ISP is not a publisher and so is entitled to use the **s 1** defence. Here, however, in the two weeks since notification of the defamatory nature of the posting, the defendant had not removed it. Therefore reasonable care had not been demonstrated and the **s 1** defence was lost.
Hulton v Jones [1910] AC 20	A fictitious newspaper article was defamatory of a churchwarden called Artemus Jones; a barrister of the same name sued in defamation.	It was possible that a jury could conclude that reasonable people would think that the article referred to the plaintiff. On this relatively strict test, the plaintiff successfully established that the article was defamatory of him.
Jameel v Wall Street Journal Europe (No 3) [2007] 1 AC 359	The defendant published an article claiming that the claimant's company was on a list of those suspected of making financial contributions to terrorism.	The '*Reynolds* defence' was described as that of 'responsible journalism'. The House of Lords was of the opinion that the defence should be applied more generously. Despite the allegation that the defendant had neglected to check carefully the background of the story, the defence was applied.
John v MGN [1997] QB 586	Following a successful defamation claim after a story that he was an enthusiast for fad diets, a jury awarded Elton John damages of £350,000.	On appeal this was reduced to £75,000. The Court of Appeal held that judges should give strong guidance to juries about the appropriate level of damages, and that parallels with personal injuries damages would be appropriate.

Case	Facts	Principle
Knupffer v London Express Newspapers [1944] AC 116	An article was defamatory of the 'Young Russian' political party which had 24 members in Britain. The plaintiff claimed that it referred to him.	In the case of 'group definition' an individual within that group can only bring a successful defamation action if something in the publication refers to him or the group is so small that reference to each member can be assumed.
Newstead v London Express Newspapers [1940] 1 KB 377	A news report of a Camberwell bigamist was the subject of a defamation action by an innocent man of the same name, also living in Camberwell.	The lack of detail distinguishing the plaintiff from the true subject of the story meant that the defendant was liable in defamation. The **Defamation Act 1996, s 2** can now provide the defence of offer of amends in such situations.
Reynolds v Times Newspapers [2001] 2 AC 127	The former Prime Minister of Ireland sued in respect of a newspaper report that he had lied to Parliament. He was successful but was only awarded one penny in damages.	The case is important because it sets out the legal principles of qualified privilege as applied to publications in the public interest. Here, his failure to print the claimant's version of the story meant that the defendant lost the '*Reynolds* defence'. See now **s 4** of the **Defamation Act 2013**.
Theaker v Richardson [1962] 1 WLR 151	A husband accidentally opened and read a letter which had been addressed to his wife, and which was defamatory of her.	On the facts, it was foreseeable that it might be read by the subject's husband and so was treated as having been published to a third party.
Tolley v Fry [1931] AC 333	An amateur golfer was portrayed in a photograph in a way which implied that he was advertising chocolate.	When the additional facts were pleaded of the golfer's amateur status in order to explain defamatory meaning, the ordinary reader would assume that he had compromised his position. This is an example of a true or legal innuendo.
Watt v Longsdon [1930] 1 KB 130	The defendant was the director of a company who told both fellow directors and the plaintiff's wife about allegations of the plaintiff's bad behaviour.	The defence of common law qualified privilege requires a reciprocal relationship and in this case defence was lost because there was held to be no 'duty' to pass the information to the plaintiff's wife.

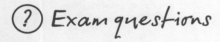
Key debates

Topic:	'Libel: Its Purpose and Reform'
Author:	D. Howarth
Viewpoint:	Considers the adequacy of libel law in terms of its objectives, particularly in relation to human rights.
Source:	(2011) 74 Modern Law Review 845.
Topic:	'Tilting at Windmills: The Defamation Act 2013'
Author:	A. Mullis and A. Scott
Viewpoint:	Analyses whether or not the law has been reformed in a way which improves the opportunities for litigants.
Source:	(2014) 77 Modern Law Review 87

② Exam questions

Problem question

Amrit tells Damien, another student, of rumours at the University of Borsetshire that Dr Lillian Lovelace, the Professor of Golf Management, has been having affairs with a number of students and then rewarding them with high marks. Toby overhears this and when the final results of their Sports degree are published, he narrowly misses a Distinction but Matthew unexpectedly gets one. Toby sends an email to Dr Noble, the Dean of Students, saying that Lillian favoured Matthew in marking his exams because of their romantic attachment.

Advise Lillian.

See the Outline Answers section in the end matter for help with this question.

Essay question

'The threat of the "chilling effect" of the English law of defamation is an illusion.'

Discuss.

Online Resource Centre

To see an outline answer to this question visit www.oup.com/lawrevision/

#15
Privacy

Key facts

- Privacy has traditionally not been directly protected in English law.

- **The Human Rights Act 1998** has opened the way for the old equitable action for breach of confidence to be adapted to regulate the publication of private information.

- The **art 8** right to respect for private and family life must be balanced with the equally powerful **art 10** right to freedom of expression.

- *Campbell v MGN* (2004) provides a detailed consideration of this area of law by the House of Lords. Here, Lord Nicholls introduced the tort he called 'wrongful disclosure of private information'.

- Privacy should be studied in conjunction with Chapter 14, 'Defamation'.

Assessment

The law relating to protection of privacy has been developing notably since the coming into force of the **Human Rights Act 1998 (HRA)**. Any answer must be based upon a sound understanding of the relationship between **arts 8** and **10** of the **European Convention on Human Rights (ECHR)**, and **s 12 HRA**, in particular.

Background

Several government committees reviewed this subject and made recommendations concerning legislation on privacy: see the Younger Committee, *Report on Privacy* (1971); the Calcutt Committee, *Report on Privacy and Related Matters* (1990).

The Calcutt Report rejected as too simplistic one American definition of privacy as 'the right to be left alone' and adopted instead as a working definition:

> The right of the individual to be protected against intrusion into his personal life or affairs, or those of his family, by direct physical means or by publication of information.

We will see later in the chapter that there are a number of different **torts** which *indirectly* address wrongful intrusion into another's privacy. However, English law has characteristically not directly protected privacy in its own right. It was the coming into force of the **HRA** which provoked significant litigation which tested the extent to which **art 8** might require courts to develop a law of privacy and, if so, how this might be accomplished. The aspect of privacy that is the main concern of the cases discussed in this chapter pertains to the *publication of private information*.

The traditional approach of English law to the question of privacy was well summarized in *Kaye v Robertson* (1991).

Kaye v Robertson [1991] FSR 62, CA

FACTS: The plaintiff, a minor celebrity, suffered serious head injuries, and while recovering in hospital in poor health was interviewed by a journalist. He later brought a legal action to prevent publication of the interview.

HELD: The Court of Appeal confirmed that there is no right to privacy in English law and rejected claims in the torts of:

- libel,
- trespass to the person, and
- passing off.

Kaye did, however, achieve limited redress under the **tort** of malicious falsehood, with the court asserting that there was a gap in the law which should be addressed by Parliament.

Looking for extra marks?

Reading the decision in *Kaye v Robertson* will provide a good overview of the common law regarding privacy prior to the **HRA**.

Human rights

The passing of the **HRA**, incorporating the **ECHR** into domestic law, enabled a new perspective on the question of protection of privacy. One matter for debate had been the extent to which the Act can be said to have *horizontal* effect, that is, to apply to actions between individuals in contrast to those brought *vertically* against public authorities. This was resolved in the important case of *Campbell v MGN* (2004) (see later in this chapter):

> The values embodied in **Articles 8 and 10** are as much applicable in disputes between individuals or between an individual and a non-governmental body such as a newspaper as they are in disputes between individuals and a public authority.

Article 8 (ECHR): Right to respect for private and family life

1. Everyone has the right to respect for his private and family life, his home and his correspondence.

2. There shall be no interference by a public authority with the exercise of this right except such as is in accordance with the law and is necessary in a democratic society in the interests of national security or the economic well-being of the country, for the prevention of disorder or crime, for the protection of health or morals, or for the protection of the rights and freedoms of others.

Article 10 (ECHR): Freedom of expression

1. Everyone has the right to freedom of expression. This right shall include freedom to hold opinions and to receive and impart information and ideas without interference by public authority . . .

2. The exercise of these freedoms, since it carries with it duties and responsibilities, may be subject to such formalities, conditions, restrictions and penalties as are prescribed by law and are necessary in a democratic society . . . for the protection of the reputation or rights of others . . .

As regards remedies under these provisions, **s 12 HRA** is important. According to **s 12(4)**, when considering relief which might affect the **art 10** right, the public interest in publication must be considered.

Breach of confidence

The primary foundation for legal developments in this area, since 2000, is the action based upon **breach of confidence**. This is a well-established cause of action, which has recently undergone a process of reinterpretation and adaptation.

Breach of confidence is a wrong, based upon the breach of a duty to keep confidence arising from a confidential situation, transaction, or relationship. Its status is unclear. Originally breach of confidence was actionable in equity and the remedy sought was an **injunction**, but now it is equally likely to result in a claim for **damages**.

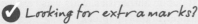 **Looking for extra marks?**

According to *Douglas v Hello!* (2005), its history indicates that **breach of confidence** was not a **tort** but a restitutionary claim for unjust enrichment, that is, to restore the gain made by a wrongful acquisition.

Traditionally, this action has been founded upon the unauthorized use of information of a confidential nature when the defendant is said to be under a duty of confidentiality, usually based upon a *relationship*.

Prince Albert v Strange (1849) De G & Sm 652

The royal family obtained an injunction prohibiting unauthorized publication of family caricatures made for family and friends by Prince Albert and Queen Victoria. Here, the information was disclosed to a printer by a servant.

Revision tip

For a modern royal action, see *HRH Prince of Wales v Associated Newspapers* (2006), later in this chapter.

Intimate aspects of a marriage were the subject of the successful **breach of confidence** action in *Duchess of Argyll v Duke of Argyll* (1967). The duty of confidentiality was seen to be intrinsic to the relationship of husband and wife.

Revision tip

You should remember that, in contrast to actions in **defamation**, those concerning issues of privacy are *not* based on allegations that the subject matter concerned is *untrue*.

Commercial relationships

In other cases, the nature of the confidential information may have commercial aspects. That was the situation when the film stars Michael Douglas and Catherine Zeta-Jones sold the exclusive rights to publish a selection of photos of their wedding to *OK!* magazine. An unauthorized photographer secretly managed to take photos of the occasion, which were later published by *OK!*'s rival, *Hello!* magazine. This gave rise to a series of legal actions.

Douglas v Hello! [2001] QB 967, CA

FACTS: The first of a number of cases arising out of the wedding of the celebrities involved the claimants' attempt to obtain an **interim injunction** to prevent the publication of wedding photos in *Hello!*

HELD: The Court of Appeal refused to uphold the interim injunction on the grounds that the claimants' interests would be adequately protected by **damages**, while the magazine would suffer disproportionate losses should the injunction be upheld. Given that the couple had already given permission for their wedding to have a certain amount of publicity, any residual interest in privacy did not warrant an injunction. The law of breach of confidence was said to cover this situation. Further, Sedley LJ believed:

> We have reached a point where it can be said with confidence that the law recognises and will appropriately protect a right of personal privacy.

For him this was an example of the common law being developed in accordance with the **HRA**, but subsequently the House of Lords, in **Campbell** (see later), rejected this sweeping assertion.

Personal relationships

The main focus of *A v B plc* was the balancing of art 8 rights as against those of art 10.

A v B plc [2003] QB 195, CA

FACTS: In an application by a footballer to prevent publication revealing adultery, an **interim injunction** was granted (and subsequently confirmed).

HELD: However, this was overturned on appeal. The Court of Appeal stressed that the remedy of injunction requires the justification of being in the public interest and here the granting of an injunction would be an unjustified interference with the freedom of the press and freedom of expression. It was significant that the claimant was a public figure. One who has 'held himself out as a role model' and 'courted publicity' must expect a degree of intrusion into his affairs in which the public will have a 'legitimate interest'.

Public interest must be balanced with private interests. A contrasting case is *CC v AB* (2006), where it was held that publication would pose a threat to the emotional well-being of the applicant's wife and to his efforts to repair his marriage and family life.

Campbell v Mirror Group Newspapers

The House of Lords' decision in *Campbell v Mirror Group Newspapers* (2004) clarified the circumstances in which there will be legal protection regarding publication of private information.

Campbell v Mirror Group Newspapers [2004] UKHL 22

FACTS: The model Naomi Campbell had publicly claimed that she did not use drugs. *The Mirror* subsequently published an article detailing Miss Campbell's 'courageous bid to beat her addiction to drink and drugs' accompanied by a photo of her leaving a Narcotics Anonymous meeting. Miss Campbell's action claiming **damages** for **breach of confidence** ultimately reached the House of Lords. The aspects of the publication which were complained of were as follows:

- the fact of Miss Campbell's drug addiction,
- the fact that she was receiving treatment,
- the fact that she was receiving treatment at Narcotics Anonymous,
- the details of the treatment, and
- the photograph of her leaving a meeting.

Accepting that each of the five aspects was of an essentially private nature, it was then necessary for the court to embark upon balancing the **art 8** right of Miss Campbell to private life with the **art 10** right of the newspaper to inform the public. The tests applied were:

- Did the publication pursue a legitimate aim?
- Were the benefits which would be achieved by publication proportionate to the harm that might be done by interference with privacy?

HELD: By a majority, her claim should succeed. A line could be drawn between the first two and the last three aspects of the claim. The fact of drug addiction and treatment was 'open to public comment in view of her denials' and not unduly intrusive. However, the disclosure of details of her treatment, accompanied by the secretly taken photograph, were more than just 'peripheral' to the main story and went beyond merely setting the record straight. This could have disrupted her therapy and so could not be justified. Miss Campbell's **damages** were reinstated.

It was concluded that although 'there is no over-arching, all-embracing cause of action of "invasion of privacy"', there can now be said to be a right against *wrongful disclosure of private information*. The test was basically a *subjective* one (based on the claimant's expectation), limited by the requirement that this expectation be reasonable and that the defendant knew or ought to have known about that expectation.

Applying the principles of Campbell

HRH Prince of Wales v Associated Newspapers [2006] EWCA Civ 1776

FACTS: Prince Charles brought an action claiming **damages** for **breach of confidence** when the *Mail on Sunday* published extracts from his personal diary concerning the handover of Hong

---

Kong to the Chinese. In a case reminiscent of *Prince Albert v Strange*, but applying the law as laid down in *Campbell v MGN*, two questions were asked in *HRH Prince of Wales v Associated Newspapers*:

1. Did the claimant have a *reasonable expectation of privacy* in relation to the information in question? The test here is an *objective* one. If so, then **art 8** would be engaged. Despite the fact that it was not of a 'highly personal or private nature' and that it had been circulated to some 20 to 75 recipients, the contents of the journal were held to raise a reasonable expectation of privacy.

2. Having accepted this 'threshold expectation', then the court had to conduct a *balancing exercise* between the **art 8** right to private and family life and the **art 10** right to freedom of expression. In carrying out the balancing exercise, the court should take the following approach:

   (a) Neither of these rights takes precedence over the other, and

   (b) any restriction or interference must be in accordance with law, and

   (c) pursue a legitimate aim (as set out in **arts 8(2)** and **10(2)**), and

   (d) meet a pressing social need, and

   (e) be no greater than is proportionate to the legitimate aim pursued.

HELD: The decision in favour of the Prince of Wales was upheld by the Court of Appeal, being of the opinion that it was significant that the material had been disclosed by an employee in breach of his own duty of confidence. Here, as in *Prince Albert*, there had been a relationship of confidence.

A modern approach to the confidential relationship was seen in *McKennitt v Ash*.

McKennitt v Ash [2006] EWCA Civ 1714

FACTS: A book was published by a former close friend of the claimant, a folk singer, revealing extensive and very personal information about the claimant.

In this **breach of confidence** action concerning disclosure of private information, two questions were required:

1. Was the information private in the sense protected by **art 8**?

2. If so, then the court must undertake a 'balancing exercise' between the claimant's right to privacy and the right to freedom of expression, with neither taking precedence.

HELD: In *McKennitt*, the answer to the first question was clearly 'yes': it would have carried a 'reasonable expectation of privacy'. Regarding the second, there was no public interest in the publication of this information, either according to the 'role model' approach of *A v B plc* or of 'setting the record straight'. As in *Campbell*, an **injunction** and **damages** were awarded.

The 'balancing exercise' which courts must undertake is further illustrated in *Re S (A Child)* (2004) and, later, *Mosley v United Kingdom* (2008). In *AAA v Associated Newspapers Ltd* (2013) which concerned revelations about the paternity of a child, the reasonable expectation of privacy had already been compromised and here was outweighed by the publisher's **art 10** rights.

Breach of confidence

✳✳✳✳✳✳✳✳✳✳✳

Photos

In *Campbell* itself, the powerful impact of visual images was noted and, for Lord Hope, the inclusion in the story of the covertly taken photos tipped the balance against upholding publication. However, according to Lord Carswell, the mere fact of covert photography was not enough in itself to make the information conveyed confidential. Photographs were a 'powerful prop to a written story', much valued by paparazzi, and thus not to be dismissed too readily as adding to the total effect of the publication.

See also *Theakston v MGN* (2002).

Privacy can also be threatened when someone is photographed in a public or semi-public space. In none of the three key cases below did the public interest in publication justify the publication of the photo in question.

Peck v United Kingdom [2003] EMLR 15

FACTS: The claimant was photographed by CCTV on a London street late at night, holding a large knife having recently attempted suicide. This footage was later broadcast widely as part of a crime prevention and detection initiative.

HELD: The European Court of Human Rights (ECtHR) found that his **art 8** rights had been breached. Despite the fact that the claimant had been photographed in a public place, public interest in demonstrating the effectiveness of CCTV in crime prevention did not warrant the extent of intrusion. Mr Peck was awarded **damages** for the distress caused by the interference in his private life.

A long-standing problem with persistent paparazzi lay behind *Von Hannover v Germany* (2004). Various German tabloid publications had published photos and accompanying articles showing Princess Caroline of Monaco in 'semi-public' places such as restaurants. Many of the photos in question had been taken in France, whose legal system is generally protective of public figures, but published in Germany, where the press are more leniently treated.

In a markedly pro-privacy decision, the ECtHR found that the German court, which had ruled against her application, had failed to take the positive steps necessary to protect her **art 8** rights. The Court noted the context, describing 'photos taken in a climate of continual harassment'. The decisive factor lay in assessing whether the photographs could make any meaningful contribution to a debate of general interest. It was concluded that because

Princess Caroline held no public office and the photos related to her private life, there was no such justification for the intrusion. Further litigation against the press by Princess Caroline culminated in *Von Hannover v Germany (No 2)* (2012). Here, she had only limited success in preventing publication of photos which were taken openly in public and were regarded not to be offensive.

Mosley v News Group Newspapers [2008] EMLR 20

FACTS: The claimant sued the defendant for **breach of confidence** and unauthorized publication of personal information contrary to **art 8 ECHR**. The *News of the World* had published photos (clandestinely taken) of him partaking in a sadomasochistic 'orgy' and these were accompanied by an interview with one of the female participants. The action was founded upon the pre-existing relationship of confidentiality between the participants, and it cited as authority *McKennitt v Ash*.

HELD: The High Court judge concluded that the claimant had had a reasonable expectation of privacy in relation to sexual activities ('albeit unconventional') carried out between consenting adults on private property. He commented particularly on the potency of visual images and carried out the now familiar balancing exercise between **arts 8** and **10** and rejected suggestions of a 'Nazi theme' which allegedly justified public interest. The judge observed that it would be extremely difficult to justify the publication of pictures of private sexual activity; further, the stimulation of 'debate of general interest' was not relevant. Mosley was awarded £60,000 damages for the distress suffered and as recognition that his right to privacy had been breached. In 2012 Mosley pursued his privacy quest to the ECtHR, where the Court refused to accept his contention that **art 8** required newspapers to give advance notice to the subjects of controversial stories.

Liability for misuse of private information—summary

- Does the information carry a 'reasonable expectation of privacy'? (There may or may not be a confidential relationship between parties.)

- In the 'balancing exercise', which has greater weight: art 8 or art 10? Public interest in publication may be the key factor.

Interim injunctions

An award of **damages**, after the fact, may well be inadequate. When the subject of a story wants to prevent its publication, time will be of the essence and an **interim injunction** may be sought, to take effect immediately. This, however, has great implications for freedom of expression and will virtually never be granted in a **defamation** case in which the defendant proposes to raise the defence of justification.

Privacy cases may be different however. You will recall that according to s 12(3) HRA, 'No . . . relief is to be granted so as to restrain publication before trial unless the court is satisfied that the applicant is likely to establish that publication should not be allowed.' This implies that the consequences will need to be very serious before an **interim injunction** can be granted. An example arose in *Venables v News Group Newspapers* (2001). Here, an injunction was granted against the world at large prohibiting publication of information which would reveal the identity and 'past, present and future' whereabouts of Venables and Thompson, the killers of James Bulger, due to fears for their physical safety. In many of these cases anonymity of the parties will also be an issue. In *JIH v Newsgroup Newspapers Ltd* (2011) the Court of Appeal clarified the considerations to be taken into account by courts in ruling on anonymity.

✅ *Looking for extra marks?*

Von Hannover is an example of the way in which some privacy cases can have multinational implications. We saw that a princess from Monaco complained about photos which were taken in France but published in Germany and the case was ultimately determined by the ECtHR in Strasbourg.

Further international comparisons can be seen in Australia (*ABC v Lenah Game Meats* (2001)), New Zealand (*Hosking v Runting and Pacific Magazines Ltd* (2004)), and the United States, where, despite a highly respected constitutional First Amendment right protecting freedom of speech, there is generally a more extensive legal protection for private information in the kinds of situations discussed here.

 ✱ *Key cases*

Case	Facts	Principle
Campbell v Mirror Group Newspapers [2004] UKHL 22	The claimant sued in respect of a story, accompanied by a photo, featuring her leaving a drugs treatment meeting.	By a majority, the House of Lords upheld her claim and set out guidelines for the tort of unauthorized publication of private information.
Douglas v Hello! (2001) QB 967	The claimants sought an injunction to prevent publication of details of their wedding by *Hello!* magazine because they had been sold to *OK!*	The injunction was not upheld but damages were awarded for this breach of confidence. The 'privacy' here had a strongly commercial element.
Kaye v Robertson [1991] FSR 62	The defendant attempted to publish an interview and photo of the plaintiff seriously injured in hospital.	The common law provided no protection for breach of privacy in itself; here the tort of malicious falsehood provided limited relief.
McKennitt v Ash [2006] EWCA Civ 1714	The defendant was a former friend who published detailed accounts of the claimant's personal life.	The information carried an expectation of confidence and there was no overwhelming public interest in their publication. The claim was successful.

Case	Facts	Principle
Mosley v News Group Newspapers [2008] EMLR 20	The claimant sued successfully for damages due to the publication of photos of his unusual group sexual activities.	**Article 8** and **10** rights were balanced and it was held that there was no general public interest in this private sexual matter.
Peck v United Kingdom [2003] EMLR 15	The claimant was photographed in a public place with a knife, having attempted suicide.	The use of his photo for anti-crime publicity constituted an unjustified infringement of his **art 8** rights.
HRH Prince of Wales v Associated Newspapers [2006] EWCA Civ 1776	Prince Charles brought an action for damages due to the publication of his personal diaries concerning political views.	The diaries had been obtained from an employee and their contents brought a reasonable expectation of privacy. The claim was successful.
Von Hannover v Germany [2004] EMLR 21	Princess Caroline brought an action against Germany for its failure to protect her privacy from journalists when she was in semi-public areas.	Germany was held to have breached its duty to her. There was no general public interest in the matters covered in the publications.

99) Key debates

Topic:	'Beyond Information'
Author:	N.A. Moreham
Viewpoint:	A consideration of the way privacy law could be extended to cover wrongful physical intrusion.
Source:	(2014) Cambs Law Journal 350

Topic:	'Injunction and the Protection of Privacy'
Author:	D. Eady
Viewpoint:	A comprehensive and practical survey of developments in privacy law, from a leading judge, with emphasis on injunctions.
Source:	(2010) CJQ 411

Exam questions

✳✳✳✳✳✳✳✳✳✳

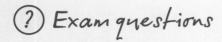

Problem question

Pete is a prominent premier league football player, who has recently been diagnosed with a serious disease. He has attempted to keep this secret, but rumours have spread. The *Daily Star*, a tabloid newspaper, is proposing to publish an interview in which his former trainer Dan talks about Pete's illness and his chances of recovery. The story is to be accompanied by a photo of him entering the hospital for a course of treatment.

Advise Pete.

See the Outline Answers section in the end matter for help with this question.

Essay question

'Freedom of expression is under serious threat from the growing number of attempts to restrain publication for reasons of invasion of privacy.'
Discuss.

To see an outline answer to this question visit www.oup.com/lawrevision/

#16
Defences and limitation

Key facts

- The main defences are

  - contributory negligence,

  - voluntary assumption of risk, and

  - illegality.

- Contributory negligence occurs when the claimant has contributed to his own damage. It is governed by the **Law Reform (Contributory Negligence) Act 1945**.

- When there is more than one wrongdoer, the **Civil Liability (Contribution) Act 1978** may permit one who is liable to claim a *contribution* from another.

- Voluntary assumption of risk (*volenti non fit injuria*) is a complete defence, on the basis that the claimant freely agreed to run the risk of damage.

- Illegality (*ex turpi causa non oritur actio*) is a complete defence, on the grounds that the law will not reward or appear to condone an illegal act.

- Limitation concerns the time limits within which legal actions must be commenced.

- The main statute regulating limitation is the **Limitation Act 1980**.

- Actions in tort must generally be brought within six years of accrual. If they involve personal injury, the time limit is three years and for defamation it is one year.

Assessment

Defences are sometimes specifically examined but more often form a crucial aspect of the answer to problem questions.

Limitation is not often examined in its own right but must be understood as it forms the context for cases such as *Letang v Cooper* (1965) discussed in Chapter 11.

Defences

Contributory negligence

When damage is suffered partly as a result of the claimant's lack of care and partly due to the **fault** of the defendant, he is liable to suffer a deduction from any compensation he is awarded.

Contributory negligence was a complete defence until the **Law Reform (Contributory Negligence) Act 1945, s 1(1)** of which provided that when it finds **fault** on the part of the claimant, the court should *apportion* **damages** according to the extent it thinks 'just and equitable having regard to the claimant's share in the responsibility for the damage'.

What sort of conduct by the claimant invokes the tort?

'fault' is defined in **s 4** as 'negligence, breach of statutory duty or other act or omission that gives rise to liability in tort'. This has been interpreted widely and in *Reeves v Metropolitan Police Commissioner* (2000) it was held to include the intentional act of suicide by the claimant's deceased husband.

It is necessary that the claimant's conduct contributed to his **loss**. It may, or may not, have contributed to the event or accident itself. This can take the form of putting himself in a situation in which harm is more likely, as in *Owens v Brimmell* (1977), where the plaintiff had accepted a lift from a drunk driver.

In many cases, the claimant has committed a *careless act* or *omitted to take precautions for his own safety*. An example of the former occurred in *Stapley v Gypsum Mines* (1953) in which a miner had continued working in unsafe conditions contrary to his employer's instructions. See also *Davies v Swan Motor Co* (1949).

Failure to take precautions, such as the wearing of safety equipment, features in a number of employers' liability cases. The courts have, however, noted that they will take into account the effect on workers of factors such as noise, distraction, tiredness, and boredom.

The most frequent application of failure to take precautions, both in practice and in exams, is the motorist who neglects to wear a seat belt or crash helmet.

Froom v Butcher [1976] QB 286
FACTS: The plaintiff's car was hit owing to the negligent driving of the defendant and his head injuries were caused by his deliberate decision not to wear a seat belt.

HELD: The plaintiff's **damages** were reduced by 20%. The court laid down guidelines for the reduction of damages according to the extent to which the **injury** would have been prevented by wearing a seat belt:

- If the whole injury, the deduction should be 25%.
- If a portion of the injury, the deduction should be 10%.
- If a seat belt would have made no difference, then no deduction should be made.

See *Capps v Miller* (1989), where similar guidelines were established for the wearing of crash helmets by motorcyclists.

Causation

You should note that it is important that the damage caused was within the foreseeable risk of the negligent conduct. In *Jones v Livox Quarries Ltd* (1952) the plaintiff was riding on a towbar on the back of a vehicle, which was forbidden by his employer. He was hit from behind by a lorry and injured. He argued that the danger from his behaviour was only of falling off, but this narrow view was rejected by the court and his damages were reduced. Had he, however, been shot while riding, then **contributory negligence** would not have applied.

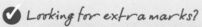

Looking for extra marks?

The *Froom* guidelines are generally adhered to, and 25% is the most common reduction, although it is varied in some circumstances; for example, in *Gregory v Kelly* (1978), where the claimant who declined to wear a seat belt knew that the car had no operative brake pedal and the reduction in his **damages** was 40%. There are certain provisions for medical exemptions. It is interesting to note that a study in 1984 revealed that **contributory negligence** was involved in 50% of all motor accidents.

Does contributory negligence apply to children?

It has generally been the case that **contributory negligence** has not been appropriate as a defence against claims made by children. See, for example, *Yachuk v Oliver Blais* (1949).

Gough v Thorne [1966] 1 WLR 1387

Here, a 13-year-old hit by a car was held not to have been contributorily negligent, although had she been an adult she would have been. A judicial view was that it would be possible for an older child to be contributorily negligent, depending on the circumstances.

When the defendant has placed the claimant in a position of some danger, leading to the claimant taking measures which injure him, then the court will be reluctant to find **contributory negligence**.

Defences

****

Jones v Boyce (1816) 1 Stark 493

FACTS: The plaintiff was a passenger on a coach which appeared to be about to crash. He jumped to save himself, breaking his leg, but in fact the crash did not occur.

HELD: His action had been reasonable in the circumstances and he was entitled to full compensation.

Apportionment

You will recall that the **1945 Act** states that the court should apportion damages according to the extent it thinks 'just and equitable having regard to the claimant's share in the responsibility for the damage'.

Cases such as *Stapley v Gypsum Mines Ltd* (1953) indicate that this will be based on a combination of blameworthiness (how far did the claimant's act fall below the standard of the reasonable man?) and **causation** (what portion of the damage was caused by the claimant's act?).

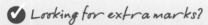 **Looking for extra marks?**

You may wish to read *Reeves v Commissioner of Police of the Metropolis* (2000), where Lord Hoffmann explored the factors to be taken into account in apportionment for **contributory negligence**.

The question often arises whether a claimant can be held to have been 100% contributorily negligent. Despite some case law which holds to the contrary, the prevailing view is that to hold a claimant 100% contributorily negligent would be contradictory because it would be equivalent to saying that the defendant had no causal role in the claimant's loss. This was the view of the Court of Appeal in *Pitts v Hunt* (1991) and was confirmed in *Anderson v Newham College of Higher Education* (2002).

When there are *multiple defendants*, *Fitzgerald v Lane* (1987) provides authority for the way in which **apportionment** should be handled.

Fitzgerald v Lane [1987] QB 781, CA

FACTS: The plaintiff carelessly stepped out into traffic on a busy road and was struck by the first defendant, and then by the second defendant who was travelling in the opposite direction. All three parties were found to have been equally responsible.

HELD: At first instance, the court reduced the claimant's **damages** by one-third, and divided the remaining two-thirds equally between the two defendants (see Figure 16.1):

Figure 16.1 *Fitzgerald v Lane* (1)

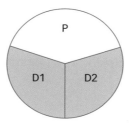

On appeal it was held that this division was wrong. It was necessary to decide first the extent of the responsibility of the plaintiff for his injuries. Here, he was as much to blame as the defendants, so his damages were reduced by 50%. Second, the defendants had been equally negligent so the remaining 50% was divided equally between them (see Figure 16.2):

Figure 16.2 *Fitzgerald v Lane* (2)

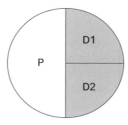

Joint and severable liability

When two or more tortfeasors combine to create a **loss** (as in Fitzgerald), the **Civil Liability (Contribution) Act 1978** provides in ss 1 and 2 that a person made liable in respect of any damage suffered by another person could recover a contribution from any other **tortfeasor** to the extent that the court finds just and equitable, taking into account each party's blameworthiness.

Revision tip

It is important not to confuse **contributory negligence** (which is concerned with the claimant's **fault**) and contribution between two or more defendants under joint and several liability.

Voluntary assumption of risk (or *volenti non fit injuria*)

The defence of *volenti* is based upon deemed acceptance by the claimant of any consequences of the defendant's unreasonable conduct. This acceptance can be express or implied. It is

Defences

✱✱✱✱✱✱✱✱✱✱✱✱

a total defence, which has diminished in importance since 1945, when **contributory negligence** provided a more flexible tool for **apportionment** of blame.

This defence requires:

- an agreement,
- voluntarily made,
- with full knowledge of the risk.

The requirement for an *agreement* means that mere knowledge of a risk is not sufficient. This was clearly stated in *Nettleship v Weston* (1971), where *volenti* failed to be accepted in the action by the driving instructor. Lord Denning explained that nothing short of an agreement, express or implied, to waive any legal claim would suffice. See also the drink driving cases of *Dann v Hamilton* (1939) and *Owens v Brimmell* (1977), where *volenti* was rejected in favour of **contributory negligence**.

The agreement must be *voluntary,* as illustrated by *Smith v Baker* (1891), where the House of Lords recognized that those working in dangerous occupations could not be said to be making a free choice to run the inherent risks. For this reason, *volenti* is rarely relevant in the employment context. See *ICI v Shatwell* (1965), a rare case of *volenti* being accepted against workers who colluded in dangerously disobeying instructions.

Full knowledge of the risk was illustrated in *Morris v Murray*.

Morris v Murray [1991] 2 QB 6, CA

FACTS: A pilot and plaintiff had been drinking all day, having consumed excessive quantities of whisky. When they took off in a light plane, the pilot was killed and the injured companion brought a **negligence** action against his estate.

HELD: The claim was defeated by *volenti*. According to the judgment, 'the wild irresponsibility of the venture is such that the law should not intervene to award damages and should leave the loss to lie where it falls'. There was no express agreement by the plaintiff but there was a deliberate collusion in the creation of the risk and this gave rise to implied agreement.

Rescuers

As was seen earlier in relation to **contributory negligence**, when the defendant has put some-one in an urgent or dangerous situation, the law is reluctant to penalize that person.

Baker v TE Hopkins and Sons Ltd [1959] 3 All ER 225

FACTS: Two employees of the defendant were working in a well when they were overcome by carbon monoxide fumes. A doctor climbed down into the well to try to save them, despite the fact that the fire brigade was on the way. All three men died.

HELD: In response to the defence of *volenti*, the Court of Appeal said it would be 'ungracious', and neither 'rational' nor 'seemly' to say the doctor freely and voluntarily accepted the risk of the rescue.

See also *Haynes v Harwood* (1935).

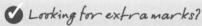 **Looking for extra marks?**

A number of US states have legislation which prohibits fire officers or other emergency personnel from bringing an action in **negligence** for injury against a party whose negligence is responsible for the emergency to which they were responding—ie the very thing which they are employed to do. *Ogwo v Taylor* (1988) indicates that there is no 'fireman's rule' in English law.

Sport

In sporting cases the issue of *volenti*, or consent, is dealt with in varying ways. Regarding a claim in **battery** or **negligence**, participants in contact sports such as rugby are taken to have consented to the sort of physical impact which would be a normal part of the game. If the standard of care between the players has not been breached, then there has been no **tort** to consent to, and so the defence of *volenti* will rarely be relevant.

Condon v Basi (1985) indicates that the standard of care will vary, so that behaviour which is held to have gone beyond the 'normal' in a Sunday league match may not do so in a profes-sional game. In **negligence** cases, therefore, the question of *standard of care* is linked to that of *volenti*.

See also *Watson v British Boxing Board* (2001).

In respect of spectators, *Wooldridge v Sumner* confirmed that *volenti* would not be applicable.

Wooldridge v Sumner [1963] 2 QB 43, CA

FACTS: A cameraman standing behind a row of tubs at the edge of a horse show was trampled by a horse which, the court found, had been allowed to gallop into a bend much too fast.

HELD: The court recognized that the reasonable spectator at such an event would know that participants would be doing as much as possible within the rules to win, and in the absence of reckless disregard for safety, there would not be a breach of duty.

Exclusion of liability

The defendant may claim that he explicitly excluded or limited liability by a notice or contractual term. As regards business liability, this will be regulated by s 2 of the Unfair Contract Terms Act 1977 (UCTA), which was discussed in regard to occupiers' liability in Chapter 13.

According to s 1(3), 'business liability' generally does not include educational or recreational entry onto business premises. The warnings and exemptions of liability at the race in *White v Blackmore* (1972) would not have been caught by UCTA because it was for charity. *volenti* was not applicable because both full knowledge and an agreement were absent. See also *Smith v Eric S Bush* (1990).

Illegality (or *ex turpi causa non oritur actio*)

The Latin phrase can be translated as 'No action can be founded upon a shameful act'. For modern purposes, the principle means that the law will not assist a claimant who has based his action on an illegal act. The defence is of uncertain scope, but it can be said that it is generally narrowly applied.

Ashton v Turner [1981] QB 137
FACTS: The plaintiff was one of three men involved in a car crash, while driving at speed after committing a burglary.
HELD: His **negligence** claim failed owing to the defence of **illegality**, with the court finding that no **duty of care** was owed to him in that context.

A second key case, illustrating the defence, is *Pitts v Hunt*:

Pitts v Hunt [1991] 1 QB 24, CA
FACTS: Here, the plaintiff had been a passenger on a motorbike, and was injured when it crashed after he had knowingly encouraged the driver to race, while drunk. His claim failed on the grounds of **illegality**.
HELD: A majority of the Court of Appeal held that it was not possible to set a standard of care. The plaintiff was also held to have been contributorily negligent, although *volenti* could not be applied owing to the **Road Traffic Act 1988, s 149**.

In both cases, the plaintiffs were involved in joint illegal enterprises.

The defence may also, of course, apply when the claimant acts alone, as in *Clunis v Camden and Islington Health Authority* (1998), where the claimant's **loss** arose directly from a homicide he had committed.

Justification

The case law reveals two varying justifications for this defence. Either:

1. that it would be an affront to the public conscience, and therefore against public policy, to allow the claimant to use the law to recover compensation in the circumstances; or

2. that in the case of an illegal enterprise it is difficult or impossible for the court to set a standard of care.

Difficulties with the latter test have been discussed, and it has been pointed out that it may be more accurate to say that the court does not wish to set a standard of care in such cases, rather than it being impossible. In the case of the former, however, it may be difficult to agree what sorts of acts are sufficiently offensive.

When will illegality apply?

Many torts, such as that of negligent driving, involve acts which are technically illegal, for example, breaking the speed limit. The defence would not generally be relevant in such cases. There must be a *close connection* between a serious illegal act and the basis for the claim.

> *Revision tip*
>
> The following hypothetical example is helpful: **illegality** would defeat a claim by a burglar injured owing to his partner's negligent handling of explosives while they were trying to break into a safe, while it would not have applied if the partner had crashed the car on the way to the job.

There is a growing line of authority in which the defence is applied to wrongs which are not criminal: see *Les Laboratoires Servier v Apotex* (2014). Here, it was stated that the degree or extent of wrongdoing is more significant than the label attached to it. A key case on **illegality** is *Gray v Thames Trains*, which arose out of the Ladbroke Grove rail crash in 1999.

> **Gray v Thames Trains [2009] UKHL 33**
>
> **FACTS:** The claimant was a formerly law-abiding passenger who suffered post-traumatic stress disorder (PTSD) and, two years after the crash, killed someone in a 'road-rage' incident. He pleaded guilty to manslaughter on the grounds of diminished responsibility and was detained under the **Mental Health Act 1983**. He sued the defendant, who had been negligent in causing the crash.
>
> **HELD:** Although the claimant was successful in respect of general **damages** for **loss** of liberty and reputation derived from his original injury, he failed in the aspects of his loss which were derived

from his crime. The speech of Lord Hoffmann is particularly helpful. His justification for accepting the defence of **illegality** in this case is that it would be inconsistent for a court to compensate a claimant for a sentence imposed owing to a criminal act for which he was responsible.

 **Looking for extra marks?**

The defence of **illegality** was considered in both 2001 and 2010 by the Law Commission. The first Consultation Paper proposed legislation in order to clarify the basis for and the scope of the defence and to get consistency. However, in 2010, the Law Commission Report concluded that it endorsed the direction in which the common law was developing, in cases such as *Gray*. (See Law Commission Report No 320, *The Illegality Defence*, 2010.)

Limitation

Limitation periods have been laid down by statute in order to restrict the amount of time within which the claimant must begin his action. It would not be convenient or workable for claimants to have an unlimited time in which to bring their **tort** claims. Evidence would be lost, memories would fade, and insurers would never be able to update or close their books.

In this complex area, you will need only to understand the basic principles. The key legislation is the **Limitation Act 1980** (see Table 16.1):

- For **tort** claims which involve personal injury caused by 'negligence, nuisance or breach of duty' (including **trespass** to the person) actions must be started within three years of the cause of action accruing (**Limitation Act 1980, s 11**).

In some circumstances the court will have the discretion to extend this period, which will be considered below.

- For **tort** claims not involving personal injury, claims must be begun within six years of the cause of action accruing (**Limitation Act 1980, s 2**). This period is not extendable.
- Some torts have special provisions. **Defamation**, for example, requires that actions must be begun within one year of **accrual** (**Defamation Act 1996, s 5**).

Table 16.1 Limitation periods in tort

Damage	Personal Injury	No personal Injury	Defamation
Time	3 years **Limitation Act 1980 s 11**	6 years **Limitation Act 1980 s 2**	1 year **Defamation Act 1996 s 5**
Extendable?	Yes	No	No

Accrual

This is the earliest time at which an action can be commenced. For instance, in the average road traffic accident, **accrual** takes place at the time of the accident, when the property and/ or personal injury takes place and damage is suffered.

Latent damage

What if a passenger sustained a type of **injury** which was not immediately apparent at the time of the accident or he learned six months later that he was suffering from depression as a result of his experience? This would be known as **latent damage** and in such cases the law may allow the limitation period to be extended. According to s 11A(4), **accrual** here is dependent on the claimant's *knowledge* of the **loss**, which is defined in s 14. (See *Ministry of Defence v AB and others* (2012), where s 14 was given a narrow interpretation.) This can also apply in non-personal injury cases.

Discretion

The court also has **discretion** to waive the limitation period for claims covered by s 11 of the Act when it is felt that it would be equitable to the claimant to do so and where the claimant has been prejudiced by the limitation provisions (**Limitation Act 1980, s 33(1)**).

Time will not begin to run against a claimant until he reaches what is known as his 'majority': his 18th birthday.

Letang v Cooper (1965) was discussed in Chapter 11, 'Intentional torts'. The plaintiff unsuccessfully attempted to bring her action in **battery** (subject to a six-year limitation) because she was no longer within the three-year period for actions in **negligence**. She was not permitted to rely on a non-existent **tort** of 'negligent trespass' in order to evade the law on limitation.

Stubbings v Webb (1993) presented a different problem. The adult plaintiff wished to bring a **trespass** action against her father and step-brother for sexual assaults over a period from 18–28 years earlier. She described her action as one for 'breach of duty', because if it could be brought under s 11 of the 1980 Act, then she could have the advantage of the latent damage provisions as well as the court's discretion to extend time under s 33.

The House of Lords held that the wrongs committed against her could only be regarded as intentional **trespass** to the person: the **tort** of **battery**. This could not be described as 'breach of duty' for the purposes of applying s 11 and thus her claim must fail. The effect of *Stubbings* has now been reversed by *A v Hoare* (2008).

The Law Commission in 2001 recommended statutory change to address the apparent unfairness that victims of intentional torts could not benefit from judicial discretion to extend. In the absence of any parliamentary response, the House of Lords took the opportunity in *A v Hoare* to depart from its earlier decision in *Stubbings* and held that 'breach of duty' under s 11 included all types of personal injury.

Key cases

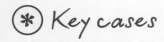

Case	Facts	Principle
A v Hoare [2008] 2 All ER 1	The plaintiff's abuse action was out of time and she sued in negligence.	The House of Lords overruled **Stubbings** and held that the same limitation period should apply to all personal injury actions.
Ashton v Turner [1981] QB 137	The plaintiff was injured in a road accident in the course of escaping from a burglary.	The defence of illegality operated to defeat his claim because no duty of care had been owed to him in the circumstances as it would be an affront to the public conscience.
Baker v TE Hopkins and Sons Ltd [1959] 3 All ER 225	The plaintiff's husband was a doctor who was killed in attempting to rescue some others from a well.	He had not consented to the risk. It is rare for 'rescuers' or those put in danger by the defendant to be defeated by **volenti**.
Froom v Butcher [1976] QB 286	The plaintiff suffered head injuries in a motor accident in which he was not wearing a seat belt.	Owing to the fact that his injuries would have been prevented by a seat belt, his damages were reduced by 20% for contributory negligence.
Gough v Thorne [1966] 1 WLR 1387	The 13-year-old child plaintiff had been careless in crossing a road, when she was hit by the defendant's car.	She was not contributorily negligent, but older children may be, in some circumstances.
Gray v Thames Trains [2009] UKHL 33	A serious injury due to the negligence of the defendant led to the claimant being sentenced for manslaughter.	The claim was based upon a criminal act for which the claimant was responsible; according to the principle of illegality, the defendant was not liable for effects of that act.
Jones v Livox Quarries Ltd [1952] 2 QB 608	The plaintiff was hit from behind while riding on the back of a vehicle. Though the most obvious risk was of falling off, he was held to be contributorily negligent.	Concerns the degree of foreseeability of causation required to establish contributory negligence.
Letang v Cooper [1965] 1 QB 232	The plaintiff was injured when the defendant ran over her legs while she sunbathed in a car park and sued in battery.	There is no tort of unintentional battery and so the claim failed. The only possible action would be in negligence.

Case	Facts	Principle
Morris v Murray [1991] 2 QB 6	The plaintiff was injured on a drunken plane flight.	He had colluded in the dangerous venture and his claim was defeated by the defence of **volenti**.
Pitts v Hunt [1991] 1 QB 24	The plaintiff's claim arose from a crash which occurred when he was riding pillion in a drunken motorcycle race.	Because it was not possible to define a duty of care in the circumstances of the joint illegal venture, the plaintiff failed.

⁹⁹ Key debates

Topic:	'The Variable Standard of Care, Contributory Negligence and Volenti'
Author:	R. Kidner
Viewpoint:	Analyses the different **tort** defences and the way that they relate to the issue of standard of care.
Source:	(1991) 11 LS 1

Topic:	'The Illegality Defence and Public Policy'
Author:	P. Davies
Viewpoint:	An analysis of the current judicial views on the **illegality** defence, with a focus on *Gray v Thames Trains*.
Source:	(2009) 125 LQR 556

? Exam questions

Problem question

Bart is racing his quad bike around his large garden, when Lisa asks if she can ride on the back. Bart agrees and offers her a spare helmet but she refuses to wear it, saying that it will spoil her hair. She then suggests that they drive down the lane to the main road and urges him to go faster. When he does, she falls off the back and breaks her leg.

Advise Lisa.

See the Outline Answers section in the end matter for help with this question.

Exam questions

✳✳✳✳✳✳✳✳✳ ✳

Essay question

'The precise basis of the defence of illegality is difficult to discern.'
Discuss.

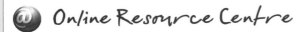 Online Resource Centre

To see an outline answer to this question visit www.oup.com/lawrevision/

#17

Remedies and principles of compensation

Key facts

- The main remedies in tort are damages and injunctions.

- Damages are compensatory and are intended to restore to the claimant what he has lost.

- Compensatory damages are divided into pecuniary and non-pecuniary damages. They are usually awarded as a lump sum.

- Tort actions (except for defamation) can survive the death of either the claimant or the defendant. The relevant statute is the **Law Reform (Miscellaneous Provisions) Act 1934**.

- Dependants have a right to sue in the case of a death when they have lost support from the victim. The relevant statute is the **Fatal Accidents Act 1976**.

Assessment

This topic is usually a subsidiary aspect of a question, that is, part of a **negligence** or **nuisance** problem question. It is important to understand the principles of remedies in **tort** because they have a direct impact on the development of the substantive law.

Introduction

The most commonly sought type of **remedy** for torts, such as **negligence**, is the award of **damages** as compensation for what the claimant has lost. The other remedy which frequently arises in tort is that of the **injunction**, which might be relevant in a **nuisance** or **defamation** action, when the claimant hopes to obtain an order that the defendant cease a particular activity. Other remedies will be briefly considered.

Damages

The main category of **damages** is **compensatory**. There are, however, three other types of damages which are non-compensatory.

Non-compensatory damages

Contemptuous

Contemptuous damages are awarded in some cases, commonly **defamation**, to indicate that although the claimant has been successful technically, the court feels that the action should never have been brought.

The claimant will usually receive the smallest coin in circulation at the time and is unlikely to have a costs award made in his favour. In *Reynolds v Times Newspapers* (2001), the former Prime Minister of Ireland was awarded 1p (and was ordered to pay the newspaper's costs) when he won his libel action.

Nominal

In some cases, the claimant will be held to have had his rights violated but will not have actually suffered any **loss**. Vindicated and not blameworthy for bringing the action, he will be awarded nominal damages, typically £2, and will not necessarily be awarded costs. In *Watkins v Secretary of State for the Home Department* (2006), the House of Lords held that the award of nominal damages would only be permissible in relation to torts which are **actionable** per se, such as **trespass**.

Exemplary or punitive

Exemplary damages are sometimes described as punitive and are imposed over and above any **compensatory** damages in order to teach the defendant that 'tort doesn't pay'. This reminds us that one of the functions of the **tort** system is **deterrence**.

In *Rookes v Barnard* (**1964**) the House of Lords itemized the restricted situations in which exemplary or punitive damages are appropriate:

- Oppressive, arbitrary, or unconstitutional actions by servants of the government. This includes not only local or central government bodies but, significantly, the police and prison officers. The torts in such cases would typically be **trespass** to the person or malicious prosecution.

Thompson v Commissioner of Police for the Metropolis [1997] 3 WLR 403

Here, some judicial limits were set on exemplary damages against the police. The usual minimum in cases where such damages are appropriate was £5,000 and £25,000 would be the usual maximum, with up to £50,000 only when high-ranking officers are implicated.

- Where the conduct has been calculated to make a profit. This typically applies in some **defamation** cases. See *John v MGN* (**1997**), in Chapter 14.

In *AB v South West Water Services* (**1993**), the Court of Appeal took a restrictive view of any possible extension of the *Rookes* categories. This restriction was rejected in *Kuddus v Chief Constable of Leicestershire Constabulary* (**2001**), where it was held that inclusion in the list depended, not upon the name of the **tort**, or of the cause of action, but the nature of the conduct involved.

✅ *Looking for extra marks?*

The Law Commission in 1997 recommended that the law regarding aggravated and exemplary damages be simplified and rationalized so that punitive damages could be awarded in an expanded range of cases, when a judge feels that this adequately reflects the conduct of the defendant. This would bring English law more in line with other common law jurisdictions in which they have a more extensive role; however, the government has shown no inclination to introduce legislation to this end.

Compensatory damages

The objective of *compensatory damages* is, as far as possible, to restore to the claimant what has been lost. This was traditionally represented by the Latin phrase *restitutio in integrum*, meaning 'restored to the original condition'. The payment of **damages** is intended to put the claimant back to his pre-**tort** position, as far as is possible (see *Lim v Camden and Islington AHA* (**1980**)).

The extent to which this can be accomplished depends very much on what the claimant has suffered. When the **loss** is a damaged car, financial means of restoration will seem more appropriate than when the loss is that of a limb or a sense such as eyesight.

Additionally, the practice of making a once-and-for-all assessment of the claimant's needs for compensation at the time of the trial has involved the need to guess what is likely to happen in the future, for instance, regarding the course of his physical condition or of his employment prospects.

Heads of damage

In personal injury cases, **damages** awarded by the judge to the successful claimant can be divided into categories or *heads of damage*: pecuniary loss (pre-and post-trial) and non-pecuniary loss (already experienced or anticipated).

Pecuniary damages

The claimant may have suffered **loss** of earnings, and incurred medical and care expenses (sometimes over a period of years) up to the date of trial. For instance, owing to a disability, his home may have required adapting. These should be capable of being specifically itemized in his claim, unlike future such monetary loss, and are required to be specifically pleaded.

The more problematic aspect of pecuniary loss is that which must be anticipated for the future but awarded at the time of the trial, owing to the 'once-and-for-all' nature of **damages** payments. These may include estimated loss of future earnings or earning capacity and the cost of future care. If the claimant's life expectancy has been shortened, damages will include loss of earnings in those 'lost years'. Any mental suffering caused by the claimant's own awareness of his reduction in life expectancy will be included under damages for 'pain and suffering' (below).

Damages can also be recovered by the claimant on behalf of others, for costs incurred in his care. (See *Hunt v Severs* (1994).)

According to the **Road Traffic (NHS Charges) Act 1999**, a central body, the Compensation Recovery Unit (CRU), will have responsibility for recovering from the wrongdoer the costs of NHS care given to his victim.

Non-pecuniary damages

Here, the court must assign costs to the physical and psychological effects of the **injury** itself. In practice, the non-pecuniary award may include compensation for:

- *the injury itself* (based upon a published tariff);
- *pain and suffering*. This is a subjective concept and it reflects what the claimant has experienced;
- *loss of amenity*. This refers to loss of the experience of life, including personal relationships, hobbies, sports, and specific physical capacities and is objectively measured.

> **Wise v Kaye [1962] 1 QB 638, CA**
>
> A victim who had been unconscious continuously since the accident was presumed to have experienced nothing of her injuries and received nothing under this head.

In *West v Shephard* (1964) it was held that a large sum would be awarded to a plaintiff who had no awareness of what she had lost.

 **Looking for extra marks?**

In 1999, the Law Commission, in *Damages for Personal Injury: Non-pecuniary Loss*, noted a gradual proportionate fall in the value of non-pecuniary damages awards due to inflation and it recommended that awards generally be increased. Subsequently, *Heil v Rankin* (2001) stipulated rises of up to 33% for the most serious injuries, tapering down to awards of £10,000, below which there would be no change. The top limit of awards for 'catastrophic injuries' was raised from £150,000 to £200,000.

Aggravated damages

These are compensatory in nature but indicate that the claimant's position has been made worse because of the defendant's malice or bad motivation. They reflect **injury** suffered to the claimant's feelings as a result of the **tort**.

They are not a separate category of **damages** but will be part of the overall compensation which the successful claimant is awarded. They have been awarded in cases of **battery**, **trespass** to the person and to land, **defamation,** and deceit, among others, but, according to *Kralj v McGrath* (1986), are not available in personal injuries actions arising out of the **tort** of **negligence**.

KD v Chief Constable of Hampshire [2005] EWHC 2550

FACTS: A police officer made sexual advances to a victim of crime. He was found liable for harassment under the **Protection from Harassment Act 1997** and for **battery**.

HELD: The claimant was awarded £10,000 in compensatory damages and an additional £10,000 in *aggravated damages*; the latter on the basis that the defendant's repeated denials had resulted in the claimant having to undergo prolonged and distressing cross-examination.

Structured settlements

Historically, **tort damages** have been paid as a once-and-for-all lump sum. Although this has the advantage of bringing finality to the proceedings for both claimant and defendant (usually an insurer), this system of payment has had a number of disadvantages:

- Because the claimant's physical and financial future cannot be known, the lump sum amount awarded at the time of trial is likely to be either inadequate or excessive.
- The impact of future inflation on the amount awarded will also be unpredictable.
- Finally, some claimants may find it difficult to handle a large sum of money in terms of saving or investment for future needs.

Damages
✶✶✶✶✶✶✶✶✶✶✶✶

Provisional damages

Since the **Senior Courts Act 1981**, courts can, in some cases, address the problem of uncertainty about the claimant's future health. **Section 32A** gives a statutory power to award *provisional damages* in cases where there is a known chance that, as a result of the **tort**, the claimant's health may suffer a 'serious deterioration' in the future. A provisional award will be made based on his current medical position at the time of the trial but allowing him to return to the court (once only) for additional compensation should the deterioration occur.

The payment of damages

These began to be utilized in the early 1990s as a way of allowing the amount of compensation to be paid on a periodical basis, which could be variable over time according to estimates of the future changing needs of the claimant. They were provided for in the **Damages Act 1996**. They were comparatively rare and restricted to the top end of **damages** awards.

Periodical payments

These were established in the **Damages Act 1996, s 2** (as amended by the **Courts Act 2003, ss 100 and 101**) and have rendered structural settlements largely obsolete. Since 1 April 2005, in all cases involving future pecuniary loss, courts must consider whether periodical payments are appropriate.

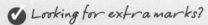 **Looking for extra marks?**

Thompson v Tameside and Glossop Acute Services NHS Trust (2008) is an important case for those interested in **damages**, as it sets out the principles for calculation (or 'indexing') of periodical payments.

Deductions

Owing to a personal injury, a claimant may receive financial benefit from sources other than **tort** compensation. The sources of these *collateral benefits* could include the claimant's own insurance, charity, employers' schemes, or, most importantly, state benefit. To what extent will they be taken into account in the calculation and payment of **damages**?

Benefits derived from a **tort** can be divided into two categories:

1. That based upon luck or the claimant's own prudence. This includes gifts and charity, his own insurance, and schemes linked to employment. Benefits from this category will *not be deducted* from **damages**.

2. This includes social security and other state benefits (received for five years following the **injury** or event) and will be deducted (or recovered if already paid). See the **Social Security (Recovery of Benefits) Act 1997**.

Property loss or damage

When property is lost or destroyed, the starting point is that the defendant will be liable for all the costs incurred in that **loss**. This will include replacement of the property at current market prices and costs incurred by the claimant, which are consequential upon, and not too remote from, the destruction; for example, the short-term hire of a replacement.

If the property is not lost but damaged, then the claimant will be entitled to the amount by which the piece of property has been diminished in value. This is usually but not always equivalent to the repair costs of the property. Again, consequential damage will be recoverable.

Injunctions

An **injunction** is an order of the court requiring the defendant either to do something (mandatory injunction) or to cease doing something (prohibitory injunction). An injunction may be appropriate in cases in which the **tort** is of an ongoing nature; for instance, **nuisance** caused by noise.

Because it is an equitable **remedy** the injunction is not available by right, but rather at the court's **discretion**. The factors which will influence how this discretion is exercised are determined by the type of injunction being sought.

Quia timet injunction

This is sought when it is anticipated that a **tort** may be committed in the future. Courts are understandably reluctant to interfere in such cases, when no wrong has yet been committed, and so will generally only grant this **remedy** if the claimant can prove that the tort is highly likely and imminent.

Interim (or interlocutory) injunction

Here, the **tort** may have already been committed but the claimant will urgently want to prevent damage until such time as the merits of the dispute can come to trial. The court will be concerned to balance the rights of both parties, on the basis that the claimant could ultimately lose the case.

In *American Cyanamid v Ethicon* (1975), the House of Lords set out the principles which are relevant to the granting of an **interim injunction**. There must be a 'serious question' to be tried and the balance of convenience must favour the granting of an injunction. Also, the claimant may be required to give an undertaking to pay **damages** and costs to the defendant should he ultimately lose the case.

Interim injunctions are rare, as was discussed in relation to publication in Chapter 15, because the courts will be aware of the public interest and the value of freedom of expression. The **Human Rights Act 1998, s 12(3)** and **(4)** are relevant to this issue.

Injunctions

✳✳✳✳✳✳✳✳✳✳✳

Revision tip

In *Douglas v Hello!* (2001), discussed in Chapter 15, the claimants were successful in obtaining an **interim injunction** against *Hello!* magazine to prevent publication of their wedding photos; however, despite this, they went on to lose the privacy case when the issue came to trial.

Final injunction

This may be granted when a judge has heard all the relevant facts and both parties have had their say in court. When an application has been made for an **injunction**, the defendant may try to convince the court that **damages** would be a preferable **remedy**. In *Shelfer v City of London Electric Lighting Co* (1895), an injunction was granted to an occupier to prevent continued noise and vibration caused by the defendant despite its significant impact upon the local electricity supply. It was held that 'damages in lieu' of an injunction would only be justified if the injury to the claimant's legal right:

- is small,
- is capable of being estimated in money,
- can be adequately compensated by a small money payment, and
- where it would be oppressive to the defendant to grant an injunction.

The extent to which courts are justified in considering the impact on the public interest in exercising their **discretion** to grant damages instead of an injunction was unclear, but *Shelfer* will not now be applied so strictly: *Coventry v Lawrence (No 1)*(2014); see Chapter 12. Note also the **nuisance** case of *Dennis v Ministry of Defence* (2003), where the interaction between the **Human Rights Act 1998** and common law nuisance was considered.

Revision tip

To better understand the use of the **injunction**, compare the **nuisance** cases of *Kennaway v Thompson* (1981), *Miller v Jackson* (1977), and *Coventry v Lawrence* (2014) in Chapter 12.

Self-help

This **remedy** basically involves the injured party taking steps on his own to address or *abate* the wrong. For instance, in a **nuisance** case (*Lemmon v Webb* (1895)) a landowner was justified in chopping off (but not keeping) branches of the defendant's tree overhanging his property.

Someone who is falsely imprisoned may attempt escape and in some circumstances can use reasonable force to protect himself from **trespass** to the person or to eject someone who is trespassing on his property. Self-help as a remedy is treated with caution by the law.

Compensation and death

The legal position following on from the death of either a claimant or defendant must now be considered.

Survival of existing cause of action

The **Law Reform (Miscellaneous Provisions) Act 1934, s 1(1)** provides that causes of action, with the exception of **defamation**, will survive the death of either party. This means that if a potential claimant has a viable cause of action against someone who then dies, he can sue the deceased's estate. Conversely, if a cause of action is in existence at the time someone dies, his estate can continue that action in respect of damage sustained before his death.

According to the **Administration of Justice Act 1982, s 1(1)(b) damages** can be recovered for the mental suffering caused by the claimant's own awareness of his reduction in life expectancy. (Certainty of an early death is not required, see *Kadir v Mistry* (2014)). However, when death is virtually instantaneous, as with the plaintiff's daughters in the crush at Hillsborough Football Stadium in 1989 in *Hicks v Chief Constable South Yorkshire Police* (1992), it was held that such a time interval is not sufficiently long to justify **damages**: the damage and the death was one and the same.

Death creating a new cause of action for loss of dependency

When a **tort** causes a fatality, there may be serious financial consequences for those close to the victim. The **Fatal Accidents Act 1976** allows those who were financially dependent on the deceased to have the benefit of a claim against the wrongdoer, providing that the deceased himself would have had a claim if he had not died.

Who count as dependants? The categories of dependants for the purposes of the Act are set out in **s 1(3)**. It includes a spouse or cohabitee, children, parents, siblings, and specific other types of relation.

There are two categories of **damages** under the Act:

- *Loss of support* is the most important, and is based upon the claimant's *reasonable expectation of support* from the deceased—either currently or in the future. The action will usually be brought on behalf of all dependants by the executor or administrator of the deceased's will.

- Second is the category known as *'bereavement'*. Spouses (including a partner or civil partner) and parents of a minor who has never married are entitled to one lump sum fixed by statutory instrument. In 2013 this stood at £12,980.

According to **s 5** of the **1976 Act** any **contributory negligence** by the deceased in relation to his death will be taken into account in the calculation of **damages**.

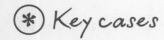

Key cases

Case	Facts	Principle
Rookes v Barnard [1964] AC 1129	A trade union was accused by the plaintiff of committing the tort of intimidation during a dispute over a 'closed shop' agreement.	The House of Lords set out the situations in which punitive damages can be awarded.
Shelfer v City of London Electric Lighting Co [1895] 1 Ch 287	A private nuisance action was brought against a utility company for the noise and vibration caused by its operations.	Initially the plaintiffs were awarded damages only but the Court of Appeal held that they were entitled to an injunction. It set out the situations in which damages could be substituted for an injunction.
Thompson v Tameside and Glossop Acute Services NHS Trust [2008] EWCA Civ 5	The claimants successfully sued the NHS for serious injuries suffered due to negligence at their birth.	The principles were set out according to which the new periodic payments authorized by the **Courts Act 2003** are to be calculated.
West v Shephard [1964] AC 516	The plaintiff had been seriously injured and was unable to appreciate or enjoy a damages award.	The loss of amenity component of a damages award for personal injuries is calculated on an objective basis and so the plaintiff was entitled to a full award.

Key debates

Topic:	**'The Structure of Aggravated and Exemplary Damages'**
Author:	A. Beever
Viewpoint:	Argues that, when analysed, exemplary damages are inconsistent with the principles of civil liability and should be abolished.
Source:	(2003) 23 OJLA 87
Topic:	**'Compensation culture reviewed'**
Author:	R. Lewis
Viewpoint:	Up to-date facts and analysis of personal injury practice and the impact of insurers on levels of claims and compensation awards.
Source:	(2014) Journal of Personal Injury Law 209

 **Exam question**

Essay question

'The award of damages in tort only partially restores to the claimant what he has lost. They are therefore inadequate.'

Discuss.

An outline answer is included at the end of the book.

Exam essentials

As with all law exam questions, your first task is to identify the area of law which is being tested. Practising this with previous questions set by your examiner is strongly advised. One characteristic of **tort** exams is that of overlap: problem questions will often include more than one possible cause of action (see later for examples). It is therefore important to go into your exam confident that you have a good grounding in all the torts—no 'question spotting' allowed!

You must always keep in mind the possible human rights implications of each tort. Tort law is based primarily on case law, although the influence of statute is growing. In both instances, it is extremely important to be up-to-date in your knowledge.

Read each question several times slowly, to make sure that you have understood it and not missed any key elements; then make a rough plan of your answer, which you can refer back to while you're writing. Plan your time carefully: remember, answering only three out of four questions will seriously affect your final mark.

The following is a brief indication of points you need to keep in mind in answering questions on the topics of the chapters of this edition of *Concentrate*.

Tort and the tort system

This area may be tested in an essay question seeking analysis of and criticism of the strengths and weaknesses of tort as a means of compensation. You should consider alternatives to tort, in our 'mixed system', as well as the possibilities of no-**fault** schemes. More advanced answers may wish to include the 'compensation culture', reforms of civil justice procedure and funding, and economic analysis of tort law.

Negligence: duty of care

Duty of care may be tested in either an essay or problem question. An essay question may require consideration of the general tests that have been used, ranging from the '**neighbour principle**' through the *Caparo* 'three-part test', and the way they have been applied in case law. A problem question may feature a defendant on whom duty has not clearly been established: for example the police. Liability for omissions and liability of public bodies must be understood. A good command of the case law will be essential here.

Economic loss

Duty of care will be problematic in this area. First, it is essential to have a clear understanding of what is included in **pure economic loss**. It will be helpful to study separately the line of cases connected to economic loss caused by negligent *acts* and that due to **negligent misstatements**. In the latter, you will note the increasing influence of *assumption of responsibility* as a determinant of the *special relationship*.

Psychiatric injury

The common law has struggled to define and limit the ambit of **duty of care** in this area. You must understand the way law developed over the course of the 20th century, culminating in the key cases of *Alcock* and *White*. You must have a clear understanding of the distinction between the primary and secondary victim, as problem questions are likely to feature a selection of these.

Breach of duty: the standard of care

This is likely to arise as part of a wider **negligence** problem question. You should be aware of the basic objective ('reasonable man') standard but also the ways in which it will vary in certain cases, particularly that of the professional defendant. Having identified the relevant standard of care, you must then decide whether, on the facts, D has breached that standard. Here you will be applying the 'risk/benefit' analysis. *Res ipsa loquitur* is a minor aspect of this topic.

Causation

As with other elements of **negligence**, this is likely to arise as one aspect of a wider problem question. You must know the basics of factual **causation**: the 'but-for' test and its exceptions. The 'asbestos' case law (eg *Fairchild*, etc.) may be significant. Causation in law (also known as remoteness) will require application of the '*Wagon Mound* test' of *reasonable foreseeability*; also relevant are the thin skull rule and intervening acts (***novus actus interveniens***).

Employers' liability

This is the particular version of **negligence** liability concerned with the **duty of care** owed by employers for the health and safety of their employees. It requires knowledge of both the common law and the **Health and Safety at Work Act 1974** and its Regulations. Recent case law features the development of employers' liability for the psychological well-being of their employees, in the 'stress' cases, such as *Hatton v Sutherland*.

Vicarious liability

This concerns the liability an employer may have for the **tort** of his employee, if it was committed in the course of employment. As such, this can be thought of as a three-party situation, and must be distinguished from employers' liability, referred to earlier, which is basically two-party. Vicarious liability can pertain to almost any tort (*Majrowski v Guys and St Thomas's NHS Trust*) and so you must be aware that vicarious liability can be tested as a discrete topic but could also arise as a minor aspect of any problem question.

Product liability

This is one of the areas of **tort** in which the common law and statute are of equal importance and *both* must be considered in any problem question. You should understand the differences and the overlap between the **negligence**-based common law and 'strict liability' under the **Consumer Protection Act 1987**. On the latter, there is relatively little case law to learn; however, the issues of 'defect' and 'the development risks defence' may be the focus of questions.

Intentional torts

Questions will test your knowledge of the ancient **'trespass'** torts: **assault**, **battery**, and **false imprisonment**. You must be clear on their key characteristics and distinguish them from **negligence** and also from the overlapping criminal actions that may be involved. Battery questions may have a medical implication and false imprisonment may raise human rights issues, as in *Austin v UK*. Also possibly included in such exam questions is the (now restricted) **tort** in *Wilkinson v Downton* and actions under the **Protection from Harassment Act 1997**.

Nuisance and *Rylands v Fletcher*

This is a prime area of **tort** in which overlap will be encountered. Many problem questions in this area will simultaneously raise possible issues in **nuisance**, **negligence**, and *Rylands v Fletcher* (**a tort of strict liability**). Although nuisance is divided into public nuisance (also a crime) and private nuisance, most tort courses focus on the latter. Statutory nuisance is of increasing practical importance, but many exams cover this in outline only.

Occupiers' liability

This is an aspect of **negligence** law, in which the **duty of care** owed by occupiers to entrants onto their property is set out and regulated by statute: the **Occupiers' Liability Acts 1957** and **1984**. This is an area in which you may observe the operation of the **Compensation Act 2006**, s 1, designed to address the worst excesses of the 'compensation culture'. Problem questions will require that you deal with liability to visitors and trespassers, and will also require that you understand the application of the **Unfair Contract Terms Act 1977**.

Defamation

Defamation is an area which will characteristically be examined on its own. It is one of the most dynamic and controversial areas of **tort** law, currently undergoing parliamentary reform, and one in which human rights law is having significant impact. Essay questions may explore the relationship, and frequent clash, between the **art 8 ECHR** right to private and family life and the **art 10 ECHR** right to freedom of expression. Defamation law contains a large amount of illustrative case law as well as procedural peculiarities. It is extremely important for you to master the defences, including the newly defined defence of honest comment and the *Reynolds* defence.

Privacy

As a **tort**, this is best understood as concerning *the misuse of private information*. It may be examined either by means of a problem or essay question. The latter may require consideration of its evolution, beginning with the origins in the action for *breach of confidence*. As with **defamation**, there have been significant developments in this area since the passage of the **Human Rights Act 1998**. The most significant case for you to master is *Campbell v MGN*. Knowledge of the scope of the **remedy** of **injunction** may also be relevant.

Defences and limitation

As with remedies and the principles of compensation, defences and the impact of basic rules of limitation must often be applied to broader problem questions. It is advisable to study defences in the context of each specific **tort**, because defences such as **contributory negligence** and **consent** do not apply consistently in all torts. The defence of **illegality** is particularly topical and somewhat problematic in scope.

Remedies and principles of compensation

These are areas which are often examined as portions of a larger problem question. You may be required to outline the way in which the court would calculate **damages** for a successful claimant, any deductions liable to be made, and the impact that the death of a party may have on litigation and compensation.

Outline answers

Chapter 1

Essay answer 1

('The objectives of the law of tort are unique.')

- Always *answer the question*.
- An understanding of the objectives of the law of tort must be demonstrated:
  - *Compensation*. What is meant by compensation in tort? Is it achievable?
  - *Deterrence*. What is meant by the deterrent function of tort law? What supports/undermines this function?
  - The *doing of justice* between the parties.

Consider whether or not these aims are unique. Compensation can be accomplished by contract law, and of course by means not requiring recourse to the legal system, primarily state benefits and personal insurance. (These means may be more efficient than tort, but less generous.) Deterrence is also one of the aims of criminal law. Doing justice between the parties might be accomplished through mediation. Strong answers will refer to the coexistence of human rights law and tort in areas such as privacy.

Conclude that perhaps the individual objectives are not unique to tort but will only be found in combination in tort.

Chapter 2

Essay answer 1

(Why, and by what means ...)

Focus is required upon duty of care as the primary 'limiting device' in the law of negligence. Other elements in the 'negligence equation' will not come into play if there is no duty of care.

Show an awareness of the history of duty of care, pre-1932, and then highlight the key case of *Donoghue v Stevenson* and the 'neighbour principle'. Explain how a duty of care has expanded and contracted post-*Donoghue* and how the neighbour principle has been redefined in *Anns v Merton* and *Caparo v*

Dickman. The 'three-stage' test of *Caparo* is now the means of determining duty in novel situations. The trend towards incremental reasoning is relevant.

Good answers will consider whether there is one duty of care, or many, depending on the interest being protected, and will also consider other jurisdictions in which control is achieved in differing ways.

Chapter 3

Problem answer

The scenario raises the issues of *duty of care* in respect of omissions and also imposition of a duty upon public services. The full answer will also involve *breach* and *causation* and they will be dealt with in Chapters 6 and 7 respectively.

Raj will want advice on whether he can sue Martin and/or Linda in negligence. You should begin by stating the elements of the 'negligence equation' and that *duty of care* is problematic in this case.

R v M: Did M owe a *duty of care* to R to take positive steps to protect R's property? Remember, he has not created the danger but arguably should be aware of that created by a third party. Relevant cases are *Smith v Littlewoods* and *Stansbie v Troman*. There has been no undertaking by M to R, although it might be argued that the employment relationship carries with it an implied duty to act. (If yes, then see Chapter 6 for whether there has been a breach.) If no duty; then no liability.

R v L: The behaviour of L must be evaluated in the light of *Kent v Griffiths*, and *duties of care* by public bodies. *Kent* may lead to the conclusion that L had a *duty* to R to notify the police, once M's call was accepted. If she did have a duty, then it may or may not have been breached. If no duty, then no liability for apparent delay.

Regarding causation: if there was a breach, was it the main cause of R's loss or can that

Outline answers
✱✱✱✱✱✱✱✱✱✱

be attributed to L or the thieves? They may be jointly liable.

Remember, you may have to deal with the issues in this case in the alternative. This will become clear when the issues of breach and causation are tackled in subsequent chapters.

Chapter 4

Problem answer

S will wish to consider if she can bring a successful action for negligent misstatement against L. It is important to identify the damage as 'pure economic loss'; S may therefore have difficulty in establishing that L owed her a relevant duty of care. The existence of a duty of care will depend on establishing a 'special relationship', based on *Hedley Byrne v Heller*, between S and L. One who can be subject to this duty, according to the minority in *Mutual Life v Evatt*, is a business person consulted in the course of business. Subject to the factual details of their conversation, it is possible that L fits this description.

The special relationship will arise if S was relying on L to exercise care, that L knew or ought to have known this, and that it was reasonable for S to so rely. There is a basic principle that this will not arise in a purely social relationship (*Chaudhry v Prabhakar* can be treated as an exceptional situation). You must argue this in the alternative, eg 'If S made it clear to L that she was requesting investment advice etc ... then there would be a special relationship.' However, 'If S did not know that L was a professional person working in the financial sector ...' (or L did not know that S was relying on her advice) then there would not be a special relationship.

On the option that there is a special relationship/duty of care, remember that you still must establish that L breached that duty and that it caused S's loss (*JEB Fasteners*).

Chapter 5

Problem answer

M and K will be considering negligence actions against the organizers of the Championship (D) for psychiatric injury (a problematic type of damage). In each case it must be established that in supplying the racehorse to W, D acted negligently. The main issue in each case will be whether D owed the claimants a duty of care in respect of their loss. Causation must also be covered.

M v D: First, is M suffering from a medically recognized psychiatric condition (*Hinz v Berry*)? Serious depression would satisfy this requirement. Is he a primary or secondary victim? According to *Page v Smith* he is a secondary victim because he views the accident from the stands, and is not in physical danger. The three *Alcock* criteria must be satisfied if there is to be a duty owed by D. M was (1) proximate in time and space to the event and (2) perceived it with his own unaided senses. The third element is whether he was in a close relationship of love and affection with W. Because she is his wife, that will be presumed. This could be challenged due to a recent affair but probably not successfully. M's injuries will then be treated as foreseeable by D. Lastly, M must prove that seeing the accident, rather than caring for W, was the cause of his depression. If so, then his claim will be successful.

K v D: K appears to be suffering from PTSD, a medically recognized psychiatric condition. The horse narrowly missed K. He was in physical danger and is therefore a primary victim. According to *Page v Smith*, psychiatric injury will be treated the same as physical injury and a duty of care is owed to him by D for both. K need not address the *Alcock* criteria although to recover he will still have to prove the causal link between the accident and his damage.

Chapter 6

Problem answer 1

The *duty* aspect applicable to this scenario was addressed in the Chapter 3 answer. The second stage of the negligence equation is: if a duty is owed, was there a *breach*? If M owed a duty to R, did he fall below the objective standard of the reasonable man in the circumstances, according to *Glasgow v Muir*? Consider the 'balancing' of risk that the alarm indicated immediate danger, as against the 'cost' (here, inconvenience) of phoning the emergency services promptly. (Relevant cases may be *Bolton v Stone, Wagon Mound No 2.*) If there is no breach, then there is no liability.

In respect of L, her delay may have been due to a reasonable assessment of the risk indicated by the alarm or by a shortage of resources. In that case, there was no breach. How would the reasonable emergency operator have acted in the circumstances? A fact-specific decision. Remember, L's behaviour was at worst an omission. Causation remains to be dealt with.

Chapter 7

Problem answer

On the assumption that (1) a duty of care was owed by M and/or L to R and (2) breach of that duty by M and/or L has been established (see earlier), it now remains to determine (3) what has been the cause of R's loss.

R must establish, on a balance of probabilities (51% or more likelihood, *Hotson v East Berkshire*) that M and/or L caused his loss of property. Apply the but-for test to the behaviour of both M and L; you may conclude that neither can be eliminated as a cause of R's loss. You must then consider whether the outcome is too remote from their breach of duty. This will not be the case, because the theft is exactly the wrong which their duty (if established) should have prevented (*Reeves v Met Police Commr*). You may then conclude that M and L are jointly and severably liable for R's loss.

Chapter 8

Problem answer

C and D will be seeking compensation for their injuries.

B owes a duty to his passengers (C) and other road users (D). It appears he is over the drink-drive limit and so has breached that duty. Did he cause their injuries? Applying the but-for test, breach would be established re C—subject to C's contributory negligence in accepting the lift (*Owens v Brimmel*) and in failing to fasten his seat belt (*Froom v Butcher*).

Causation is more complicated re D: *Fitzgerald v Lane* would indicate that, if E was driving negligently, B and E would be jointly liable as having provided cumulative causes, subject to possible contributory negligence by D. The possible negligence of the doctor, M, would not have causative effect on D's injuries because she had not had a better than 50% chance of avoiding the outcome (*Hotson v E Berks*).

The possibility of A being vicariously liable, having delegated the task of driving her car to B as her agent, would not apply due to B's diversion (*Morgans v Launchbury*).

Chapter 9

Problem answer 1

The question, as with many (but not all) employers' liability questions, requires consideration of both common law and statutory liability.

The main authority for the former derives from *Wilson and Clyde Coal v English*: outline the four aspects of the common law duty. J will bring a negligence case against T who owes her a duty as her employer. The standard of care is that of the reasonable employer. She will argue that they have breached the duty to provide competent staff (D should not have ignored her and used the hoist when untrained; see also *Hudson v Ridge*), to provide a safe system of working (to give nurses adequate training), and to provide adequate plant and equipment.

Also possible is T's vicarious liability for D's negligence—outline the ingredients, his standard of care being that of the reasonably competent trained nurse (*Wilsher v Essex*).

You should consider the possibility that the hoist itself is defective. In that case, the **Employer's Liability (Defective Equipment) Act 1969, s 1** dictates that the breach will be that of T.

There will be a breach of statutory duty by T if it does not provide the trained staff to enable the hoist to be used when it is required.

Contributory negligence may be invoked against J in trying to catch V, but would fail: *Jones v Boyce*.

Outline answers

✱✱✱✱✱✱✱✱✱✱

Chapter 10

Problem answer

All product liability questions must be approached in terms of:

1. common law negligence liability, then

2. statutory liability under the Consumer Protection Act 1987.

Bugs R Us will be treated as D. Conclusions will involve hypotheses of factual findings.

L v D:

1. Duty of care owed by D to L is established by the narrow ratio in *Donoghue v Stevenson*. The question of breach will be a matter of fact and appears to be satisfied, as long as L is not acting unforeseeably in the way he is using the product. L's most difficult task will be establishing the causal link between the product and his illness (on balance of probabilities), again a factual question. If this is satisfied then he will have a successful cause of action against D.

2. CPA: the insecticide is a product for the purposes of the Act (s 1(2) and s 45(1)), D is a producer under s 1(2), and L has suffered physical damage (s 5). He must prove the causal link to the product (see previously in no. 1) and that the product is defective, ie whether the safety of the product is not what the public are entitled to according to the factors of s 3 (considering expected use of the product and protective measures). The defences under s 4 must be considered, potentially s 4(1)(e).

B v D:

1. D will owe a common law duty of care to B under *Donoghue* as a user of the product. It will be helpful to take the question of causation next. B will want to establish breach in terms of whatever caused her burns: whether it was the canisters or the insecticide, combined with possible inadequacy of the protective equipment. The question of breach will then turn on who supplied the canisters, why they burst, and whether it was reasonably foreseeable that the insecticide could burn a user's arms.

2. Producer and damage established as previous point. The product may be the insecticide or it may be the canisters if supplied by D. In either case, defect (s 3) and defence (s 4) must be considered in relation to both.

C v D:

1. D will owe a common law duty of care to C under *Donoghue* as a user of the product. It appears unlikely that there has been any breach in relation to C's sunburn; similarly a lack of causal link with the sunburn.

2. Product and producer already established. Product unlikely to be defective in relation to C; similarly lack of causal link with the sunburn.

Good answers will mention that B may also have a negligence action against L for employers' liability, in terms of the possibly inadequate canisters and protective equipment.

Chapter 11

Problem answer

Consider chronologically the actions (and defences) possible in relation to each event.

G v E: the shoving could constitute the tort of battery by E (the intentional and immediate application of physical contact to another). 'Hostility' (*Wilson v Pringle*) no longer required, but must be beyond ordinary social contact and unwanted (*Collins v Wilcock*). The defence of self-defence would not be of assistance as the response appears to be disproportionate (*Lane v Holloway, Ashley v Chief Constable of Sussex*).

E v G: These blows also constitute battery and again, self-defence would not apply (see G v E previously).

E v R: Pushing him through the window would not be actionable in battery owing to lack of intention. The only action would be negligence: if E suffered recognized damage, causation would appear to be present but breach of duty would need to be established according to the 'reasonable man' standard.

Locking him in the house would constitute false imprisonment (unlawful and total restriction of freedom of movement), whether or not E knew that he was detained (*Meering v Grahame-White Aviation*). It is possible that R would have the defence of lawful authority in making a citizen's arrest, if she could satisfy the conditions of PACE 1984, s 24A.

G v R: The pushing through the window would be treated as with E v R, previously.

Giving G first aid while he was unconscious would constitute the tort of battery, as outlined previously. R may have the defence of necessity, if she reasonably believes she is acting in G's best interests, as G temporarily lacks capacity to consent to treatment. (See also the Mental Capacity Act 2005.)

Chapter 12

Problem answer

Remember that all questions apparently involving nuisance may additionally raise issues in *Rylands v Fletcher* and negligence.

T and C have suffered the following types of damage: (1) smell, loss of enjoyment of land, and property damage due to Arthur's activities on the allotment; (2) the seeding of marijuana plants on their land; and (3) inability to use the jetty.

In respect of (1), they would hope to bring an action in private nuisance. To do so, they must have an interest in land and you may deduce that both T and C are either tenants or owners. Owing to the smoke, they have suffered an appropriate type of damage for private nuisance: physical injury to property and substantial interference with the enjoyment of their land. They are likely to sue A as the creator (briefly consider landlords' potential liability). Is the interference 'unlawful' (ie unreasonable)? All the relevant factors would need to be considered in balancing the rights of the claimants and defendant (duration, frequency, abnormal sensitivity, etc.), but note that locality is not relevant when there is physical damage to property (the umbrellas) (*St Helen's Smelting v Tipping*). When A doubles the bonfires, malice comes into play (*Christie v Davey*) and makes a finding of nuisance more likely. Consider A's possible defences, noting that 'coming to the nuisance' is not a valid defence. They would be seeking damages and an injunction.

In respect of (2), the marijuana seeds raise the possibility of an action by T and C in *Rylands v Fletcher*—owing to the factors of collection of something not normally on the land and escape onto their land. They would have to identify who was the source of the marijuana seeds and there would be strict liability for

this. The problem would be the non-natural user requirement, which is unlikely to be fulfilled (*Transco v Stockport*).

In respect of (3), the blockage of the jetty may be actionable against 'Rocks' as the creators of public nuisance, for which T and C have suffered particular damage, as in *Tate & Lyle v GLC*. The planning permission for the quarry would not be relevant in public nuisance (*Gillingham BC v Medway*, *Coventry v Lawrence*: private nuisance).

Chapter 13

Problem answer

There are five potential claimants in this occupiers' liability question. The first thing to do is to establish the status of each (occupier or trespasser?) and then the potential defendant (the 'occupier' in relation to the loss each sustains).

Mrs B has broken her ankle. She has express permission to be at the poolside and so is a visitor: OLA 1957 applies. Who is the occupier? Oasis plc are the tenants and appear to have sole control over the operation of the Park, as reinforced by the sign they have displayed. It should be noted that the exemption notice is invalid in respect of personal injury and death: UCTA 1977, s 2(1).

Has O breached its 'common duty of care' to Mrs B? Wet tiles are an inherent feature of swimming pools and an obvious danger; additionally she was running, despite the sign posted. Depending on details this may be treated as a warning under s 2(4)(a). It is unlikely that the duty has been breached.

Norman, like his mother, is a visitor. His vomiting, if caused by the toxic gas, may be actionable. O may be liable (see s 2(3)(a)), or less likely, Pools4U (vicariously liable, if F and G have been negligent), if breach of duty is established in relation to escape of gas. See s 2(4)(b) re independent contractors. It should be argued that O was unreasonable in permitting the filter work to take place during opening hours.

F and G are visitors. It appears likely that O will not be liable for their illness (see s 2(3)(b)). They are exercising their calling and

Outline answers

✶✶✶✶✶✶✶✶✶✶

should have taken precautions concerning the gas (*Roles v Nathan*).

M is a trespasser (see OLA 1984). It is probable that OLA will not apply, as there is no indication that the accident was due to the state of the premises (*Tomlinson v Congleton BC*, *Keown v Coventry*). (Note that the damage to the iPod would not be covered in any event by the OLA 1984.) You should, however, outline the provisions of the 1984 Act, concerning whether a duty was owed according to s 1(3) and, if so, whether it was breached: s 1(4). M's case is similar to *Ratcliffe v McConnell* and the likely conclusion is that M voluntarily encountered the risk, ie the defence of *volenti* in the common law (or no breach of duty under OLA 1984, *volenti* preserved in s 1(6)).

Chapter 14

Problem answer

Approach all defamation problem questions following the three required elements of defamation. L v A: (1) Has there been a defamatory statement? Would A's allegation that the Professor had affairs with students and then rewarded them with high marks, lower her in the eyes of right-thinking members of society (*Sim v Stretch*). Section 1(1) of the Defamation Act 2013 requires the claimant to establish that publication of the statement caused or was likely to cause him serious harm. The answer is almost certainly yes. (2) Did the statement refer to L? Apparently it did. (3) Was it published to a third party? Yes, in that A told D. A has also published to T if it was foreseeable that he would overhear (*Theaker v Richardson*). Note that this was slander and so would require proof of damage to be actionable, unless it comes within one of the four exceptions. It does: imputation of professional unfitness, Defamation Act 1952, s 2.

It is always important to consider relevant defences. First: truth (2013 Act, s 2). Note that there are two 'stings' here and both must be true if the defence is to succeed. The other relevant defence is qualified privilege (legal, moral, or social duty/interest). Depending on the facts, this is unlikely to apply in that A is only passing on rumours. Malice, ie lack of honest belief in the statement, will defeat

qualified privilege (*Horrocks v Lowe*). Offer of amends (Defamation Act 1996, ss 2–4) could be mentioned, though it is unlikely to be of much assistance here.

L v T: (1) Yes, the allegation is defamatory (see previously) (2) It refers to L. (3) It has been published to Dr N.

Defences: Truth. Qualified privilege is more likely to apply to this action, subject to the question of malice.

Good answers will also consider the possibility of an action by M against T.

Chapter 15

Problem answer

This raises the issue of privacy (allegation probably not defamatory and in any case it is true). Begin with a brief introductory paragraph explaining no common law right to privacy as such (*Kaye v Robertson*), the expansion of breach of confidence and the limited protection of private information under HRA 1998.

The key case in this area is *Campbell v MGN* and the facts are not dissimilar. Health matters are generally treated as confidential in nature, so the information has the quality of confidence. Further, it has been disclosed by D who, according to *McKennitt v Ash*, was under a duty of confidence to P. *McKennitt* suggests balancing arts 8 and 10: there is no evidence that DS can claim to be 'setting the record straight', ie in relation to P's assertions about his health (*Campbell*). Therefore, despite P being a public figure, there appear to be no strong public interest arguments to be made by DS. The accompanying photo aggravates the misuse of private information (MPI) (*Campbell*, *Von Hannover v Germany (No 1)*). P is likely to be successful in obtaining an injunction, subject to s 12(3) HRA.

Chapter 16

Problem answer

L is going to bring an action in negligence against B. In order to discuss defences, you must first briefly establish the case in negligence. B owes a duty to L as his passenger (*Donoghue v Stevenson*); arguably he has breached the duty of the reasonable driver (*Nettleship v Weston*) in driving too fast and driving down steps; and, but for his negligence, her injury is unlikely to have occurred, so causation is established.

What defences are available to B?

First you may consider *volenti*, or consent by L. According to the RTA 1988, s 149, *volenti* does not apply when third-party insurance is required, but that would not be the case here as it is private land. It is a complete defence, very limited, and the requirements are unlikely to be satisfied here, despite her behaviour (*Morris v Murray* was an extreme situation).

Next, contributory negligence should be considered, and its requirements under the Law Reform (Contributory Negligence) Act 1945. L has contributed to her damage by her refusal to wear a seat belt (according to *Froom v Butcher*, up to 25%) and, arguably by her encouragement of B to speed. Her damages will be reduced 'as is just and equitable'.

The defence of illegality (*ex turpi causa*) is unlikely to apply. Even if B's activity is technically illegal, the injury was not intrinsic to a joint criminal activity.

There has been no attempt by B to limit or exclude damage.

Chapter 17

Essay answer

The main objective of damages in tort is to restore the claimant, as far as possible, to the position he was in before the tort was committed (*Lim v Camden and Islington AHA*). This question requires that you consider first the extent to which this is possible and then, what other, secondary, objectives damages may have.

Compensatory damages can only be quantified in financial terms. They can provide for loss of earnings, present and future, medical and care costs, and repair or replacement of property. Because damages are normally paid once, in a lump sum, estimation of future loss is likely to be inaccurate. Provisional damages are possible (**Administration of Justice Act 1982, s 6**) as are periodical payments (**Damages Act 1996, s 2**).

If damage is physical, money cannot restore a lost eye, limb, or life, as recognized in *West v Shephard*. Non-pecuniary damages, for loss of amenity or pain and suffering (describe these), cannot truly compensate for the damage and the former is objectively calculated, even if the claimant is unaware.

Secondary objectives of damages are punishment, deterrence, and doing justice or righting a wrong. The ways in which the law of tort approaches these objectives should be discussed. In relation to the first, punitive damages and *Rookes v Barnard* should be outlined; for the second, the role of tort law in determining behaviour should be outlined along with strengths and weaknesses (eg employers' liability and product liability); lastly, the doing of justice (eg illustrated with the torts actionable *per se*) and nominal damages, then the role of insurance should be cited. You should conclude as to whether or not damages can be said to be inadequate, given the wider aims of tort.

Glossary

Accrual The earliest time at which a cause of action, for instance a claim in negligence, can be brought by a defendant.

Actionable *per se* The claimant need not prove damage or loss as a result of the tort, eg trespass torts and libel.

Apportionment A proportionate allocation of a gain or loss, eg as done by the court in relation to legal responsibility in cases of joint and several liability.

Assault The tort of causing the claimant to reasonably apprehend the infliction of a battery on him by the defendant.

Assumption of responsibility One justification for the imposition of a duty of care, particularly in respect of pure economic loss.

Battery The tort of intentional and direct application of force to another, without his consent.

Breach of confidence Formerly an equitable action, this is now a tort used to protect private information.

Causation The essential factual and legal link between the defendant's wrong and the claimant's loss.

Compensatory The most common type of damages in tort, which aim to put the claimant back in the position he or she would have been in had the tort not occurred.

Conditional fee agreement (CFA) A way of funding access to legal services, whereby legal fees are reduced or eliminated if an action is unsuccessful but subject to an 'uplift' if successful.

Contributory negligence The failure of a claimant to take adequate care to prevent his loss. This will result in the judge reducing damages to an extent which is just and equitable under the **Law Reform (Contributory Negligence) Act 1945**.

Damages Payment by a defendant, agreed or legally imposed, for an infringement of a claimant's interests. Damages in tort are primarily compensatory.

Damnum sine injuria A wrong suffered which is not legally actionable.

Defamation The tort, comprising libel and slander, which protects the interest in reputation.

Derogation Acting in a way which departs from or diminishes the objective of a law.

Deterrence The process of discouraging someone from doing something, usually predicting undesired consequences.

Discretion The power or right to decide or act according to one's own judgment.

Duty of care The relationship between the claimant and the defendant which is the first element in establishing potential negligence liability.

Ex gratia Voluntarily given, rather than out of duty or legal obligation.

Fault The extent to which a defendant has failed to fulfil his or her duty of care to a claimant.

Foreseeability The extent of likelihood that a certain outcome will occur.

Illegality A defence to negligence based upon the fact that the claimant's action was founded on his involvement in an illegal enterprise. The Latin term is *ex turpi causa not oritur actio*.

Injunction A remedy whereby the court orders someone to do, or refrain from doing, a certain act.

Injury An alternative word for the loss or damage which is the subject of a duty of care.

Interim injunction An injunction given on the urgent application of one party, which is temporary pending a full trial of the issue.

Jointly and severally liable When two or more independent wrongdoers cause a single indivisible loss to the claimant, each can either be totally liable for the loss or alternatively may seek a contribution from the others.

Justiciable Able or appropriate to be determined by a court.

Latent damage Physical damage which is delayed in becoming apparent. For instance, defective building foundations leading to subsidence after ten years.

Loss Like damage, the basis of the claimant's tort action against the defendant.

Negligence A major category of tort which requires the elements of duty of care, breach of duty, and causation of a legally recognized form of damage which is not too remote.

Negligent misstatement Carelessly given information or services which may be the basis of a tort action for pure economic loss, as described first in *Hedley Byrne v Heller*.

Neighbour principle The general rule for determining when there is a duty of care in negligence, as set out by Lord Atkin in *Donoghue v Stevenson*.

Novus actus interveniens An intervening act (by the claimant, a third party, or natural) which breaks the 'chain of causation' and makes the result too remote to be actionable.

Nuisance The area of tort which is concerned with injury to the use and enjoyment of land.

Objective standard An expectation of behaviour which is imposed by law, regardless of the individual characteristics or situation of the defendant.

Pearson Commission The Royal Commission on Civil Liability and Compensation, established in 1973 to study and evaluate the tort system, and reporting in 1978.

Policy The non-legal considerations (eg economic, political, ethical and social), which may have a role in judicial decision-making.

Prima facie On the face of it, or at first sight.

Privilege A defence to defamation based upon a special situation or relationship.

Proximity The extent of closeness between two parties or two events.

Pure economic loss Financial loss not derived from personal injury or property damage, eg loss of prospective profit or the acquisition of a defective product.

Quantum An amount, particularly of damages.

Remedy What is sought by the claimant as recognition of, or to 'make good', the tort committed against him or her.

Res ipsa loquitur An evidential rule which may be applied when a claimant has difficulty establishing that a defendant has breached the duty of care owed.

Strict liability Liability without the establishment of fault by the defendant, eg under the Consumer Protection Act 1987 or *Rylands v Fletcher*.

Striking out action A procedural tactic whereby a party applies to the court to discontinue a legal action because it discloses no cause of action or possibility of defence.

Tort A civil wrong in which the claimant's interest is protected from the world at large, rather than based upon contract.

Tortfeasor One who commits a tort, or civil wrong.

Trespass The oldest category of tort, which is actionable without proof of damage and is based upon a direct and intentional act.

Ultra vires A public law concept indicating the acting outside of legally given powers, usually statutory.

Volenti The Latin term which describes consent by the claimant, which is a complete defence.

Index

abatement 148, 222
absolute privilege 180
accountants
negligent
misstatements 41, 42
services 41
accumulation
causation 81–2
Rylands v Fletcher rule
151
actionable *per se*
defamation 2, 128, 173
false imprisonment 128,
132
libel 173
trespass to the person 128,
132
aggravated damages 219
ambulance services
omissions and 25
amends, offers of 175, 183
amenity, loss of 142, 143,
146, 218
apologies
defamation and 183
apportionment 202, 204–5
asbestos 8
apportionment of
damages 82–3
assault 128
criminal law 131
direct and immediate
application of
force 130–1
harassment 130
reasonable apprehension
of force 130
speech 130
stalking 130
assumption of risk *see*
voluntary assumption of
risk
Attorney General
relator action 148
auditors 41

barristers
cab-rank rule 15
immunity 15
battery 128, 129–30, 134
consent 129–30
directness 128, 129
force, application of 129
intention 129
medical treatment, consent
to 130
negativing battery 130
social touching 130
transferred intent 129
bereavement damages 223
blood products 121, 124
Bolam test 66, 67
borrowed or hired out
employees 110
breach of confidence 192–8
commercial
relationships 193
damages 192, 194, 195–7
freedom of expression
193–4, 197
freedom of the press 193–4
harassment 196–7
Human Rights Act
1998 193–4
husband and wife 192
injunctions 192, 193, 195,
197–8
personal relationships 193
photographs 193, 196–7, 198
privacy 192–8
private information,
publication of 194–5,
197, 198
proportionality 194
public figures 192–7
public interest 193, 195,
196, 197
reasonable
expectation 194–5, 197
restitution for unjust
enrichment 192

threshold expectation 195
Wilkinson v Downton, tort
in 196
breach of statutory duty 107,
108
burden of proof
causation 77
defamation 178, 183
negligence 71
'but for' test 76–8, 80, 90

cab-rank rule 15
Calcutt Committee 190
causation
accumulation 81–2
apportionment 82–3
asbestos 82–3
burden of proof 77
'but for' test 76–8, 80, 90
Compensation Act 2006 83
consecutive causes 83–5
contributory
negligence 203
cumulative causes 81–2
duty of care 18, 76
fact, causation in 75–88,
85, 90
foreseeability 71
intervening acts 85, 90–3,
97
joint and several
liability 78, 83
law, causation in 18, 94–7
loss of a chance 77, 79–80
material contribution 81–2
material increase in
risk 81–2, 83
medical negligence 76–7, 82
negligent misstatements 39
product liability 120
psychiatric injury 52–4,
81, 105
remoteness 18, 85, 90, 94–6
several liability 78, 83
standard of care 63

Index

causes of action
death of party 223
chance, loss of 77, 79–80
charities 7, 220
children
allurement 161–2
congenital disabilities 29
contributory
negligence 203–4
occupiers' liability 161–2,
164, 165, 166
remoteness 96
standard of care 65
unborn children as
claimants 29
claimants
characteristics 17–18
remoteness 18
unborn children 29
unforeseeable 17–18
clinical negligence *see*
medical negligence
common employment,
doctrine of 102, 103
companies, defamation
of 177
compensation
Compensation Act
2006 8–9, 70, 83
compensation culture 7–8,
70
compensation orders 4
Compensation Recovery
Unit 218
Criminal Injuries
Compensation
Authority 7
defamation 183
ex gratia 7
Motor Insurers' Bureau 7
no fault liability 6
product liability 122
single issue compensation 7
standard of care 70
see also **damages**
Compensation Act 2006 8–9
causation 83
occupiers' liability 164
standard of care 70
complex structure theory 37

conditional fee agreements
(CFAs) 8, 185
confidentiality *see* **breach of**
confidence
congenital disabilities 29
consent
battery 129–30
medical treatment 130
occupiers' liability 164, 166
Rylands v Fletcher, rule
in 152
trespass to the person 134
voluntary assumption of
risk 206
consequential loss 35, 221
contemptuous damages 216
contract 4, 12–13, 108–9
see also **unfair contract**
terms, exclusion clauses
and
contractors 160
contribution 78
contributory negligence
apportionment 202, 204–5
carelessness 202
causation 203
children 203–4
conduct, types of 202–3
crash helmets 202–3
damages, reduction in
203–5, 223
death 223
drivers' failure to take
precautions 202–3
employers' liability 202
fault 202
foreseeability 203
intervening acts 91
joint and several
liability 205
occupiers' liability 164, 165
precautions 202–3
seat belts 202–3
trespass to the person 136
voluntary assumption of
risk 206
control test 108
costs 183, 185, 218, 221
criminal law
assault 131

comparison with tort 4
compensation orders 4
convictions as evidence in
tort 70
Criminal Injuries
Compensation
Authority 7
defamation 173
homicide 208, 209
intervening acts 92
nuisance 148
objectives of criminal law 4
public bodies 28–9
self-defence 135
third parties, acts of 92
vicarious liability 112
wrongs which constitute
crimes, examples 4
see also **police**

damages
aggravated damages 219
alternate routes 6–7
apportionment 82–3
bereavement damages 223
breach of confidence 192,
194, 195–7
causation 82–3
charities 7, 220
collateral benefits 220
Compensation Act 2006
8–9, 70, 83
compensation culture 7–8,
70
Compensation Recovery
Unit 218
compensatory 184, 217–19
consequential loss 221
contemptuous 216
contribution 78
contributory
negligence 223
costs 218, 221
death 223
deductions 220
defamation 4, 179, 184, 185,
216
dependency, loss of 223
deterrence 6, 8
diminution in value 221

Index

****

damages (*Cont.*)
exemplary damages 216–17
false imprisonment 128, 132
fatal accidents 223
first party insurance 7
future loss 218, 219–20
gifts 220
government bodies, punitive or exemplary damages against 217
harassment 219
harm or loss, types of 2
heads of damage 218–19
inflation 219
injunctions 147, 216
insurance 7, 220
investment 219
Law Commission 217, 219
life expectancy 218, 223
loss of amenity 218
loss of earnings 218
loss of support, damages for 223
lost years 218
lump sums 219
Motor Insurers' Bureau 7
NHS care, recovery of costs of 218
no fault liability 6
nominal damages 216
non-compensatory damages 216–17
non-pecuniary damages 218–19
nuisance 146, 147–8, 153
objective 6
pain and suffering 218
pecuniary damages 218
periodical payments 220
personal injuries 218, 219
police or prison service, damages against 217
profit, conduct intended to make 217
property loss or damage 221
provisional 220
psychiatric injury 50–1
punitive 4, 6, 184, 216–17

social security 7, 220
structured settlements 219–20
trespass to the person 128
types of harm covered 2–3
vaccine damage 7
vicarious liability 107
see also **compensation**
damnum sine injuria
definition 2
dangerous situations, creation of 24, 26, 92
death
bereavement damages 223
contributory negligence 223
damages 223
defamation actions 223
dependency, loss of 223
duty of care 12, 13
fatal accidents 223
loss of support, damages for 223
occupiers' liability 161, 165
survival of existing causes of action 223
deceit 37
defamation 172–88
absolute privilege 180
abuse 174
actionable *per se* 2, 128, 173
amends, offers of 175, 183
apologies 183
burden of proof 178, 183
companies 177
compensation 183
compensatory damages 184
conditional fee agreements 185
contemptuous damages 216
context 174
copying 183
costs 183, 185
criminal offence, imputation of 173
damage, proof of 2
damages 4, 179, 184, 185, 216

death of party 223
Defamation Act 2013 173–4, 177, 178, 182
defamatory statements, definition of 173–4
defences 177–83
European Convention on Human Rights 172, 175, 177, 185
executive privilege 180
exemplary damages 184
fair comment 179
foreseeability 176
freedom of expression 172, 175, 177, 185
genuinely and honestly held view 179–80
group or class defamation 175
honest opinion 177, 179
human rights 172, 175, 177, 185
injunctions 184–5
innocent dissemination 183
innuendo 174
Internet 176–7, 185
judicial proceedings 180
juries 174, 184, 185
justification 178, 197
libel, definition of 173
limits 177
local authorities 177
malice 178, 180, 182, 183
mechanical distribution 183
mistaken identity 175
opinions based on true facts 179–80
parliamentary privilege 180
pictures 175
policy 185
political speech 177, 183
public bodies 177
public figures, actual malice and 183
public interest 177, 181–3
publication 175–6
punitive damages 4, 184
qualified privilege 180–1

radio broadcasts 173
refer to claimant,
    defamatory statements
    which 174–5
remedies 4, 183–5, 216
repetition 176
reputation 2
responsible
    journalism 181–3
Reynolds privilege 181–3
secondary publishers 176
serious harm 173
single publication rule 177
slander, definition of 173
special damage, proof
    of 173
strict liability 175
theatre performances 173
third parties,
    communication to 175–6
truth 177, 178
TV 173
unfitness or incompetence,
    imputation of 173
writing 173
defective liability *see* product
    liability
Defective Premises Act
    1972 168
defences 202–14
compliance with EU
    obligations 122
contributory negligence 91,
    136, 164, 165, 202–5, 223
defamation 177–83
development risks or state
    of the art defence 122–3
exclusion of liability 208
illegality 208–10
justification 209
limitation periods 210–11
nuisance 146
occupiers' liability 164
product liability 122–3
Rylands v Fletcher, rule
    in 152
trespass to the
    person 135–6
voluntary assumption of
    risk 205–7

dependency, loss of 223
deterrence 6, 8
detours, vicarious liability
    and 111
development risks or state of
    the art defence 122–3
diminution in value, damages
    for 221
disclaimers 38, 45–6
diversions, vicarious liability
    and 111
drivers
contributory
    negligence 202–3
crash helmets 202–3
illegality 208, 209
insurance 5, 7, 206
learner drivers, standard
    of care of 64–5
Motor Insurers' Bureau 7
precautions 202–3
seat belts 202–3
duty of care 11–32
barristers, immunity of 15
blind persons 18
causation 18, 76
characteristics of
    claimants 17–18
contract 12–13
controlling function 13, 18
death 12, 13
economic loss 13, 15, 37–45
fair, just and reasonable
    test 16–17, 26, 42, 43,
    44, 104
floodgates problem 15
foreseeability 14, 16–17, 71
incremental approach 17
negligence 12–13
negligent
    misstatements 37–45, 70
neighbour principle 13–17,
    119
novel situations 14, 16, 18
occupiers' liability 159–60,
    165–6
omissions 14, 16, 23–6, 28
personal injuries 12, 13
police, immunity of 16,
    28–9

policy 14–15, 16, 17
proximity 14–17, 28
psychiatric injury 13
public bodies as
    defendants 16, 26–9
remoteness 18
standard of proof 70
striking out applications 18
'three-stage' test 16–17,
    40, 42
'two-stage' test 14
types of cases 13
unborn child as claimant 29
unforeseeable
    claimant 17–18
see also standard of care

earnings, damages for loss
    of 218
economic loss
complex structure
    theory 37
consequential loss 35
contract 4
Defective Premises Act
    1972 37
defective property 36–7
duty of care 13, 15, 33–48
floodgates problem 34
historical background 34–5
negligent misstatements 4,
    37–45
nuisance 149
physical damage 34–7
property damage 34–7
pure economic loss 34–7,
    40–1, 122
effective remedy, right to 27
eggshell skull rule 96–7
employment
asbestos claims 8, 82–3
breach of statutory duty 107
common employment
    doctrine 102, 103
common law 102–3
competent workforce 103
contributory
    negligence 202
defamation 173
employers' liability 102–7

Index

✳✳✳✳✳✳✳✳✳✳✳

employment (*Cont.*)
employment
relationship 108–10
equipment 104
fair, just and reasonable
test 104
financial loss 104
Health and Safety at Work
etc. Act 1974 106–7
history of employers'
liability 102
immunity 27
instructions 104
insurance 5
omissions 27
plant and equipment 103–4,
107
precautions 202
psychiatric injury 27, 57,
105–6
safe place of work, duty to
provide a 104
safe system of work 104
standard of care 107
statutory regulation 106–7
stress at work 51, 105–6
training 104
vicarious liability 102
voluntary assumption of
risk 206, 207
warnings 104
see also **vicarious liability**
**European Convention on
Human Rights**
comparison with tort 4–5
defamation 172, 175,
177, 185
effective remedy, right to
an 27
European Court of Human
Rights 4–5
freedom of expression 3,
172, 175, 177, 185, 191,
193–4, 197
Human Rights Act
1998 4–5
inhuman or degrading
treatment 27
liberty and security, right
to 131

peaceful enjoyment of
possessions 145
private and family life,
right to respect for 145,
191, 193–4, 196–7
public bodies 26–7
ex gratia **or single issue
compensation schemes** 7
ex turpi causa
defence 208–10
Law Commission 210
exclusion of liability 45–6,
164
defence 208
negligent misstatement 38
occupiers' liability 168
**executive privilege in
defamation actions** 180
exemplary damages 216–17
expression, freedom of *see*
freedom of expression

failure to act *see* **omissions**
**fair comment, defamation
and** 179
**fair, just and reasonable
test** 16–17, 42, 43, 44,
45, 104
omissions 26
false imprisonment 6
actionable *per se* 128, 132
arrest 132
damages 128, 132
defences 132–3
definition 131
escape, means of 131
knowledge of
imprisonment 132
lawful authority 132–3
liberty and security, right
to 131
necessity defence 133
omissions 132
police 132–3
prison authorities 133
quantum of
compensation 132
restraint must be
complete 131–2
self-help 222

trespass to the person 128,
131–2
use of force 222
fault 145, 202
fire
fire services, omissions
and 25
Rylands v Fletcher, rule
in 152–3
floodgates problem
duty of care 15
economic loss 34
policy 15, 50, 56
psychiatric injury 50, 56
pure economic loss 34
force *see* **trespass to the
person; use of force**
foreseeability
causation 71
contributory
negligence 203
defamation 176
duty of care 14, 16–17, 71
intervening acts 93
negligent
misstatements 38, 40, 44
nuisance 145
omissions 24, 26
psychiatric injury 52–3, 105
reasonableness 94
remoteness 94–6
Rylands v Fletcher, rule
in 150, 151
unforeseeable
claimant 17–18
freedom of expression
breach of confidence 193–4,
197
confidentiality 3
defamation 172, 175,
177, 185
injunctions 221
privacy 191
reputation 3
freedom of the press 193–4
future loss, damages for 218,
219–20

gifts 220
government bodies

punitive or exemplary
damages against 217
group or class
defamation 175

harassment
alarm or distress
causing 134
assault 130
breach of confidence 196–7
course of conduct 134
damages 219
stalking 130
trespass to the person 134
harm, different types of 2–3
Health and Safety at Work
etc. Act 1974 106–7
highway
obstruction of, or damage
to 149
hired out employees 110
homicide 208, 209
human rights/Human Rights
Act 1998
breach of confidence 193–4
comparison with tort 4–5
defamation 172, 175, 177,
185
entry into force 4
injunctions 221, 222
nuisance 145–6
privacy 191, 197
private and family life,
right to respect for 196–7
public bodies 26–7
see also **European**
Convention on Human
Rights

illegality (*ex turpi causa***
defence)** 208–10
immunity
barristers 15
police 16, 28–9
indemnities
vicarious liability 113
independent contractors 108,
109, 163–4
inequality of bargaining
power 45–6

inhuman or degrading
treatment 27
injunctions
breach of confidence 192,
193, 195, 197–8
costs 221
damages 147, 221, 222
defamation 184–5, 216
discretion 221
final 222
freedom of expression 221
Human Rights Act
1998 221, 222
interim or interlocutory
injunctions 221–2
mandatory 221
nuisance 3, 141, 144, 146,
147, 153, 216, 221, 222
privacy 197–8
prohibitory 221
public interest 221, 222
quia timet injunctions 221
innocent dissemination 183
innuendo 174
instructions 104, 111, 121
insurance
compulsory insurance 5
damages 7, 220
deterrence 6
employers' compulsory
liability insurance 5
first party 7
independent
contractors 164
motor insurance 5, 7, 206
Motor Insurers' Bureau 7
Pearson Commission 5
integration test 109
intention
battery 129
trespass to the person 128
vicarious liability 112
Internet
defamation and 176–7, 185
intervening acts
actions by the
claimants 90–1
breaking the chain 93
'but for' test 90
causation 85, 90–3, 97

chain of causation 90, 93
contributory negligence 91
criminal acts by third
parties 92
dangerous situations,
creation of 92
definition 90
foreseeability 93
natural events 90, 93
policy 93
reasonableness 91
rescuers 92
suicide 91
third parties 90, 92–3

Jackson review 8
joint and several liability 78,
83
contributory
negligence 205
judicial proceedings,
defamation and 180
justice, aim of tort 6
justification defence 209

knowledge
false imprisonment 132
negligent
misstatements 38, 41
occupiers' liability 166, 168
product liability 122
scientific and technical
knowledge, state of 122
standard of care 65
voluntary assumption of
risk 206

landlords
defective premises 168
nuisance 143
occupiers' liability 168
Law Commission
damages 217, 219
illegality defence 210
limitation periods 211
psychiatric injury 57–8
learner drivers, standard of
care of 64–5
libel
definition of 173

Index

✱✱✱✱✱✱✱✱✱✱✱✱

**liberty and security, right
to** 131
**life expectancy, damages for
loss** 218, 223
limitation periods
accrual 211
discretion 211
extension of period 210
knowledge 211
latent damage 211
Law Commission 211
nuisance 146
prescription 146–7
product liability 124
sexual abuse 211
trespass to the person 211
losses
amenity, loss of 142, 143,
146, 218
chance, loss of 77, 79–80
consequential 35, 221
damages 218
dependency 223
earnings, loss of 218
future loss, damages
for 218, 219–20
lost years 218
spreading 107
support, loss of 223
types of loss 2–3
vicarious liability 107
see also **economic loss**

malice
defamation 178, 180, 182,
183
malicious falsehood 190
media
defamation 181–3
freedom of the press 193–4
responsible
journalism 181–3
medical negligence
battery 130
best interests of the
patient 130
best practice 67–8
'but for' test 76–7
causation 76–7, 82
consent 130, 134

experience 66
necessity 135
omissions 23
standard of care 66, 67–8
vicarious liability 108
warnings 80
misstatements *see* **negligent
misstatements**
motor insurance 5, 7, 206

National Health Service care
recovery of costs of 218
natural events
intervening acts 90, 93
nuisance 144–5
necessity 135–6
false imprisonment
defence 133
negligence
contract 4
definition 2
overlapping interests 3
Rylands v Fletcher, rule
in 3
see also **contributory
negligence; duty of care;
medical negligence;
negligent misstatements**
negligent misstatements
accountants 41, 42
advice 37, 45
auditors 41
causation 39
context 39
contract 4
deceit 37
disclaimers 38, 45–6
duty of care 37–45, 70
economic loss 4, 37–45
exemption clauses 38,
45–6
fair, just and reasonable
test 42, 43, 44, 45
foreseeability 37, 40, 44
indirect statements 39–40
inequality of bargaining
power 45–6
information, provision of 37
knowledge 38, 41
proximity 37, 41, 43

pure economic loss 37,
40–1, 42, 43
purpose of statement 41
reasonableness 38, 40, 44
references 37–8, 43
reliance 38, 40, 41, 43–5
services 37, 42, 44
silence 39
skill and judgment 38
social relationships 39
special relationships 37–9,
42
surveyors 40
third parties 43–5
threats 39
'three-stage' test 40, 42
unfair contract terms,
exclusion clauses and 38,
45–6
voluntary assumption of
responsibility 41–4
warn, failure to 39
wills, solicitors' duty to
beneficiaries of 44
neighbour principle 13–17, 119
nervous shock *see* **psychiatric
injury**
New Zealand
no fault system in 6
NHS care
recovery of costs 218
no fault liability 6
no-win no fee *see* **conditional
fee agreements (CFAs)**
noise 143, 145, 146, 153
nominal damages 216
novus actus interveniens see
intervening acts
nuisance
abatement 148, 222
anti-social behaviour 143
Attorney General, relator
action 148
claimants 142, 148–9
coming to the
nuisance 146
continuing state of
affairs 141
continuous interference
with use of land 141

creators of nuisance 142, 149

crime, public nuisance as a 148

damages 146, 147–8, 153

defences 146

definition 141

economic loss 149

environmental pollution 153

fault 145

foreseeability 145

fumes 141

human rights 145–6

injunctions 3, 141, 144, 146, 147, 153, 216, 221, 222

interference with use and enjoyment of land 141–2

landlords 143

locality 143, 146

loss of amenity 142, 143, 146

malice 144

motive 144

nature, positive duties arising from acts of 144–5

noise 142, 143, 145, 146, 153

number of individual events 149

obstruction of the highway 149

occupiers of land 142

one-off incidents 141

overlapping interests 3

peaceful enjoyment of possessions 145

personal injuries 142, 149

physical damage 141, 143, 149

planning permission 143–4

possessory or proprietary interests 142

prescription 146–7

privacy 3, 145

private nuisance 141–8, 149, 153

proof of damage 141

property interests 2

public bodies 147

public nuisance 148–53, 153

reasonableness 141, 144

relator action 148

remedies 3, 147–8, 153

Rylands v Fletcher, rule in 3, 153

self-help 148, 222

sensitivity of claimants 144

smell 142, 143

special damage 148

statutory authority 147

statutory nuisance 153

television, interference with 142

trees, encroachment of 145, 148, 222

unlawful interference with land 141

utility of defendant's conduct 144

warning notices 161, 162–3, 166

who can be sued 142–3, 149

who can sue 142, 148–9

objectives of tort law 4, 6

obstruction of the highway 149

occupiers' liability 158–71

activity duty 159, 165

allurement 161–2

children 161–2, 164, 165, 166

common humanity, duty of 164

Compensation Act 2006 164

consent 164, 166

contractors 160

contributory negligence 164, 165

control of premises 159–60

death 161, 165

Defective Premises Act 1972 168

defences 164

duty of care 159–60, 165–6

exclusion of liability 160, 164, 167

independent contractors 161, 163–4

insurance 164

interests in land 160

invitees 159, 160

knowledge 166, 167

landlords 168

licensees 160

limitations 160

obvious risks, warnings and 163, 166

occupancy duty 159, 165

occupier, definition of 159–60

Occupiers' Liability Act 1957 159–64

Occupiers' Liability Act 1984 162, 164–8

omissions 161

permission 160

personal injuries 161, 165

premises, definition of 160

property damage 165

rights of way 160, 165, 168

skilled visitors 161, 162

standard of care 160–1, 165, 166–7

trespassers 159, 160, 164–7, 167

unfair contract terms, exclusion clauses and 164

visitors 159, 160–4, 167

warning notices 161, 162–3

offers of amends 175, 183

omissions

ambulance services 25

control, existing relationship of 24, 25

creation of or failure to remove a danger 24, 26

definition 23

duty of care 14, 16, 23–6, 28

fair, just and reasonable test 26

false imprisonment 132

fire services 25

foreseeability 24, 26

medical negligence 23

occupiers' liability 161

police, immunity of the 28–9

Index
****

omissions (*Cont.*)
  proximity 24, 26
  public bodies 24–5
  rescuers 23
  voluntary assumption
    of responsibility 24–5
operational/policy
  distinction 26

pain and suffering, damages
  for 218
parliamentary privilege,
  defamation and 180
peaceful enjoyment of
  possessions 145
Pearson Commission 5, 6
periodical payments 220
  indexing of 220
personal injuries
  damages 218, 219
  duty of care 12, 13
  nuisance 142, 149
  occupiers' liability 161, 165
  psychiatric injury 49–61
  Rylands v Fletcher, rule
    in 151
plant and equipment 103–4,
  107
police
  arrest 132–3
  crime control 28–9
  damages against 217, 219
  duty of care 16, 28–9
  immunity 16, 28–9
  omissions 28–9
  operational/policy
    distinction 28
  policy 28–9
policy
  defamation 185
  definition 14–15
  duty of care 14–15, 16, 17
  floodgates problem 15,
    50, 56
  intervening acts 93
  operational/policy
    distinction 28
  police immunity 28–9
  psychiatric injury 50, 56
  public bodies 26–9

  standard of care 64
political speech 177, 183
post-traumatic stress
  disorder (PTSD) 50, 55
precautions 68
  employers' liability 105
  failure to take 202–3
prescription 146–7
press, freedom of the 193–4
prison service 133, 217
privacy 189–200
  anonymity 198
  background 190–1
  breach of
    confidence 192–8
  Calcutt Committee 190
  definition 190
  European Convention on
    Human Rights 191
  freedom of
    expression 190–1
  horizontal effect 191
  Human Rights Act
    1998 190–1, 197
  injunctions 197–8
  malicious falsehood 190
  media intrusion 2
  nuisance 3, 145
  photographs 193, 194,
    196–7, 198
  private and family life,
    right to respect for 145,
    191, 193–4, 196–7
  public bodies 191
  public figures 190
  United States 198
  vertical effect 191
  Wilkinson v Downton, tort
    in 134
  Younger Committee 190
private nuisance 141–8, 149,
  153
privilege in defamation
  actions 180–3
product liability 118–26
  blood products 121, 124
  burden of proof of
    defence 124
  causation 120, 122
  common law 119–20, 123

  compensation 122
  compliance with EU
    obligations 122
  consumer expectation
    test 121
  Consumer Protection Act
    1987 120–4
  defences 122–3
  definition of products 120
  development risks or state
    of the art defence 122–3
  exclusions 122
  importers 120
  instructions 121
  intermediate
    examination 119–20
  manufacturers 119, 120
  marketing 121
  neighbour principle 119
  own branders 120
  producers 120, 124
  Product Liability
    Directive 120, 124
  pure economic loss 122
  scientific and technical
    knowledge, state of 122
  strict liability 120, 121
  suppliers 121
  time limits 124
  warnings 121
provisional damages 220
proximity
  duty of care 14–17, 28
  negligent
    misstatements 37, 41, 43
  omissions 24, 26
  psychiatric injury 54
  public bodies 28
psychiatric injury 49–61
  bad news, breaking 57
  bystanders 50–2, 55, 56, 58
  causation 52–4, 81, 105
  controlling factors 50–8
  damages 50–1
  distress 134
  duty of care 13
  employment 27, 57, 105–6
  floodgates problem 50, 56
  foreseeability 52–3, 105
  fortitude policy 53, 56

grief 50–1
immediate aftermath 51, 54, 58
imprisonment 57
Law Commission 57–8
love and affection, relationships of 54, 56, 58
material contribution 81
medically diagnosed psychiatric conditions 133
physical injury 50, 52
police 55
policy 50, 56
post-traumatic stress disorder 50, 55
primary victims 51–8, 105
proximity 54
recognised psychiatric illness 50
reform 57–8
relationship to primary victims 53–4, 58
rescuers 55
secondary victims 51–8, 105
stress at work 51, 57, 105–6
sudden events 51, 57
thin skull rule 53
unique factual situations 55–6
voluntary assumption of responsibility 57
Wilkinson v Downton, tort in 133–4
witnesses 50, 51, 55, 58
public bodies
ambulance services, omissions and 25
Anns test, crime control 28
damages 217
defamation 177
defendants, as 16, 26–9
duty of care 16, 26–9
effective remedy, right to 27
employees, psychiatric injury to 27

European Convention on Human Rights 27
fire services, omissions and 25
Human Rights Act 1998 26
inhuman or degrading treatment 27
justiciability 26, 27
local authorities, defamation of 177
nuisance 145, 147
omissions 24–5, 28
policy 26–9
policy/operational distinction 26
prison service 133, 217
privacy 191
proximity 28
punitive or exemplary damages against 217
standard of care 27
ultra vires 26
see also **police**
public figures
breach of confidence 192–7
defamation 183
malice 183
privacy 190
public interest
breach of confidence 193, 195, 196, 197
children 96
defamation 177, 181–3
direct consequences test 94
duty of care 18
foreseeability 71, 94–5
injunctions 221, 222
privacy 191
res ipsa loquitur 63, 70–1
standard of care 69
thin skull rule 96–7
'three-stage' test 95
public nuisance 148–53, 153
punitive damages 4, 6, 184, 216–17
pure economic loss 34–7
floodgates 34
negligent misstatements 37, 40–1, 42, 43
product liability 122

qualified privilege in defamation actions 180–1
quia timet **injunctions** 221

reasonableness
breach of confidence 194–5, 197
fair, just and reasonable test 16–17, 26, 43, 44, 45, 104
foreseeability 94–5
intervening acts 91
negligent misstatements 38, 40, 44
nuisance 141, 144
standard of care 64–8
unfair contract terms, exclusion clauses and 164
references 37–8, 43
relationships
breach of confidence 193
love and affection 54, 56, 58
negligent misstatements 37–9, 42
psychiatric injury 53–4, 58
social relationships 39
special relationships 37–9, 42
reliance on negligent misstatements 38, 40, 41, 43–5
remedies
defamation 4, 183–5, 216
effective remedy, right to an 27
nuisance 3, 147–8
see also **compensation**; **damages**; **injunctions**
remoteness
causation in fact 85, 90
causation in law 18, 94–6
children 96
direct consequences test 94
intervening acts 90
res ipsa loquitur
burden of proof 71
standard of care 70–1
rescuers 23, 55, 92, 207
restitution for unjust enrichment 192

Index

Reynolds privilege in
 defamation actions 181–3
right to liberty and
 security 131
right to respect for private
 and family life 145, 191,
 193–4, 196–7
rights of way 160
 occupiers' liability 165, 168
risk *see* voluntary assumption
 of risk
Rylands v Fletcher, rule
 in 150–1
 accumulation 151
 act of stranger 152
 Acts of God 152
 common benefit 152
 consent 152
 defences 152
 escape 150, 151
 fire 152–3
 flooding 152
 foreseeability 150, 151
 negligence 3
 non-natural user 150
 nuisance 3, 153
 overlapping interests 3
 personal injuries 151
 physical damage 149
 property interests 2
 statutory authority 152
 strangers, act of 152
 third parties 152

self-defence 135
self-help 147–8, 222
several liability 78, 83
single issue or *ex gratia*
 compensation schemes 7
single publication rule 177
skill
 negligent misstatements 38
 occupiers' liability 161
 standard of care 65–6, 67
 visitors 161, 162
slander, definition of 173
smell 142, 143
social security 7, 220
solicitors' duty to
 beneficiaries 44

spectators, voluntary
 assumption of risk
 by 207
sports liability 66, 207
stalking 130
standard of care
 balancing factors 63, 68–70
 best practice 67–8
 Bolam test 66, 67
 breach of duty 62–74
 causation 63
 children 65
 common practice 67
 Compensation Act 2006 70
 'compensation culture' 70
 costs of running or avoiding
  risk 68–9
 employers' liability 107
 experience 66
 illegality 208–9
 illness 65
 importance of activity 68, 69
 knowledge 65
 learner drivers 64–5
 magnitude of risk 68
 medical negligence 66, 67–8
 objective approach 64–6
 occupiers' liability 160–1,
  165, 166–7
 policy 64
 precautions, costs of 68
 professional skills 67
 public bodies 27
 reasonable person test 64–8
 res ipsa loquitur 63, 70–1
 restricted resources of
  defendant 68
 scientific and technical
  expertise 65
 skill 65–6, 67
 social utility of purpose 69
 special standards 66–7
 sports 66
 subjective approach 64, 67
 warn, duty to 80
standard of proof 70
 causation 77
state of the art or
 development risks
 defence 122–3

statutory nuisance 153
stress at work 51, 57, 105–6
strict liability 120, 121, 175
striking out applications 18
structured settlements 219–20
suicide 91
surveyors 40
survival of existing causes
 of action
 death 223

thin skull rule 53, 96–7
third parties
 criminal acts 92
 defamation 175–6
 intervening acts 92
 motor insurance 206
 negligent
  misstatements 43–5
 Rylands v Fletcher, rule
  in 152
 voluntary assumption of
  risk 206
'three-stage' duty of care
 test 16–17, 40, 42, 95
transferred intent 129
trees, encroachment of 145,
 148, 222
trespass *see* trespass to land;
 trespass to the person
trespass to land 134
trespass to the person
 actionable *per se* 128, 132
 assault 128, 130–1
 battery 129–30, 134
 consent 129–30, 135
 contributory negligence 136
 criminal law 131
 damages 128
 defences 135–6
 direct and indirect
  trespass 128
 false imprisonment 128,
  131–2, 222
 harassment 130, 134
 injunctions 222
 intention 128
 lawful authority 135
 medical treatment 130
 necessity 135–6

physical safety 2
self-defence 135
speech 130
Wilkinson v Downton, tort
 in 133–4
'two-stage' duty of care test 14
types of loss or harm 2–3

ultra vires
 public bodies 26
unborn children as
 claimants 29
unfair contract terms,
 exclusion clauses and
 business liability 208
 disclaimers 38, 45–6
 negligent
  misstatements 38, 45–6
 occupiers' liability 164
 reasonableness 45, 164
 warnings 208
unforeseeable claimant 17–18
unjust enrichment,
 restitution for 192
unreasonableness *see*
 reasonableness
use of force
 voluntary assumption of
  risk 207
 see also **trespass to the**
  person

vaccine damage 7
vicarious liability 107–13
 borrowed or hired out
  employees 110

breach of statutory duty in
 employment context 108
carelessness 110
close connection 112–13
composite test 109
contract for services 108
contract of service 108
control test 108
course of employment 110
criminal acts 112
damages 107
diversions and
 detours 111
employers' liability 102
employment
 relationship 108–10
identifiability 108
indemnities 113
independent
 contractors 108, 109
instructions, acting
 contrary to 111
integration test 109
intentional acts 112
justifications 107–8
loss spreading 107
medical negligence 108
motive of employees 110
travelling to and from
 work 111–12
visitors, occupiers' liability
 and 160–4, 167
volenti non fit injuria *see*
 voluntary assumption of
 risk

voluntary assumption of
 responsibility
 negligent
  misstatements 41–4
 omissions 24–5
 psychiatric injury 57
 rescuers 207
 spectators 207
 sport 207
 standard of care 207
 unfair contract terms,
  exclusion clauses and 208
voluntary assumption of risk
 consent 206
 contributory
  negligence 206
 employment 206
 knowledge 206
 third party motor
  insurance 206

warnings
 medical negligence 80
 negligent misstatements 39
 obvious risks 163, 166
 occupiers' liability 161,
  162–3, 166
Wilkinson v Downton, **tort**
 in 133–4, 196
wills, solicitors' duty to
 beneficiaries of 44

Younger Committee 190